Auto/Biography in the Americas

Auto/Biography in the Americas: Relational lives brings together scholars from disparate geographic regions, cultural perspectives, linguistic frameworks, and disciplinary backgrounds to explore what connects narrated lives in the Americas. By interweaving scholarship on Afro-diasporic subjectivities, gendered narratives, lives in translation, celebrity auto/biographies, and pedagogical approaches to teaching auto/biographical narratives, this volume argues that connections between the contrasting locations of the Americas may be found in a shared history of diasporic movement that causes a heightened awareness of the need to belong and to thereby define the self in relation to others.

Read together, the essays in this collection suggest that identities across the Americas are constructed with an emphasis on intersubjectivity and relationality. This transnational approach to reading life writing beyond the borders of the Americas—pertinent to comparative American studies and hemispheric studies as well as life writing and auto/biography studies—also demonstrates an interdisciplinary, international, and multilingual model for collaborative research in the humanities and social sciences. The scholars included in this volume work in the fields of anthropology, sociology, history, literature, and education, and furthermore, this book marks the first time that many of these scholars have had their work translated into and published in English. This book was originally published as a special issue of *a/b: Auto/Biography Studies*.

Ricia Anne Chansky is an Associate Professor of Literature at the University of Puerto Rico at Mayagüez, Puerto Rico. She is the co-editor of the scholarly journal, *a/b: Auto/Biography Studies*, and the editor of the forthcoming volumes, *The Routledge Auto/Biography Studies Reader* and *Auto/Biography across the Americas: Transnational Themes Life Writing*. She founded the International Auto/Biography Association—Chapter of the Americas.

T0347510

Auto/Biography in the Americas

Relational lives

Edited by
Ricia Anne Chansky

Routledge
Taylor & Francis Group

LONDON AND NEW YORK

First published 2016
by Routledge

2 Park Square, Milton Park, Abingdon, Oxfordshire OX14 4RN
711 Third Avenue, New York, NY 10017

Routledge is an imprint of the Taylor & Francis Group, an informa business

First issued in paperback 2017

British Library Cataloguing in Publication Data
A catalogue record for this book is available from the British Library

ISBN 13: 978-1-138-64104-4 (hbk)
ISBN 13: 978-1-138-30947-0 (pbk)

Typeset in Perpetua
by diacriTech, Chennai

Publisher's Note
The publisher accepts responsibility for any inconsistencies that may have arisen during the conversion of this book from journal articles to book chapters, namely the possible inclusion of journal terminology.

Disclaimer
Every effort has been made to contact copyright holders for their permission to reprint material in this book. The publishers would be grateful to hear from any copyright holder who is not here acknowledged and will undertake to rectify any errors or omissions in future editions of this book.

For my grandmothers:

Ann Sancinito
Lillian Chansky
Sylvia Ruback

Contents

CONTENTS

Citation Information

The chapters in this book were originally published in *a/b: Auto/Biography Studies*, volume 30, issue 1 (Spring 2015). When citing this material, please use the original page numbering for each article, as follows:

Foreword
30 Years (and Counting)
Ricia Anne Chansky and Emily Hipchen
a/b: Auto/Biography Studies, volume 30, issue 1 (Spring 2015) pp. 1–2

Introduction
Moving beyond Borders
Ricia Anne Chansky
a/b: Auto/Biography Studies, volume 30, issue 1 (Spring 2015) pp. 3–16

Chapter 1
Finding Enslaved Children's Place, Voice, and Agency within the Narrative
Colleen A. Vasconcellos
a/b: Auto/Biography Studies, volume 30, issue 1 (Spring 2015) pp. 17–30

Chapter 2
On Racial Silence and Salience: Narrating "African Things" in Puerto Rican Oral History
Jocelyn A. Géliga Vargas
a/b: Auto/Biography Studies, volume 30, issue 1 (Spring 2015) pp. 31–52

Chapter 3
Roots and Routes: The Biographical Meshwork of Saint Josephine Bakhita
Maria Suely Kofes
a/b: Auto/Biography Studies, volume 30, issue 1 (Spring 2015) pp. 53–66

CITATION INFORMATION

For any permission-related enquiries please visit:
http://www.tandfonline.com/page/help/permissions

Notes on Contributors

Bella Brodzki is a Professor of Comparative Literature at Sarah Lawrence College, Yonkers, NY, USA. She is the co-editor of *Life/Lines: Theorizing Women's Autobiography* (1989), and she is also the author of *Can These Bones Live? Translation, Survival, and Cultural Memory* (2007). She co-edited a special issue of the journal *Comparative Literature Studies* (2011), and is co-editing the forthcoming special issue "Translating Memory across Cultures and Disciplines" for the journal *Translation*.

Ricia Anne Chansky is an Associate Professor of Literature at the University of Puerto Rico at Mayagüez, Puerto Rico. She is the co-editor of the scholarly journal, *a/b: Auto/Biography Studies*, and the editor of the forthcoming volumes, *The Routledge Auto/Biography Studies Reader* and *Auto/Biography across the Americas: Transnational Themes Life Writing*. She founded the International Auto/Biography Association—Chapter of the Americas.

Elizeu Clementino de Souza is a Researcher at the National Council for Scientific and Technological Development, Brazil. He is also a Professor in the Graduate Program in Education and Contemporaneity at the Universidade do Estado da Bahia, Brazil; Coordinator of the Group of (Auto)Biographical Research, Education, and Oral History; a member of the board of directors of the International Association of Life Histories and Biographical Research in Education; an Associate Researcher at the EXPERICE Laboratory at the University of Paris, France; and President of the Brazilian Association of (Auto)Biographical Research.

Jocelyn A. Géliga Vargas is an Associate Professor in the Department of English at the University of Puerto Rico at Mayagüez, Puerto Rico, and Coordinator of the English Writing Center. Her publications include journal articles and book chapters on identity studies and film studies, with a focus on Puerto Rican/Caribbean cinema and Puerto Rican representations in Hollywood films, and collaborative and participatory research methods in oral history and ethnography. She is currently working on a book-length manuscript based on Afro-Puerto Rican oral history.

Donna P. Hope is a Director and a Senior Lecturer of the Institute of Caribbean Studies and Reggae Studies Unit at the University of the West Indies, Mona, Jamaica. Her two award-winning books, *Inna di Dancehall: Popular Culture and the Politics of Identity in Jamaica* (2000) and *Man Vibes: Masculinities in the Jamaican Dancehall* (2010), draw from research undertaken over many years on Jamaican music and dancehall culture, cultural/creative industries, youth development, black masculinities, black popular culture, gender, identity, and power. She has also published two edited collections: *International Reggae: Current and Future Trends in Jamaican Popular Music* (2013) and *Reggae from Yaad: Traditional and Emerging Themes in Jamaican Popular Music* (2015).

Maria Suely Kofes is a Professor of Anthropology in the Institute of Philosophy and Human Sciences at Universidade Estadual de Campinas, Brazil. Her research deals with the construction, legitimation, and reproduction of cultural identities, and draws on ethnography and biographical perspectives, anthropology, cultural studies and social theory, the processes of differentiation and identity recognition, and studies of race and gender. She created, with the Department of Social Anthropology at UNICAMP, the Anthropological Laboratory for Word and Image, which explores the points of intersection between narratives and images.

Joycelyn K. Moody is a Chair in American Literature at the University of Texas at San Antonio, TX, USA. She is currently co-editing special issues on black print-culture studies for the journals *American Periodicals* and *MELUS: Multi-Ethnic Literatures of the United States*. She is also currently editing and writing the introduction to *A History of African American Autobiography*. She is the author of *Sentimental Confessions: Spiritual Narratives of Nineteenth-Century African American Women* (2003) and *Teaching with the Norton Anthology of African American Literature* (1997), as well as the editor of a recent edition of the *Memoirs of Elleanor Eldridge* (2014). She is also the founding Director of the UTSA's African American Literatures and Cultures Institute and, with John Ernest, the co-editor for the West Virginia University Press series *Regenerations: African American Literature and Culture*.

Gabriel Jaime Murillo Arango is a Professor of Pedagogy in the Department of Education at the Universidad Nacional de Colombia, Medellín, Colombia. He has published several essays and books on his research on the role of auto/biography in teaching and curricular development, especially in relation to social justice and national memory, including *Maestros contadores de historias: Narra en red pedagogica* (2008), *Palabras y cosas de maestros* (2010), and *Las Historias de vida: infancias y memoria* (2013). His current work, on a Colombian national curriculum of memory, remembering, and mourning, links oral and written narratives with visual art, music, and film-making.

Colleen A. Vasconcellos is an Associate Professor of History at the University of West Georgia, Carrollton, GA, USA. While her teaching focuses on the African diaspora and the Atlantic world, her research concentrates on enslaved children in the Americas. Her first book, *Slavery, Childhood, and Abolition, 1788–1838*, was published by the University of Georgia Press in 2015 as part of its *Early American Places* Series.

Julia Watson is a Professor Emerita of Comparative Studies and the former Associate Dean of Arts and Sciences at The Ohio State University, Columbus, OH, USA. She and Sidonie Smith have co-written *Reading Autobiography: A Guide for Interpreting Life Narratives* (2010), co-edited five collections of essays, and published several co-authored essays, most recently on testimony and authenticity, and online self-presentation. She has also recently published essays on graphic memoir, posthumanism, and autoethnography.

Acknowledgements

I am grateful to my parents, Patricia and Howard Chansky, for instilling in me their unwavering belief that all things are possible. As always, my husband, Eric D. Lamore, showed great patience, kindness, and a sense of humor as I worked on this project. He was particularly generous in his willingness to act as a consulting editor on the special issue of *a/b: Auto/Biography Studies* (30.1) that grew into this volume.

This book would not be possible without the collaboration of the scholars who participated in the 2013 symposium, "Auto/Biography across the Americas: Reading beyond Geographic and Cultural Boundaries." I find myself continually impressed by the widespread outpouring of enthusiasm and encouragement offered by this international community of researchers.

This initial conference received generous funding from The Autobiography Society, under the guidance of William L. Andrews, and from the Zentrum für Interkulturelle Studien, directed by Alfred Hornung. I am extremely appreciative of both of these individuals for demonstrating their faith in this project. The University of Puerto Rico at Mayagüez has also consistently supported my research, for which I am indebted.

Additionally, several editorial assistants and interns who have worked for *a/b: Auto/Biography Studies* over the years have invested their time and energy in this undertaking. I would be remiss if I did not recognize the contributions made by Krista E. Roberts, Wanda Ortiz Hernández, Kate Peterson, Karla Marie Rodríguez Acosta, and Daysha Pinto.

I am also lucky to work with the talented editorial team of *a/b: Auto/Biography Studies*, and I thank them for sharing their intelligence, insights, and friendship with me. Thank you to Emily Hipchen, Becky and Joe Hogan, Tanya Kam, Emily Woster, Sarah Brophy, Eva Karpinski, Laura Beard, and Tim Feeney for making projects like this one possible.

The abstracts included in this volume have been translated from English into Spanish by Karla Marie Rodríguez Acosta, Wanda Ortiz Hernández, and Daysha Pinto.

30 Years (and Counting)

Dedicated to Rebecca and Joseph Hogan

In 1985, James Olney convened a conference in auto|biography studies at Louisiana State University: "the International Symposium on Autobiography and Autobiography Studies." This meeting turned out to be a momentous occasion for the field of life narrative and for our journal. Not only was a seed sown in several like-minded colleagues who would build this robust field into the remarkable site of scholarly activity that it is today, but Barbara Sher, Rebecca Hogan, and Timothy Dow Adams met and joined together to publish a small newsletter that grew into the international journal *a/b: Auto/Biography Studies*. In these early years of the journal, a collaborative group of enthusiastic scholars worked diligently to keep *a/b* in print. William L. Andrews generously arranged for funding for the journal, while Tom Smith, Tim Adams, and Becky and Joe Hogan each took year-long turns producing and distributing it. In 1988, Becky and Joe assumed editorship of the journal at the University of Wisconsin-Whitewater and, beginning with issue 5.2, Bill took over all matters related to production and subscription, first at the University of Kansas and then the University of North Carolina at Chapel Hill.

After the Hogans retired in 2012, we became the journal's editors and, in 2014, *a/b* became a member of the Routledge Literature portfolio of journals. We have subsequently spent much of this past year moving all of our production and distribution to Routledge. As the new editors, we work to uphold the tradition of publishing vital scholarship on narrated lives while expanding our emphasis on methodology, interdisciplinarity, and global perspectives. In order to meet these objectives, we have expanded the work of the journal to include convening symposia, leading collaborative research projects, developing a book program, creating micro-documentaries to accompany special issues, and funding and mentoring graduate students and scholars from underrepresented communities.

This special issue is particularly apropos to the occasion of our thirtieth anniversary, as "Auto|Biography across the Americas" is an example of one project that has grown from these editorial objectives. This issue stems from a conference of the same name that we convened in 2013. Through the International Auto|Biography Association (IABA) Chapter of the Americas, we have developed this conference into an ongoing collaborative research project that fosters scholarship and deliberately crosses geographic, cultural, linguistic, and disciplinary boundaries.

Our anniversary festivities will continue with the forthcoming publication of *The Routledge Auto/Biography Studies Reader* in December 2015 and at the 2016 IABA conference in Cyprus. In honor of our thirtieth anniversary, we are also introducing two prizes: the Timothy Dow Adams Award, to be presented in the form of a travel grant to an IABA conference, and The Hogan Prize, for an outstanding essay published in a special issue of the journal. Routledge has also published a special digital collection of essays assembled from our archives: "30 Years | 30 Essays." This collection is free through December 2015 and can be accessed from our website at tandfonline.com/raut.

For thirty years, *a/b: Auto/Biography Studies* has been a leading voice in the expanding body of scholarship on auto|biographical narratives. As we celebrate three decades of publishing exemplary scholarship on auto|biographical narratives, we would like to express our gratitude to those who were integral in founding both the field and our journal, as well as our editorial board and the many scholars, students, and practitioners who continue to read, contribute to, and volunteer their time for *a/b: Auto/Biography Studies*. Thank you for being a part of our first thirty years, and we hope to see you over the next thirty!

RICIA AND EMILY

Moving beyond Boundaries

By Ricia Anne Chansky

This essay proposes that the historic or contemporary movement of peoples to, in, and from the Americas—forced or chosen—underlies the ways in which identity is constructed in this contested space. Such an understanding of the importance of movement within narratives of the Americas leads to considerations of belonging steeped in the strata of performativity, relationality, and intersubjectivity. Rather than suggest that a transnational approach to auto/biographical narratives of the Americas is only that which charts a subject's movement across national borders, the idea of movement, and the resultant quest for belonging, is read as a transnational theme that motivates and provides a cohesive discursive point among these auto/biographical narratives.

Este ensayo propone que los movimientos históricos o contemporáneos de las personas hacia, dentro y desde las Américas -voluntarios o involuntarios- delínean las formas en las cuales la identidad es construída en este espacio. El entendimiento de la importancia del movimiento dentro de las narrativas de las Américas lleva a consideraciones de pertenecia dentro de la estrata de performatividad, relacionalidad e intersubjetividad. En vez de sugerir que un enfoque transnacional hacia las narrativas auto/biográficas de las Américas es sólo aquello que traza el movimiento de un sujeto a través de las fronteras nacionales, la idea de movimiento y de la búsqueda subsequente de pertenecer es leída como un tema transnacional que motiva y proveé un discurso cohesivo entre estas narrativas auto/biográficas.

In the summer of 2013, the editors of *a/b: Auto/Biography Studies* convened a conference in San Juan, Puerto Rico, titled "Auto|Biography across the Americas: Reading beyond Geographic and Cultural Divides." As the new editors of *a/b*, we wanted to define what auto|biography studies in the twenty-first century meant to us by placing an emphasis on international dialogues, collaborative research, interdisciplinary practices, multimodal narratives, and the exploration of diverse methodologies. This conference was our way of constructing a space in which to begin exploring these ideas with our colleagues. To that end, this symposium brought together thirty scholars of life narrative from North America, the Caribbean, and South America for four days of presentations and extended discussions. Our objectives were to develop a community of collaborative researchers in the western hemisphere and to foster discourse on moving beyond limiting geographic, cultural, linguistic, and disciplinary boundaries to explore the connections present in our research on auto|biographical narratives of the Americas.

We had noted, like many of our colleagues, that the programs from the International Auto|Biography Association (IABA) conferences did not fully reflect the diverse vitality of international discourse on narrated lives. I was particularly concerned about the underrepresentation of my colleagues from the Caribbean and Latin America. A review of the programs from the three IABA conferences directly preceding the inception of our project reflects a dearth of participants from these regions: the 2010 IABA conference program lists five participants from universities in Latin America and two from the Caribbean; the 2008 conference program lists one participant from Latin America and no participants from the Caribbean; and the 2006 program lists no participants from Latin America and none from the Caribbean.[1] We believe that this underrepresentation stems from linguistic and financial factors, as the common language of the IABA is English and the conferences can be expensive to attend, especially if one does not receive monetary support from one's home institution.

Logistically, we realized early on that we would have these linguistic and financial concerns to surmount in our undertaking. While we are still learning a great deal about building international research communities, we strove to make this conference an affordable and welcoming space for all attendees. To this end, we created a multilingual space in which all abstracts were published in at least two languages, translators were available onsite, and presentations were delivered in the presenter's language of choice with translations available for the audience. Attending scholars were informed of this available translation support at the time of invitation. Additionally, we were fortunate enough to obtain a grant that allowed us to waive registration fees for all invited participants and to provide most meals and coffee breaks. Originally, we had conceptualized these meals as a money-saving means for participants; however, they quickly surpassed our expectations by also functioning as an extension of the conversations that began in the more formal spaces of the conference, and they further allowed conference participants to develop personal relationships beyond the work of scholarship. Of course, the size of this conference contributed to the camaraderie that grew in these small corners.

Another practical aspect of this undertaking for us to consider was the interdisciplinary nature of the scholars assembled. The presenters at this conference were trained as scholars in the disciplines of literature, linguistics, art history, history, political science, sociology, anthropology, pedagogy, and communications and media studies. They have published, and continue to do so, in the areas of auto|biography studies, American studies, Canadian studies, Latin American studies, Caribbean studies, African diasporic studies, Native American |Indigenous|Aboriginal studies, Latino|a studies, critical race theory, the Early Black Atlantic, transnational and transatlantic studies, post colonial studies, translation studies, oral history|*testimonio*, gender studies, cultural studies, visual culture, new media and the digital humanities, musicology, and rural and class studies, among other modes of inquiry. Of course, each of these subject areas and specializations utilizes different vocabularies, rhetorical strategies, and research methodologies. We were, therefore, charged with considering multilingualism from the additional perspective of appropriately capturing and conveying disciplinary terminology and subject-specific norms. Through a programmatic emphasis on methodological approaches, as well as an effort to discuss disparate terminologies, the assembled scholars worked together graciously to surpass these disciplinary divides. Maintaining an attentive eye on the crossroads and meeting places of identity construction in the Americas, the attendees strove to learn from the diverse subject positions, rhetorical stances, and methodological approaches of their colleagues.

These efforts continue under the auspices of the IABA Chapter of the Americas, which was founded at "Auto|Biography across the Americas," and through the continuing work of the journal to foster international and interdisciplinary dialogues. The first biennial conference of the IABA Chapter of the Americas, titled "Encounters across the Americas: Archives, Technologies, and Methodologies," was convened in 2015 by Sidonie Smith and Julia Watson at the University of Michigan at Ann Arbor. This conference included the presentation of the first annual Timothy Dow Adams Awards, conferred by *a|b*. The prize will be made in the form of a travel grant to the conference. In addition to this special issue of the journal, we are in the process of editing a forthcoming book of essays, *Auto|Biography across the Americas: Transnational Themes in Life Writing*, which also emerged from the work of the conference. Additionally, we are working on several grant projects and developing curricular training workshops and other projects to facilitate collaborative research in the Americas.

For the purposes of this conference, we specifically asked the presenters to share papers related to the micro-themes of language, translation, and trust; modes, multimodality, and genres; race, ethnicity, and diasporic communities; or the contested body. The focus of the conference was intentionally structured in this broad manner because we wanted macro-themes to evolve from the work of this international, multilingual, multidisciplinary conference, rather than have them be defined from our singular subject positions. We hoped that some of the ways in which auto|biographical narratives of the Americas suggest that identities in the western hemisphere are interconnected would be brought into clearer focus through this gathering, and that the delegates at this meeting would work collaboratively to deliberate these ideas of constructing identities of the Americas beyond boundaries. Our intention was not to suggest that the assembled scholars were individually transnational, or that their scholarship was necessarily focused on the fluidity of movement that signifies a geographically transnational text. Rather, we wished to explore what themes might be emergent as transnational, thereby underlying identities constructed in the western hemisphere. Thus, by eschewing more traditional definitions of the transnational, we wanted to consider what themes might be fluid enough to transcend the national, cultural, and linguistic boundaries of the Americas.

Informing the thematic structure of this conference were some of the concepts being explored in life writing and American studies that encouraged us to consider what a "global subject" is (Smith 567). In her 2011 presidential address, the then president of the Modern Language Association, Sidonie Smith, suggested that auto|biographical narratives encourage scholars and readers "to comprehend how we are no longer only national but also global subjects," further stating that "the flow in narrated lives also becomes a means for increasing numbers of people around the globe to imagine themselves as global citizens" (567). We were quite taken with the idea of global citizenship and wondered what it might mean to be a citizen of the Americas, beyond our geographically bound concepts of nationalism and national identity.

Also of interest to us were conversations emerging from new American studies, comparative American studies, and transnational American studies. Shelley Fisher Fishkin asked in her 2004 American Studies Association presidential address, "What roles might comparative, collaborative, border-crossing research play in this reconfigured field? If national borders no longer delimit the subject of our study, then how can we allow them to delimit the scholarship that demands our attention?" (22). These questions became woven into the fabric of our undertaking as we worked to construct definitions of the term transnational that would reflect our thinking and consider the ways in which scholars of auto|biographical narratives across the Americas might adapt such a reconfigured research model that emphasized border crossings.

Furthermore, John Carlos Rowe's call for a comparatist approach to American studies that "take[s] into account at the very least the different nationalities, cultures, and languages of the Western hemisphere" shaped our thinking regarding the composition of our event (169). Concerned by the lack of representation of our colleagues from the Caribbean and Latin America at relevant international meetings, in research projects, and in publications, we determined that the conversations we wanted to engage in about identity in the Americas needed to include scholars and scholarship from different parts of the western hemisphere. Our interpretation, then, of Rowe's comparatist approach was to place scholars with diverse vantage points in conversation with one another in order to develop such comparisons from multiple subjectivities.

As the presentations and discussions of the conference unfolded, we took note of the thematic repetitions that reverberated across languages, cultures, geographies, and disciplines. On reflection, we see these themes converging under the interrelated headings of movement, belonging, and relationality. Our initial conclusions rest on the observation that the historic or contemporary movement of peoples to, in, and from the Americas—forced or chosen—underlies the ways in which identity is constructed in this contested space. Such an understanding of the importance of movement to narratives of the western hemisphere leads to considerations of belonging steeped in the strata of performativity, relationality, and intersubjectivity. Rather than suggest that a transnational approach to auto|biographical narratives of the Americas is only that which charts a subject's movement across national borders, then, we read the idea of movement, and the resultant quest for belonging, as a transnational theme that motivates and provides a cohesive discursive point among narratives of the Americas.

These observations on movement as underlying identity constructions in the western hemisphere grow from a consideration of Sandra Pouchet Paquet's work on narrated lives of the Caribbean. She suggests that "any pan-Caribbean paradigm is immediately qualified by the thematics of diaspora" and that these "themes of diaspora…are complicated because Caribbean writers and scholars have been at great pains to represent the region, historically and culturally, as diasporic space" (6). "Diasporic space," she adds, "represents the Caribbean in specific histories of conquest and settlement, population movements, exile and migrations" (6). This point suggests that historic movements—and a resultant sense of belonging to more than one location—motivate the construction of identities in the Caribbean. Our premise extends Pouchet Paquet's work to suggest that historic movement to the Americas is a core element of narrated lives throughout the Americas, which leads to an emphasis on the struggle for belonging. The forthcoming book, *Auto/Biography across the Americas: Transnational Themes in Life Writing*, focuses on the concepts of movement and belonging as themes underlying auto|biographical narratives of the Americas. This special issue is, therefore, dedicated to exploring relationality and intersubjectivity in narrated lives. It is our intention that these two texts will provide the foundation for future investigations of identity studies in the western hemisphere.

Sidonie Smith and Julia Watson's concise overview of relationality as applied to life writing articulates that "the subject is always the subject of the other, constituting and constituted by heterogeneous social discourses. The very words through which the story is 'spoken' or written are the language of the other" (216). They suggest that "relationality characterizes all autobiographical writing" (279). Stemming from our proposal that lives narrated in the Americas have at their root a history of displacement and movement, however, advocates that relationality may be deeper or uniquely fashioned in these narratives. Bart Moore-Gilbert observes that "[p]ostcolonial women's life-writing" can be read as demonstrative of "enhanced…attributes of relationality" (18)—a sentiment that I further clarify in my mind as extending beyond the female to the feminized. Smith and Watson further point to Françoise Lionnet's "theory of auto-biographical textuality as a *métissage* of disparate voices in subjects whose cultural origins and allegiances are multiple and conflicting" (217). Considering reading strategies that place the self in relation to "cultural origins and allegiances" that "are multiple and conflicting" may be one that we feel more comfortable applying to narratives struggling more overtly with the legacies of colonialism, rather than with approaches that include the US and Canada. However, as many other scholars have noted in multiple variances, legacies of internal displacement and movement abound in both nations as well as continuing migration and lingering connections to countries of origin.

Beginning with historian Colleen Vasconcellos's "Process" piece, this special issue opens with a grouping of essays that explore the African diaspora from diverse vantage points across the Americas; the cluster considers some of the ways in which this forced migration motivated, and continues to motivate, understandings of identity constructions. Vasconcellos's reflective essay, "Finding Enslaved Children's Place, Voice, and Agency within the Narrative," charts her experiences reconstructing the narratives of enslaved children from Jamaican archival resources. Using abolitionist documentation, legal archives, plantation records, and personal papers such as diaries and letters, Vasconcellos first maps planters' changing attitudes to enslaved children as the transatlantic slave trade, and subsequently the institution of slavery, was threatened by new laws; she then demonstrates that many of the recorded crimes that these enslaved youths were accused of may be read as both a resistance to slavery and as exemplary of their reactions to the traumatic experiences of enslavement. Ultimately, Vasconcellos's recreation of the lives of enslaved children from her archival research shows that they "struggled to survive and identify with the world around them" in an attempt "to negotiate their place within the plantation complex through acts of violence, theft, self-destruction, and even murder. Forced into adulthood before their time, enslaved children in Jamaica would never escape the traumas they faced on a daily basis".

Vasconcellos's work, however, also calls into question the lack of interest in studying children's narratives in scholarship on the transatlantic slave trade. Her project suggests that, until we recover and read the historically silenced voices of enslaved children, we cannot begin to understand the full weight that the legacies of slavery have placed on identity constructions emergent from Afro-diasporic communities.

Jocelyn Géliga Vargas's essay, "On Racial Silence and Salience: Narrating 'African Things' in Puerto Rican Oral History," also addresses themes of silence and silencing. In her essay, she proposes that the narrated life may also construct a separation from such affiliations when they are deemed unwanted by a particular subject. Rather than the enforced silences explored in Vasconcellos's piece, Géliga Vargas suggests that "[r]ace talk [in Puerto Rico] is regarded as impolite, and racial identities are considered irrelevant, foreign, and incongruous with our formation as a mixed *pueblo* that has shaped itself and come of age in a balmy climate of racial harmony" (33). Drawing on her ongoing collaborative oral-history project to support her argument, she contends "that the apparent silencing of racial discourse and racial identities in Puerto Rico has indeed contributed to the internalization of a logic of (de)racialized domination that reveals the multivalent, unstable, and fragmentary nature of silences" (32). In this context, Géliga Vargas discusses the "systematic purging of blackness and Africanness from the national character and territory that the narrators' apparent dissociation from Afro-diasporic identities and allegiances must be gauged" (37). One of her interviewees even admits that he "feared marrying a black woman because I didn't want my children to be black...I didn't want to marry someone like me because I didn't want my children to be lowbred" (44). As Géliga Vargas suggests, however, these *testimonios afropuertorriqueños* may be read as separating themselves from one form of racialization in order to evoke "the collectivities that the Self has recourse to, and inform it as a Self in the making. The intersubjective and partial truths that are thus registered enrich our understanding and appreciation of Afro-Puerto Rican memory as living histories" (48).

Whereas Vasconcellos and Géliga Vargas discuss the silencing and voicing of Afro-diasporic identities, Maria Suely Kofes focuses on the manipulation of one such voice in her contribution to this special issue, "Roots and Routes: The Biographical Meshwork of Saint Josephine Bakhita." Kofes contends that biographical representations of Bakhita as the first formerly enslaved person to be canonized by the Catholic Church "have been utilized to present, re-present, and represent the saint for multiple purposes: as a link between Europe, Africa, and Latin America; as a model of African Catholicism; as a critique of slavery and racism; as a mediation between Islam and Christianity; and as a successful model for Afro-diasporic and Afro-Brazilian peoples to follow in the struggle for equality" (54). According to Kofes's reading of the multiple biographical narratives of Bakhita's life, this "brown saint" is positioned as a figurehead for several trajectories of thought without a clear articulation of her own subject position. Exemplary of Kofes's reflections on biographical manipulations, this essay maintains that Bakhita's life has been voiced through imagined affiliations to certain belief systems that are wholly unsupported by any factual evidence.

In opposition to Vasconcellos's archival research, the biographies that Kofes discusses are noteworthy for their lack of research and validation, which allows for these unsubstantiated associations. For Kofes, however, of more value to her anthropological study than the factual elements of the emergence of transatlantic Bakhita biographies is the convergence of the lines of this "African saint" or, as she refers to it, the "meshwork." As she explains, unfolding as expanded lines, "[t]he name of Bakhita is the agent of a minimal biographical composition that is also a political metaphor—that of the liberated Africa. In one of its lines there is liberation through Christianity, while another refers to the struggle of Afro-Brazilians" (65). The contemporary manifestations of the Bakhita story, therefore, may be read as biographical narratives of exaggerated connections and overextended parallelisms, created to foster imagined relationships that did not necessarily exist.

Joycelyn Moody extends the discussion on voice and agency in her essay "Tactical Lines in Three Black Women's Visual Portraits, 1773—1849," which scrutinizes the representational significance of the frontispieces crafted for texts related to three African American women: Elleanor Eldridge, Phillis Wheatley, and Jarena Lee. The images in question may be read as another means of influencing voice in Afro-diasporic communities, both for author and for publisher gain. Moody argues that "[a] national obsession with representing one's inner essence...played a key role in the inclusion of author images in narratives by or about a good many formerly enslaved and other free(d) black people" (75). Contemplating the question of "[h]ow much...agency...could a black woman sitter exert over the rendering of her image...in the late eighteenth century and into the nineteenth" (73), she indicates that the presentation and manipulation of these images of "African womanhood" shape how readers, historical and contemporary, approach and engage with their texts, suggesting that the medium, visual grammar, and artist affiliation of each portrait influence readers. At a time of prephotographic iconography, Moody argues, these three frontispieces helped shape understandings of black women as subjects different than white women and black men, while still reflecting the complex negotiations between authors, artists, editors, and publishers.

In her essay "(Un)Translatability and the Autobiographical Subject in Maryse Condé's *La vie sans fards*," Bella Brodzki continues this notion of the complex negotiation for agency between those invested in crafting text through her reflection on the relationship between Condé and her husband and translator, Richard Philcox. Considering Condé's narrative of her years living in West Africa, *La vie sans fards*, Brodzki provides a concise overview of the author's quest for an understanding of an Africa that turns out "to be more foreign than she ever imagined" (101); Condé searches for an African identity that may not be hers to access. Adding to the dimension of displacement felt by this Guadeloupian author searching for self-recognition in Africa is the articulation that Condé felt her work to be untranslatable: translation, for her, is "at best...a mechanistic exercise or practical necessity, not a creative practice worthy of her serious attention" (104). While Philcox's translation "has meant that her work has exceeded its linguistic and cultural bounds, and lived beyond its own temporal and spatial borders" (103), Condé labels the translation as a separate text and an inauthentic imitation, despite its contribution to her "pre-eminent status as a global Caribbean writer" (103). This essay, then, considers the self as one caught between geographic and linguistic identities, suggesting that the denial of a self in translation—a self in more than one language and in more than one location—can act as a claim for agency through the rejection of a translated self: both one written into a second language and one caught in a foreign space.

Similarly, Donna Hope, in her essay "Exploring Narratives of Contested Gender Identities in Jamaican Dancehall," analyzes the rejection of an Other as a means of reifying the self. Through a careful examination of the lyrics of Jamaican dancehall music, Hope argues that constructions of masculinity are being built through articulations of hypermasculinity in opposition to a feminized male subject position; she states that "[t]he male body in dancehall culture remains a central site of contested discourses of gender identity" (108). As Hope explains, "dancehall culture's fantasies of masculinity are interwoven with multiple identity debates that flit across the stages of dancehall culture. In this regard, dancehall's ritual performances of heterosexual masculinity are very prominent and often feature graphic and explicit lyrics" (110). These "graphic and explicit lyrics" that perform hypermasculinity onstage and elsewhere reinforce heterosexuality through the degradation of other men and of homosexuality. Hope's work suggests, though, that underlying the binary opposition of the "Badman" and the "Chi Chi Man" present in auto|biographical dancehall lyrics is the "Fashion Ova Style" man—a masculine identity that "highlights the development of transitional and transgressive sites of male identity formation and signals a form of borderline identity" (118). This point suggests that prolonged considerations of the self in relation to an Other may allow for the creation of a self that contains elements of both the self and the Other.

Contemplations of extended relationality are further developed in Julia Watson's essay, "Patti Smith Kicks in the Walls of Memoir: *Just Kids.*" Growing from her analysis of Smith's "note" at the end of the paperback version of her narrative—which explains that the memoir of her years with Robert Mapplethorpe "was obliged to wait until I could find the right voice" (135) —Watson explores the "transpersonal and intersubjective voice" (136) that is "shuttling between Patti and Robert, and speaking as 'our story'" (136). She further calls attention to the exchange between the two transcribed in the "note" that "move[s] their two voices in sentences without quotation marks, fuses indirect discourse with sentences of recollected dialogue, suggesting their emotional reciprocity. Its flow, without demarcation or quotation marks separating the speakers, creates a shared 'third' voice" (135). Ultimately, this essay suggests that this time in Smith's life was (and is presently remembered as) so intertwined with Mapplethorpe's that she cannot write *her* memoir without finding an adequate voice of inclusion for him; therefore, the self explored in this memoir is so entangled with an Other that to narrate one story is to recount both stories. Furthermore, this consideration of

Just Kids as a "polyphonic performance" that enables us to "observe the play of personal voice within, and against, the narrative genres" (145) blurs the contours of exceptionalism and the tradition of privileging the idea of an individual voice over a communal or collaborative one.

Two essays that dovetail auto|biographical narratives with pedagogical theory close this special issue: "Public Memory and Public Mourning in Contemporary Colombia," by Gabriel Jaime Murillo Arango, and "(Auto)Biography in Pre-Service Teacher Training: Rural Education in Bahia, Brazil," by Elizeu Clementino de Souza. In his contemplation of curricula that move beyond the last decade of "La Violencia" in Colombia, Murillo Arango uses the Centro Nacional de Memoria Histórica as a starting place to develop his pedagogical approach to healing the nation through teaching. His work considers how a curriculum of recording and sharing personal narratives could build a national memory and memorialize those who have been disappeared, dispossessed, overlooked, or forgotten, especially the NNs (No Names) who have been recovered from anonymous mass graves. Murillo Arango argues that "[u]nderstanding the political function of historical narrative means understanding that there are also multiple narratives of war," (158) further advising that "[t]he role of historical narrative in this political scenario…takes the form of a medium that is used to construct coexistence and achieve national peace" (158). Drawing on visual artists whose work focuses on memory, remembering, and memorializing, he proposes that a countrywide crusade for the articulation of memory through *empalabramiento* ("rewording," "re-voicing," or "silence-breaking") in schools and public spaces stands as a viable means for national healing. In this case, Murillo Arango's work advocates that, in the wake of war and national tragedy, the self cannot progress without attention to the lost Other.

While Murillo Arango's pedagogical theories respond to national mourning with the suggestion of curricular development on a nationwide scale, Clementino de Souza's essay delineates how detrimental the application of a region-specific curriculum can be when it is applied to all the schools of a given nation. Discussing his collaborative research project on rural education, he explains that the focus on urban populations in Brazil has been disadvantageous to students of rural schools, as urban pedagogies are being unilaterally applied in rural locations without an understanding of the students' differing needs. Many of the rural schools that Clementino de Souza discusses are *unidocente* classrooms, with all levels of students grouped together in one class with only one teacher who is wholly untrained to teach under such circumstances. He argues that the inclusion of self-reflexive pedagogical autoethnographies in pre-service teacher training offers an exemplary way to prepare teachers for these rural classrooms. He states that "[o]f paramount importance…is the production of self-reflexive (auto)biographical texts by the enrolled pre-service teachers, as both a means of preparing teachers to work in multigrade classes and a biographical methodology for researchers to study the preparation of these teachers" (175-6). This imposition of urban identities on rural students implies that concerns over one facet of the nation may become superimposed onto a national identity erroneously; occupation with the slums of certain Brazilian cities has translated, in this case, into a faulty assumption that this is a national reality instead of a localized problem. The resulting countrywide pedagogy fails to take into account a multifaceted national identity.

The essays of this special issue all consider the ever-present Other as a central factor in auto|biographical narratives. Some of them consider relationality as a demarcation of the African diaspora in the following ways: the process of re-voicing the erased and overlooked enslaved children of the transatlantic slave trade; the move *to* erase and separate one's self from African and Afro-diasporic identities and communities; the manipulation of a formerly enslaved person's identity through biographical representations that align her with different sociopolitical and sociocultural ideologies which she may not necessarily have endorsed or even seen in her lifetime; the fraught navigations for agency between authors, artists, and editors in the quest for the unique representation of black women, separate from both white women and black men; and the layers of untranslatability between the languages and locations that contribute to one's identity constructions.

Other essays in this special issue consider relationality as both a rejection and a consummation of the Other. This idea is extended to the gendered commentary offered in dancehall lyrics, in which identity definitions rest as firmly on the denunciation of one type of masculinity as on the acceptance of another. This discourse is further protracted through reflections on intersubjectivity in lives so intertwined within a narrative of hyperaffiliation that to tell one's life is also to share the life of another, if one can "find the right voice" to do so. The concluding essays, which bring these theories into practice in the classroom, explore national pedagogies that are reliant on auto|biographical narratives—one as a means of using memory and life stories to promote national healing, the other to develop more fully a national identity that extends beyond limiting discourse of the nation as solely an urban site laden with poverty and overcrowding.

Taken together, all of the essays included in this special issue look to relationality as a core element in narratives of the western hemisphere, signifying that identity formation in the Americas is driven by underlying ideas of movement that simultaneously promote the interrelated idea of belonging. These essays have been grouped together to promote discussion on what might connect narratives of the western hemisphere. This special issue, our forthcoming book, and the work of the IABA Chapter of the Americas begin to open the door to a long overdue conversation on what connects us and underlies our lives and experiences in the Americas.

Acknowledgments

We are grateful to William L. Andrews and Alfred Hornung for their initial and ongoing support of this project. We are also indebted to The Autobiography Society, the Zentrum für Interkulturelle Studien at the Johannes Gutenberg

University in Mainz, Germany, the University of Puerto Rico at Mayagüez, the University of West Georgia, and the management of the Sheraton Old San Juan Hotel for their contributions to the success of the conference.

Disclosure Statement

No potential conflict of interest was reported by the author.

Note

1. Marijke Huisman has noted, "Only a small number of participants from outside the Anglo-American world...have participated in the biennial conferences organized by IABA" (12).

Works Cited

Fisher Fishkin, Shelley. "Crossroads of Culture: The Transnational Turn in American Studies—Presidential Address to the American Studies Association, November 12, 2004." *American Quarterly* 57.1 (2005): 17—57. Print.

Huisman, Marijke. "Introduction: *Life Writing Matters in Europe*." *Life Writing Matters in Europe*. Ed. Huisman et al. Heidelberg: Universitätsverlag Winter, 2012. 9—19. Print.

Moore-Gilbert, Bart. *Postcolonial Life-Writing: Culture, Politics and Self-Representation*. London: Routledge, 2009. Print.

Pouchet Paquet, Sandra. *Caribbean Autobiography: Cultural Identity and Self-Representation*. Madison: U of Wisconsin P, 2002. Print.

Rowe, John Carlos. "Postnationalism, Globalism, and the New American Studies." *The Futures of American Studies*. Ed. Donald E. Pease and Robyn Wiegman. Durham: Duke UP, 2002. 167—82. Print.

Smith, Sidonie. "Presidential Address 2011: Narrating Lives and Contemporary Imaginaries." *PMLA* 126.3 (2011): 564—74. Print.

—, and Julia Watson. *Reading Autobiography: A Guide for Interpreting Life Narratives*. 2nd ed. Minneapolis: U of Minnesota P, 2010. Print.

The following scholars delivered presentations at the 2013 "Auto|Biography across the Americas: Reading beyond Geographic and Cultural Divides" conference:

Rose Mary Allen, University of Curaçao
William L. Andrews, University of North Carolina at Chapel Hill
Leonor Arfuch, Universidad de Buenos Aires

Sergio Barcellos, Brazilian Ministry of Education
Laura Beard, University of Alberta
Bella Brodzki, Sarah Lawrence College
Sarah Brophy, McMaster University
Ricia Anne Chansky, University of Puerto Rico at Mayagüez
Elizeu Clementino de Souza, Universidade do Estado da Bahia
Jocelyn Géliga Vargas, University of Puerto Rico at Mayagüez
Leigh Gilmore, Harvard Divinity School
Joel Haefner, Illinois Wesleyan University
Emily Hipchen, University of West Georgia
Donna Hope, University of the West Indies, Mona
Alfred Hornung, Johannes Gutenberg Universität
Craig Howes, University of Hawai'i at Manoa
Cynthia Huff, Illinois State University
Eva Karpinski, Glendon College, York University
Suely Kofes, Universidade Estadual de Campinas
Eric D. Lamore, University of Puerto Rico at Mayagüez
Joycelyn K. Moody, The University of Texas at San Antonio
Gabriel Jaime Murillo Arango, Universidad de Antioquia
Gerardo Necoechea Gracia, Escuela Nacional de Antropología e Historia
Cruz Miguel Ortíz Cuadra, University of Puerto Rico at Humaçao
Sandra Pouchet Paquet, University of Miami
Julie Rak, University of Alberta
Sidonie Smith, University of Michigan, Ann Arbor
Linda Warley, University of Waterloo
Julia Watson, The Ohio State University
Gillian Whitlock, The University of Queensland
Kari J. Winter, State University of New York at Buffalo

Finding Enslaved Children's Place, Voice, and Agency within the Narrative

Documentos relacionados a niños en los archivos de esclavos en Jamaica

By Colleen A. Vasconcellos

In this essay, I discuss the methodologies behind examining the nature of childhood within Jamaican slavery. By exploring children's experiences through lenses like family, resistance, and culture, I argue that we give them a voice and agency by examining how they carved a place for themselves in the slave community.

En este ensayo, discuto las metodologías envueltas en la examinación de la naturaleza de la niñez dentro del contexto de la esclavitud Jamaiquina. Mediante la exploración de las experiencias infantiles a través de enfoques como la familia, resistencia, y la cultura, argumento que les otorgamos una voz y agencia al examinar cómo ellos han establecido un lugar para ellos mismos dentro de la comunidad esclava.

Children traditionally find themselves on the fringes of historical discourse. Not only was childhood itself a largely unrecognized stage of life until the early modern era, historians generally prefer to examine topics with greater archival meat. As would be expected, source material for any study of childhood can be limited when children are confined to the periphery. Sifting through archival sources for any bit of information can be laborious, time-consuming, and a bit like trying to find a needle in a haystack. As a result, children largely remain silent players in the annals of history.

Source material for a study of the children of slaves is even more elusive. Already part of a marginalized group of people, enslaved children, for the most part, have been lost within the traditional treatments of Atlantic-world slavery—ones that categorically depict the enslaved as victims or voiceless statistics. Because most slaves were illiterate, only a minute fraction put their memories to paper. Furthermore, the complexities of history and memory being what they are, as well as the biases of the abolitionists who collected and helped to publish their stories after their freedom, the validity of those few narratives that we do have is questionable. The quantity and quality of evidence suffers even more from gaps in documentation, age, and environmental deterioration. Outside of accounts written (or related) by Mary Prince, Frederick Douglass, Ottobah Cugoano, and Olaudah Equiano, among others, we really do not have much to go on when reconstructing the experiences of enslaved children and youth. Needless to say, the majority of our sources are from the planters' point of view.

Until the mid-eighteenth century, planters generally viewed the enslaved children on their estates as financial burdens because they had to be supported without any reciprocal contribution to the plantation economy. Planters largely believed that children were a huge risk with little to no investment potential, given the incredibly high infant- and child-mortality rates endemic on plantations throughout the Atlantic world. To estate bookkeepers, who often recorded only the overall number of slaves in their annual reports, enslaved children were an afterthought. Only when the abolitionist movement began to threaten the slave trade, and later slavery itself, did more children begin to appear in the inventories and tax rolls. Even then, children were merely commoditized and catalogued in their own column below a long list of adults.

This kind of attitude from a society that justified a system of race-based slave labor as a "necessary evil" is expected. Planters chose to see only numbers and profits, investments and trade potential, opting to inventory and stratify enslaved Africans and their descendants into groupings based on age, gender, occupation, and degrees of blackness. To them, enslaved children were a nuisance—that is, until the institution of slavery became increasingly threatened by the abolitionist movement, beginning in about the 1750s. Despite the fact that planters began to place more importance on the children laboring in their fields, the white community did not see children. They saw only chattel.

What is surprising, and also incredibly disappointing, is that historians largely ignore these children as well, refusing to see enslaved children as anything more than members of slave families and kinship groups. Cecily Jones has called this troubling gap in the historiography "striking" (92), and I agree. When children are discussed, their stories are mere postscripts to their mothers' experiences as slaves. Not only does this fail to acknowledge that enslaved children have a unique story compared to their mothers', families', or even their kinship group's narrative, but this coopting ultimately fails to recognize that these stories are significant to the study of the African diaspora in their own right. Such disregard for children's experiences as slaves keeps their voices silent and perpetuates their position on the periphery.

By using enslaved children in Jamaica as a case study, this essay discusses how to find their agency in an effort to bring their experiences to the forefront and help them step out of the periphery. Whether African-born or creole, these children lived in an environment that constantly reinforced their status as chattel—a status defined by the nature of their work. If we look, however, we can see a life outside of that labor and begin to piece together a picture of their childhoods, albeit one surrounded by suffering, brutality, and death. We also begin to see how these children struggled and fought for survival in a world that refused to acknowledge and protect their childhoods, and how many children reacted to their enslavement through acts of resistance and violence. Ultimately, this essay examines the various ways in which enslaved children as a whole coped with the hardships of slavery and the realization that they were slaves by considering how they developed physically and psychologically within the plantation complex.

Finding Place

Despite the fact that our knowledge of child development in the slave villages is limited, archival sources do offer glimpses into the experiences of enslaved children on Jamaican estates during the slave era. What these sources reveal are experiences defined by instability, immense poverty, overwork, and death—experiences not unlike those suffered by the adults living and working alongside them. Enslaved children were expected to work twelve- to fifteen-hour days in the hot tropical sun or even longer in the great house, just like enslaved adults. When their work was slow, they suffered the lash just like adults. And they resisted their enslavement and their owners just like enslaved adults when they acted out, stole food, ran away, burned crops, destroyed equipment, and poisoned their owners.

As enslaved children transitioned from the nursery to the field at age five or six, from the children's gang to the second gang at age eight or nine, and eventually to the first gang by age fifteen, the tasks they performed were designed to socialize progressively and acclimate them to their lives as slaves. As members of the children's gang, they picked grass, tended livestock, carried cane husks from the boiling houses to the trash, washed clothes in lye, worked in hot kitchens, served meals, and waited on their masters' every whim. Children who survived long enough to move to the second gang harvested sugar cane and other cash crops, dried tobacco, boiled cane juice into molasses, and refined this substance into sugar. On their transition to the first gang, enslaved children were expected to perform the same work at the same pace as the adults working alongside them.

Uncovering their childhoods within this narrative is no easy task, and that is probably the main reason why their experiences and stories have been over-looked. Beginning in September 2002, I spent ten months searching for their narratives in the archival collections held at three principle holdings in Jamaica: the National Archives of Jamaica in Spanish Town, the National Library of Jamaica in Kingston, and the West India Collection at the University of the West Indies at Mona. The majority of my time was spent pouring over the numerous plantation inventories and letter books, registries, manumission decrees, tax rolls, and Assembly records housed at the National Archives. I spent a month looking through the various collections of folklore and music found at the National Library, in addition to its impressive cache of newspapers and periodicals from the slave era. Another two months were devoted to the examination of the rare books, diaries, and journals housed within the West India Collection at the University of the West Indies at Mona. For nearly a year, I immersed myself in ephemera and inventories, carefully constructing forgotten childhoods by separating the experiences of enslaved children from the larger narrative on slavery in Jamaica. I had no particular methodology in selecting sources; I simply requested materials that fell between the years 1750 and 1838, my specific years of study, and carefully skimmed each source, looking for anything and everything I could find on enslaved children.

Walking into the archives, my main questions concerned the specific nature of childhood within the slave community and how it changed over time. I wanted to tell these children's stories and give them a voice—one that was unique from the adults who lived and toiled beside them. My only plan was to look beyond the obvious and let the sources guide me. For example, following the names of enslaved children who appeared and then disappeared in the Regis-try of the Returns of Slaves confirmed the widely held argument that extremely high infant- and child-mortality rates were endemic on the sugar and coffee plantations in every parish on the island. However, there is much more to the registries than easily observable quantitative evidence. Beginning in 1817, the Assembly of Jamaica required triennial returns from each slaveholder, listing each slave's name, sex, age, color, and country of origin, and any additional remarks, including the mothers' names, if known (Registry 1B|11|7; *Reasons* 40, 56, 64; *Review* 9, 20—21). Once I began to examine these returns in the

National Archives, I instantly saw the wealth of information listed therein and knew that I needed to look much more closely for glimpses of everyday life outside of the work that defined them as slaves.

Immediately after opening the first registry book, I began to see the presence of West African naming traditions among Jamaican-born creoles. Page after page listed enslaved creole children, often of creole parentage, with traditional West African day names, like Quamin and Cudjoe, as well as children with names like Friday and Tuesday, January and December. One afternoon spent with the 1817 returns resulted in the discovery of two creole women of African parentage on two different estates in the parish of Westmoreland who named their children Eboe and Fantee (1B|11|7|9). In the parish of St. George, these same returns listed a twenty-eight-year-old creole woman named Banda (1B|11|7|22). Not only did this information indicate that enslaved children in Jamaica continued to receive West African day names, as was customary in Akan, Ga, and Ewe cultures, some ten and even twenty-five years after the abolition of the transatlantic slave trade, but it also showed that the slave community placed great significance on the names that they gave to their children. Names like these not only passed down West African naming practices to other generations, but they gave enslaved children an individuality outside of their identity as slaves and educated them about their past. Furthermore, this practice showed that the slave community regularly used enslaved children to sustain their national identity in Jamaica and to ensure that it was protected from the destructive process of slavery—proof that their childhoods had meaning.

Outside of the retention and reinvention of African cultural identity in Jamaica, names offer even more complex information when one examines them in the context of family structure. While reading through the Radnor Estate Letter Book at the National Library in Kingston, I found a collection of documents that proved to be very useful not only in describing the nature of children's work in the fields and great house, but also in shedding light on the complex familial formations of the slave villages. In January 1824, for example, a Radnor Estate bookkeeper noted in the estate's inventories that George and Grace's young daughter, Moriah, died of worms. The following year, an enslaved woman named Elfrida gave birth to a daughter, who she named Moriah. Interestingly, I remembered reading that just two years earlier, in 1823, the bookkeeper noted that Elfrida's daughter Grace had died of yaws. I searched the remaining pages in the letter book and observed that the inventories did not duplicate the names of any of the slaves living on the estate like many others in the archives. However, nowhere in the letter book did the bookkeeper state whether Grace and Elfrida were related. That was not surprising, since most bookkeepers did not bother to list such information. Most had no clue about the complex nature of family and kinship in the slave villages. While it could mean that the Radnor Estate managers or owners had a decided interest in the names

Grace and Moriah, the names of these children do propose the real possibility that some sort of bond existed between their families.

While this commentary is merely a snapshot of the lives of two families and their children, other archival sources allowed me to piece together entire lives. While examining the Votes of the Assembly of Jamaica at the National Archives, I was introduced to Molly Matthews, a recently baptized infant born in 1764 to an unnamed slave woman belonging to the Clarendon parish rectory. According to the parish rector, little Molly was the reputed daughter of a white man named David Matthews. Four years after her birth, Matthews applied for Molly's manumission and provided a new slave woman in exchange for her freedom. Unfortunately for Matthews and his daughter, the parish rector stole Molly's replacement and left the parish before her manumission paperwork could be processed. The two were never seen again, and the Clarendon Vestry rescinded the order until Matthews provided a new slave. Matthews never supplied the parish rectory with another enslaved woman, so little Molly remained enslaved. Thirty years later, a more sympathetic Clarendon Vestry championed Molly's case and petitioned the Assembly for her freedom in November 1794. This time, with little debate, the Assembly manumitted Molly and her four children. Interestingly, the Assembly did not require the customary replacement slaves for Molly or her children, and the thirty-year-old mother of four walked out of the Clarendon rectory with her family to begin her life as a free woman (Votes fols. 79–80, 119).

Life histories like Molly's are extremely rare because most information about enslaved children comes in small bits of information that must be assembled together like a puzzle. The fact that I found evidence of both Molly's childhood and adulthood was monumental, and I was hard-pressed to find more than a handful of life histories during my time in the archives. Furthermore, Molly's manumission experience is unique and certainly a result of her connection to the Clarendon rectory. Enslaved children rarely had a champion, including the abolitionists who waxed poetic from across the ocean about freedom. That said, her life experiences are exemplary of what many enslaved children in her situation faced in Jamaica during this period. Molly's status as a mulatto, or the child of an enslaved woman and a white man, was one that set her apart from the rest of the slave community. In addition to having manumission opportunities that most enslaved children only dreamed of, some enslaved children like Molly enjoyed certain benefits from being a child of mixed parentage. Furthermore, although her father attempted to secure her freedom while she was a child, her experiences with the manumission process illustrate the difficulties and setbacks that many people of color faced while trying to attain their freedom. While Molly was lucky to gain the support of the Clarendon Vestry in her adulthood, many progressed through their childhood without even a sliver of hope for freedom.

As I started piecing stories like these together, a pattern began to form and I began to see a link between the changing nature of childhood, the changing nature of slavery, and the growth, influence, and impact of the British abolitionist movement during my period of study. Planters and members of the British Parliament modified their definitions of value, risk, and investment as attitudes toward abolition and abolitionists changed. Simply put, the abolitionist movement forced the planters to re-evaluate the economic viability of enslaved children. Before abolitionist sentiment threatened the slave trade, children were nothing more than a risk and a hindrance to Jamaican planters and overseers. Once the abolition of the slave trade became a possibility, however, children, in the minds of Jamaican planters, changed from a risk to a necessity as they began to envision children as a means of delaying the inevitability of abolition. Planters' ideas of child worth expanded as they gradually came to recognize enslaved children as a means of securing the profitability of their estates. As a result, Jamaican planters soon depended on slave youth just as they had depended on the slave trade before English abolitionists threatened the slave supply.

Needless to say, enslaved children became more visible in the archival sources once they became more important to the planters. They were not just slaves; they were sons and daughters, members of complex familial units and kinship groups, cultural agents, and contributors to their own household economies. The abolitionist movement provided an excellent opportunity for me to see how their childhoods changed over time, as well as how these changes affected the quality of life for Jamaica's enslaved children. The more archival texts I found, the more I began to understand childhood as not only an important concept defined by planter opinion and manipulation, but one also affected by the institution of slavery. These children were fighters, and they continued their struggle for survival despite the increased pressures put upon them. Yet, at the same time, children inadvertently gained leverage from the abolitionist movement, using it as a window of opportunity to negotiate their own place and voice as historical agents.

Finding Voice through Agency

One can only surmise how children's experiences as slaves shaped or obstructed their psychological development, but the archival sources do suggest that children acted out their frustrations in many ways. While examining issues of the *Royal Gazette* and the *Kingston Chronicle* housed at the National Library, I was impressed by the number of enslaved boys and girls whose names appeared in the runaway lists as having "absconded" from their estates. One particular boy named John appeared a few times within the available issues, and I was struck not only by his bravery, but also by his tenacity. I first ran across John in an announcement of a public auction in Spanish Town, where he was sold in

August 1781 (*Royal Gazette* 19 Aug. 1781). I recorded the information in my notes, mostly in an effort to compare the fluctuations in market prices for enslaved children. However, I saw John appear again in another issue: six months after his purchase at public auction, John's new owners included him in the runaway lists, believing that he was "lurking around" Spanish Town in search of his mother, who lived there as a slave (*Royal Gazette* 2 Mar. 1782).

Most runaway advertisements simply list the name and, occasionally, the estimated age of the slave in question. They usually appear in a grid of boxes, with or without the obligatory sketch of a chained slave en route or the cartoonish "Sambo" profile, filling the first few pages of each edition of the newspaper. Every so often we are lucky to find an advertisement that lists certain characteristics or descriptors, included by the owners to help better identify the runaway if found. This advertisement for John was extremely rare in that it added familial information, giving me much more insight into who he was and his reasons for running away. This added insight helped me construct a backstory that I was rarely privy to as a historian. While the archival sources do not indicate whether John was reunited with his mother, this was not the last time I saw John's name appear in the lists, suggesting that he had not found her. Or perhaps he did and he ran away from time to time to visit her, which was common among slaves, regardless of their age. Sadly, the National Library had a limited number of issues of the *Royal Gazette*, and I was left wondering how John's story turned out. What was clearly evident, however, was John's refusal to accept his status as a slave or his separation from his family.

Small acts of resistance like running away and destroying tools and property pepper the Jamaican archival sources, indicating to me that enslaved children reacted to their situation as slaves just like enslaved adults. Some children resorted to alcohol as an escape, a habit that many believe was encouraged by parents. The manager of Egypt Estate, Thomas Thistlewood, noted one instance in his diaries where a boy named Jimmy "was very drunk, with Rum he Stole out of the Bottle" (7 July 1754). As I scanned the few surviving logs from the plantation hospitals, I wondered whether the children I saw listed among the patients were there because they were sick or because they were feigning sickness like they had seen many adults do over the years. I suspect it was a little bit of both, but the plantation doctors never offered an opinion, probably preferring to believe that children were incapable of such deception—or they simply did not care.

Records of slave courts are one of the few places that enable scholars to learn about how slaves voiced their opinions on and feelings toward the institution of slavery and its eventual abolition, thereby making them vital in understanding how children reacted to their situation as slaves. While enslaved children frequently appeared before the island's slave courts for committing various acts of theft, violence, vandalism, and arson, and disturbing the peace, other children appeared for directing "Violent and Indecent language in the

Public Street" toward free and white residents (Port Royal; St. Ann). Although the courts defined these acts as "crimes," it is more likely that they were merely acts of resistance from the perspective of the children themselves. In other words, some enslaved children turned to "crime" as an outlet for their frustrations.

While examining a copy of Matthew "Monk" Lewis's well-known *Journal of a West Indian Proprietor* in the West India Collection at the University of the West Indies at Mona, his account of one girl who appeared before the Westmoreland Slave Court sometime between 1815 and 1817 piqued my interest. Lewis, owner of the Cornwall Estate in Westmoreland, described the case of a fifteen-year-old girl named Minetta, who allegedly attempted to murder her owner with some poisoned brandy. In her defense, he recounted, Minetta argued that she had added the substance at the direction of her grandmother, who never indicated that it was poison. Although the girl pleaded with the court that it was an accident, Lewis described a sociopath who had "stood by the bed to see her master drink the poison," witnessing his death "without one expression of surprise or pity" (178—79).

Unfortunately, the Westmoreland Slave Court records have not survived and are not available in any of the holdings on the island, so I had to take Lewis at his word. However, the story is still useful. Enslaved children like Minetta did appear before the slave courts for more serious crimes, indicating that they were capable of resisting their situation as strongly as adults. Furthermore, Minetta's story helps to dismantle the common reaction we have to a child appearing before a court of law for murder. We prefer to see a child who is harmless, innocent. It is a natural reaction to believe the girl's suggestion that she was merely a puppet controlled by her grandmother. We want to see her as a victim too. But what happens to a child when they are in a situation that forces them into adulthood at an extremely early age? What happens when they are forced to survive that situation by any means necessary? What happens to a child when they begin to fight back?

This set of questions brings me to Sally. I first met Sally during my time in the West India Collection at the University of the West Indies at Mona, where I spent nearly three weeks combing through the diaries of Thomas Thistlewood, the second son of an English tenant farmer who had come to the island in 1751 in search of his fortune. Unlike most Englishmen who came to the Caribbean, Thistlewood stayed until his death, working first as a hired manager for Vineyard Pen and later as an owner of Egypt Estate in Westmoreland. More importantly, Thistlewood kept a detailed, frank diary of those thirty-seven years spent in Jamaica, leaving us fourteen thousand pages of his daily thoughts on and observations of plantation life. His diaries are impressive to say the least, and they provide us with the rare opportunity to read about the innermost workings of the plantation complex.

According to the diary, Thistlewood purchased Sally, a young Congolese girl of about nine or ten years of age, in April 1762 from a local attorney in Savanna-la-Mar, intending for her to work as a seamstress on Egypt Estate (Thistlewood 1 Apr. 1762; Burnard 218). He did not note how long she had been on the island or under what conditions she lived before he purchased her. Research on the horrors of the middle passage gave me an idea of what she had been through, and I knew that she was lucky to have survived the traumas of the trans-Atlantic slave trade. I could only imagine the fragile psyche of this young girl, who had been ripped from her family and homeland only to be taken to a place where most Africans died within three to five years of their arrival.

As I read further into the diary, Sally's life story unfolded, and I began to understand her as a survivor. Sally's sale to Thistlewood was perhaps the worst place she could have gone. The epitome of sadism, he took immense pleasure in torturing and punishing his slaves in horrific ways, such as the Derby's Dose—a punishment of his own invention that involved having one slave defecate in the mouth of another (Hall 104; Burnard 31). In addition to his infamous brutality, the man was a vile and highly sexed predator with unlimited access to a pool of women and girls who were often powerless to defend themselves from his advances; typically, he recorded these encounters in some detail. In 1751 alone, Thistlewood had frequent sexual liaisons with at least twelve of the twenty-six women and six of the nine girls belonging to the estate (Burnard 28). Throughout the pages of his diaries, he boasted of his virility and prowess, cataloguing each rape in sordid detail, usually in Latin, right alongside the minutiae of the everyday. It would not be until 1816 that the Assembly of Jamaica would attempt to protect girls of Sally's age from men like Thistlewood by enacting a law stipulating that any carnal knowledge of a female slave below the age of ten was punishable by death (Laws of Jamaica). Unfortunately, with the exception of historian Trevor Burnard, scholars have been more interested in Thistlewood's antics and sexual exploits than the slaves he terrorized on a daily basis. The fact that children like Sally entered into this macabre lifestyle never occurs to them.

Within a month of her purchase, Thistlewood apprenticed Sally to Doll, his master seamstress. According to Thistlewood's plan, young Sally would work under Doll's tutelage as an apprentice until she had sufficiently learned her trade and could be listed in the slave inventories as a seamstress in her own right. In October 1765, three years later, a frustrated Doll sent young Sally back to him because she was not minding her work and was unable to develop the skills that Thistlewood desired from her. Incensed, Thistlewood put the girl in the stocks as punishment for wasting his time and money; then, after an appropriate time that he deemed necessary, Thistlewood released her and sent her to the fields as punishment for her inability to learn the specialized trade he had intended for her (Thistlewood 2 May 1762; Hall 137; Burnard 218–21).

After her release from the stocks and her return to the fields, Sally became quite the troublemaker. This behavior was undoubtedly a response to her situation and to Thistlewood's frequent sexual attacks, and she ran away with some degree of regularity. In fact, the first instance occurred not long after being released from the stocks, at the young age of twelve or thirteen. Even as a child, Sally refused to accept her situation. Burnard gives an excellent but sad account of Sally's troubled life on Egypt Estate, painting the picture of a girl who was so consumed by anger at her situation that eventually she was even shunned by the slave community itself. Unable to deal with her frequent running away, acts of theft, fights with fellow slaves, and self-destruction, Thistlewood transported Sally off the island in November 1784, and that is when we lose track of her (Hall 137; Burnard 218—21; Vasconcellos 111n94).

So what does all of this commentary tell us? Sally's story is one of a girl who refused to accept her status as a slave. Sally was angry, incensed at the life that fate had given her, and she acted out consistently as a result. Not only did she resist, she fought. Furthermore, while this example is a rather extreme ending to only one enslaved girl's experience under plantation slavery in Jamaica, Sally's story does shed light on the nature of slavery in Jamaica and the children who were part of this system. It was not uncommon for an enslaved child of Sally's age to be given the opportunity to escape the back-breaking labor of the fields and improve their station in life by learning a more skilled craft or trade. Yet, they undoubtedly lived with the knowledge that their apprenticeship was a tenuous one, and they could return to those fields in the blink of an eye if their work was faulty, slow, or unacceptable in the eyes of their owners. Some children, like Sally, refused to go back without a fight.

As Jamaican planters placed increasing responsibility on enslaved children to lead them toward the economic stability and profitability they craved, enslaved children in Jamaica continued their struggle for survival. Forced to grow up at an extremely early age, enslaved children in Jamaica would never escape the traumas they faced on a daily basis, despite their acts of resistance and violence. Although we will never know the extent of how their experiences as slaves damaged their psychological and emotional development, one can imagine how a life filled with death, disease, and harsh labor affected these children. One can engage with certain archival documents to see glimpses of how they reacted to that life.

As the nature of slavery and childhood changed on the island during this period, we see how enslaved children struggled to survive and identify with the world around them. For Jamaican planters, childhood was an economic investment; for enslaved children in Jamaica, childhood was a rushed and contested process filled with immense poverty, hard labor, familial separation, and death. As these children moved from gang to gang, however, we see enslaved children attempting to negotiate their place within the plantation complex through acts of violence, theft, self-destruction, and even murder. Forced into adulthood before their time, enslaved children in Jamaica would never escape the traumas they faced on a daily basis. As a result, their short childhoods ended almost as soon as they began.

That said, their childhoods were, and are, important, and their experiences add depth to an already prolific historiography on the African diaspora. Although many of our archival sources chart changes in the childhood of a slave from a planter's point of view, exploring children's experiences as slaves through lenses like family, resistance, culture, status, and labor gives them a voice by examining how they carved a place for themselves in the slave community. In doing so, we give them agency, as well as learning a great deal about their childhoods from the inside, along with more about slavery in the Atlantic world. What is revealed is a more textured, complex, and succinct explanation of how the childhoods of slaves progressed and changed throughout the eighteenth and nineteenth centuries. In the end, we can tell the story of an overlooked childhood—one that was often defined by the Jamaican planters, but always contested and redefined by the enslaved children themselves.

University of West Georgia

Disclosure Statement

No potential conflict of interest was reported by the author.

Works Cited

Assembly of Jamaica. Laws of Jamaica. 57 George III, c. 25 (1816). Natl. Archives of Jamaica, Spanish Town.
—. Votes of the Assembly, 1794—1795. Natl. Archives of Jamaica, Spanish Town.
Burnard, Trevor. *Mastery, Tyranny, and Desire: Thomas Thistlewood and His Slaves in the Anglo-Jamaican World*. Chapel Hill: U of North Carolina P, 2004. Print.
Hall, Douglas. *In Miserable Slavery: Thomas Thistlewood in Jamaica, 1750—86*. 2nd ed. Mona: U of the West Indies P, 1999. Print.
Jones, Cecily. "'If This Be Living I'd Rather Be Dead': Enslaved Youth, Agency and Resistance on an Eighteenth-Century Jamaican Estate." *History of the Family* 12.2 (2007): 92—103. Print.
Lewis, Matthew Gregory. *Journal of a West Indian Proprietor: Kept During a Residence in the Island of Jamaica*. London: John Murray, 1834. Print.
Port Royal Summary Slave Trials, 1819—1834. Natl. Archives of Jamaica, Spanish Town.
Radnor Estate Letter Book, 1822—1826. Ms. 180. Natl. Lib. of Jamaica, Kingston.

Reasons for Establishing a Registry of Slaves in the British Colonies. London, 1814. Print.

Registry of the Returns of Slaves, 1817—1832. 1B|11|7. Natl. Archives of Jamaica, Spanish Town.

A Review of the Reasons Given for Establishing a Registry of Slaves in the British Colonies. London: Hachard, 1816. Print.

Royal Gazette [Kingston] 19 Aug. 1781. Microfilm.

Royal Gazette [Kingston] 2 Mar. 1782. Microfilm.

St. Ann Slave Court, 1787—1814. Natl. Lib. of Jamaica, Kingston.

Thistlewood, Thomas. Thomas Thistlewood Diaries, 1751—1786. Monson 31|1—31|35. West India Collection, U of the West Indies at Mona.

Vasconcellos, Colleen A. *Slavery, Childhood, and Abolition in Jamaica, 1788—1838*. Athens: U of Georgia P, 2015. Print.

On Racial Silence and Salience: Narrating "African Things" in Puerto Rican Oral History

Sobre silencio y prominencia racial: Narrando "cosas africanas" en la historia oral de puertorriqueña

By Jocelyn A. Géliga Vargas

Puerto Rican identity has been constructed on the myth of racial harmony—the supposedly harmonious *mestizaje* of Taíno, Spanish, and African roots. While the ideology of *mestizaje* has been replaced with a more balanced multiculturalism in other parts of Latin America, the silencing of Afro-Puerto Ricanness has remained entrenched in the culture. Afro-Puerto Rican oral histories can counter discursive silence with salience. Afro-Puerto Rican Testimonies: An Oral History Project in Western Puerto Rico collected the oral histories of Afro-Puerto Rican narrators who bring to the fore the complex operations of situated Afro-diasporic memory work.

La identidad puertorriqueña ha sido construida a base de mitos de harmonía racial, el supuesto mestizaje harmonioso del Taíno y las raíces españolas y africanas. A pesar de que la ideología del mestizaje ha sido remplazada por un multiculturalismo más balanceado en otras partes de American Latina, el silenciamiento de la afropuertorriqueñidad se ha mantenido atrincherado. Testimonios afropuertorriqueños: Un proyecto de Historia Oral en el Oeste de Puerto Rico recopiló las historias orales de narradores afropuertorriqueños que ponen delante las complejas operaciones situadas en el trabajo de memoria Afro-diásporo.

Lynching is unknown in Puerto Rico, the legal system makes no distinction along color lines and everyone marries or "shacks up with" whoever his carnal desire dictates. This was a contributing factor to the disappearance of the Indian, whose blood was gradually diluted through *mestizaje*. The same phenomenon has been occurring with African blood .... In Puerto Rico we barely have any remaining pure blacks, except in some limited areas in the coastal region. (Blanco 122)

Tomás Blanco's now canonical treatise on racial prejudice in Puerto Rico has been credited with legitimizing and popularizing a conciliatory narrative about racial difference in Puerto Rican history. Cultural critic Arcadio Díaz Quiñones argues that it renders a vision, a set of historical myths and social and spiritual values, which has endured in dominant cultural and political discourses (qtd. in Blanco 16). Blanco's views on race relations and his scientistic rationale for heralding racial unity in Puerto Rico encapsulate a history of racialization and its silencing that merits critical interrogation in the present. This essay draws from an Afro-Puerto Rican oral-history project conducted from 2007 to 2010 in two western Puerto Rican towns. This collaborative research initiative project collected thirty-three extensive oral-history interviews with a diverse group of narrators.[1] My objective is to call into question the trope of silence around issues of race, racial difference, and racial hierarchies in contemporary Puerto Rican history, and to examine the production and performance of Afro-diasporic narrations composed in the interstices of memory and experience in order to reveal, rearticulate, and restore the significance of race in contemporary Puerto Rico.

In the first part of the essay, I address the issue of racial silence in Puerto Rico in order to contextualize the oral-history project. The second part examines the imbrications of racial silence and racial salience in an effort to unveil their complex and complicit relation. I engage with the life stories of Afro-Puerto Ricans to argue that the apparent silencing of racial discourse and racial identities in Puerto Rico has indeed contributed to the internalization of a logic of (de)racialized domination that reveals the multivalent, unstable, and fragmentary nature of silences. As Rodríguez-Silva succinctly puts it, silences are both "tools of domination and a means of survival" (13). Silences, that is, cede voice to the force of domination but also uncover its tensions, contradictions, and fissures, and, most importantly, ignite the possibility of resistance (14). By tapping into the repositories of individual and collective memory, I examine how the (self-)negation of racial difference coexists with its affirmation in ways that reveal the "contextual, contested, and contingent" (Scott 36) nature of Afro-Puerto Rican identities. Moreover, I discuss how, by remembering their lives, the narrators engage in a semantic and political power struggle that unlatches nuanced forms of racialized difference in terms that can be empowering, validating, and redemptive. Highlighting the relational nature of oral history—and of life writing in general—I also address how self-narration is not a means of revealing the Self, but of rendering it meaningful to oneself and to others in the vexed process of imagining community and staking belongingness.

On Racial Silences

It is an often-stated platitude that open discussions about race are taboo in Puerto Rico. Race talk is regarded as impolite, and racial identities are considered irrelevant, foreign, and incongruous with our formation as a mixed *pueblo* that has shaped itself and come of age in a balmy climate of racial harmony. The study of race in Puerto Rico is but a marginal area of inquiry in academia, which has made few inroads into curricular design at both the basic and higher education levels, and has left no trace in public-policy debates. Publicly voicing a racialized sense of Self (especially in terms that do not assert whiteness) is generally regarded as a sign of psychosocial maladjustment and|or ideological belligerence.

Yet notions of race, ethnicity, culture, history, and nationality have clashed and collided in efforts to characterize and plot the path of the Puerto Rican *pueblo* in modern history, especially since the transformations effected by the US's occupation of Puerto Rico in 1898. Surely, these complex processes of nation formation in a colonial context have not engendered a singular, unitary narrative of *la puertorriqueñidad* ("Puerto Ricanness")? Competing and conflicting notions of our national identity have vied for legitimacy in public and collective memory, and in official and popular discourses and practices.[2] However, they converge in their determination to deflect attention from race as an organizing principle in Puerto Rico's social, political, economic, and cultural history.

In the introduction to *Beyond Slavery*, Darién J. Davis notes that the ideology of *mestizaje*, or the racial mixing of indigenous, European, and African traits and legacies, became official dogma in most of Latin America in the first decades of the twentieth century (11). In their introductory chapter to their comprehensive anthology on blackness in Latin America, Arlene Torres and Norman E. Whitten qualify this ideology as an "explicit master symbol" in the region (7), which—as Wade (*Race*), Miller, and others have demonstrated—acquired a variety of interpretations and representations in national narratives across the region. In the case of Puerto Rico, this symbol has been invariably depicted as the gradual, progressive, and harmonic fusion of three signs: Taínos (regarded as the original inhabitants of Borikén—today, Puerto Rico), Spanish (a synecdoche for European colonizers and settlers), and Africans (generally represented as slaves bereft of any history prior to their arrival in the New World and belonging to a homogenous national group). Redolent with scientistic rhetoric, this additive logic refers to these groups as the three "elements" or "roots" that converged in the formation of the Puerto Rican subject. The enthusiastic stirring of this melting pot, however, stems from the attribution of particular flavors to each foundational ingredient. These attributes have been historically and strategically ordered in a value-laden hierarchy that tends to romanticize Taíno ancestry, enshrine Spanish genealogy, and debase and distance African heritage.[3]

The reification of European ancestry and the ejection of African ancestry are firmly entrenched edicts in Latin American and Hispanic Caribbean nation-building projects (Davis; Andrews; Torres and Whitten). More recent research suggests that the Eurocentric ideology of monocultural *mestizaje* has given way to ideologies of multiculturalism that have made Afro-descendant populations visible in parts of Central America, the Andes, and Brazil (Rahier 1). In Puerto Rico, however, the ideology of *mestizaje* cannot be memorialized as a past historical moment; in fact, a growing body of research confirms that Hispanophilia stands strong as one of the master lessons disseminated across the public education system.[4]

The displacement of African ancestry in spatial and temporal planes and its concomitant denial of the power dynamics that gave rise to African presence in the national territory are conspicuous, if not concerted, attempts to block consciousness about the undoubtedly racialized (Afro-)Puerto Rican experience. However, these official maneuvers to suppress race talk, repress racialized memory, and erase race as a marker of identity (and difference and inequality) enact a silence that speaks. The story of our harmonious fusion is bound to register the tones it orchestrates and thus to encounter the polyphony, if not the cacophony, of its score. Michel Foucault urges us to think of silence as plural and to conceive of silences as an integral part of the strategies that underlie and permeate discourses. "There is no binary division to be made between what one says and what one does not say; we must try to determine the different ways of not saying such things, how those who can and those who cannot speak of them are distributed, which type of discourse is authorized, or which form of discretion is required in either case" (Foucault 27). This insight, along with Foucault's understanding of silence as a situated speech act that can be understood only within particular discursive practices inscribed in specific socio-historical contexts, compels us to map the ways in which the technologies of silence in Puerto Rican history operate to retrace and reinstate the salience of race.

Literary and cultural workers have been among the most prominent figures in challenging the Hispanophilic *mestizaje* ideology and forefronting the salience of race. In a seminal article about a field he coined "Afro-Puerto Rican Cultural Studies," Juan Giusti Cordero critically assesses the disruptions enacted by two Afro-Puerto Rican cultural and political movements in the twentieth century: *cultura negroide* and *antillanismo*. The former spanned the period from the 1920s to the 1960s and highlighted, against the grain of canonical literature, Afro-Puerto Rican cultural manifestations, even if it constructed them "Eurocentrically, as unique, primitive, erotic and irrational" (Giusti Cordero 69). Its successor, *antillanismo*, gained momentum in the 1960s and was influenced by the Puerto Rican community in the US. According to Giusti Cordero, *antillanista* cultural expressions more explicitly engaged Africa and the African diaspora in the Caribbean. But they did not regard African presence as constitutive of a heterogeneous Puerto Rican social culture in the present, but displaced it as a past legacy connected to slavery and slave resistance (63). For the author, the ways in which *cultura negroide* and *antillanismo* erupted in the identitarian discourse in Puerto Rico effectively racialized cultural discussion, but, revealing the multiplicity of silences iterated by Foucault, blocked consideration and discussion of "the various social groups that shaped and were shaped by Afro-Puerto Rican tradition," and thus failed to advance a concrete and historical sense of *afropuertorriqueño* culture (71).

In a different register, renowned Nuyorican poet Víctor Hernández Cruz brought to the fore the complex issues of the silence and salience of race, and of African descent, in his autobiographical poem "African Things." He does so by summoning his grandmother to "speak to me & tell me of african things" (Hernández Cruz line 10). His choice of interlocutor evokes the classic poem by *cultura negroide* forefather Fortunato Vizcarrondo, "¿Y tu agüela a'onde ejtá?" ("And Yo' Granma, Where She At?"), which criticized the refusal of Puerto Ricans to disclose or admit to African ancestry. The poetic image of the grandmother as the bearer of Afro-diasporic memory is not exclusively a Puerto Rican phenomenon, but in this context it becomes a transgression of the paternalistic racial myth of the Great Puerto Rican Family, with the Hispanic patriarch at the helm, upon which our national history and identity have been officially built. Hernández Cruz's poem thus issues a transgressive call for the embodied voicing of silenced, complicit Afro-Puerto Rican memory: "dance & tell me black African things | i know you know" (lines 15–16).

Over the last two decades, the study of race in Puerto Rico has received increased scholarly attention. Important volumes have reappraised the centrality of race in, and the maneuvers to displace it from, the narrative of the nation.[5] However, few interventions offer a sustained rejoinder to the poetics and politics voiced by Hernández Cruz and Giusti Cordero in the sense of examining Afro-Puerto Ricanness as a living phenomenon—as an embodied history that is a constitutive element of who we are and who we might become.

Employing oral history not just as a set of methodological techniques, but as a collaborative engagement in life narration, our research collective embarked on the project of collecting the life stories of contemporary Afro-Puerto Ricans. Even though oral history in the Puerto Rican archipelago is often associated with decolonizing projects (Díaz Royo), our intent was not to document how Afro-Puerto Ricans have challenged the silencing effects of nationalist ideologies, but to record Afro-Puerto Rican memories as an active and relational process of the creation of meanings about the experience of racialization in Puerto Rico. In other words, taking stock of the claims raised by Giusti Cordero, Hernández Cruz, and others, we set out to make inroads in the study of Afro-Puerto Rican histories and cultures, in the inevitably plural and partial ways in which these are remembered and narrated.

The section that follows examines the perimeters of racial silence and the conditions on which racial salience is articulated in our attempt to document contemporary Afro-Puerto Rican histories.

On Racial Salience

A caveat is in order before proceeding to discuss the oral-history project. Although a genealogy of the term *afropuertorriqueño* has yet to be established, its appearance is certainly more recent than that of equivalent terms in other Caribbean and Latin American nations—notably Cuba, where anthropologist Fernando Ortiz coined the term *afrocubano* in the 1910s, and Brazil, where the term *afro-brasileiro* was popularized by Gilberto Freyre in the 1930s. Giusti Cordero rightly noted in the 1990s that the term *afropuertorriqueño* was not a universally accepted term in Puerto Rico. Over the past two decades, scholars and cultural workers in Puerto Rico and the diaspora have gradually adopted the term *afropuertorriqueño* as a substitute for "black" Puerto Ricans, Puerto Ricans "of color," or Puerto Ricans who are presumed to have, or manifest having, "African descent."[6] However, for the general population, the term remains elusive, if not foreign.

Thus, when we launched our oral-history project under the title "Testimonios afropuertorriqueños: Un proyecto de historia oral en el oeste de Puerto Rico,"[7] we placed our prospective narrators in a racial category that was not their own, but was indebted to contemporary scholarly, cultural, and policy debates in Puerto Rico, the Spanish Caribbean, and that slippery region scholars refer to as Afro-Latin America.[8] In our project's effort to challenge the entrenched myths of harmonious racial *mestizaje*, we strategically but problematically imposed an Afro-diasporic identity onto our so-called "oral informants." Interestingly, the life narratives that were thoughtfully composed over the course of multiple encounters, engaged conversations, and complicit relational exchanges expressed a minimal sense of connection and, indeed, almost no reference to the polysemic referent of Africa, the dislocation of the Afro-diaspora, Afro-descendants at large, or African ancestry at home.

As I discussed in the preceding section, the metanarrative of the Puerto Rican *pueblo* has emphasized racial harmony as the fait accompli of our modern colonial society, while tuning out our connection to Africa and the African diasporas as a vestige of a distant past. Godreau has demonstrated that this temporal dislocation of Afro-descendents in contemporary Puerto Rico operates in tandem with a spatial dislocation that conceptualizes blackness (and thus African ancestry) "as a singularity, as an exception" ("Folkloric" 179), which can be found only in ever-shrinking sectors of the nation regarded as traditional or, to borrow Linda Tuhiwai Smith's term, as a "primitive" residue in our historical development (30). A deliberate decision in our methodological design is worth mentioning for its likely impingement on the narrators' processes of racial (self-) construction. In an effort to challenge the entrenched circumscription of African ancestry and blackness in Puerto Rico to particular regions in the north-eastern part of the archipelago, we conducted our study in two western towns (Aguadilla and Hormigueros), which are not considered locales of significant black presence in the archipelago. It is in the context of this systematic purging of blackness and Africanness from the national character and territory that the narrators' apparent dissociation from Afro-diasporic identities and allegiances must be gauged. Moreover, oral history's ability to record the processes through which subjects come to self-knowledge and self-narration allows us to explore the extent to which the Afro-diasporic, or, specifically, lo afropuertorriqueño, might be less contingent on reconstructions of a common past or passage than on the recognition of particular scripts which shape the stories of the Self that racialized subjects create in the varied and variable locations they inhabit. According to Judith Butler, "the 'I' who begins to tell its story can tell it only according to recognizable norms of life narration" (52), and thus must circuit its narration through an externality. Disentangling the operations of these norms of life narration, as well as their confines and fissures in the process of narrating the Self, enables us to track Other Afro-diasporic stories and identities that have remained not untold, but certainly unheard in the pursuit of historical coherence and progress.

In what follows, I focus on the oral histories of three narrators from Hormigueros to discuss three central themes that traverse the narratives as the narrators reflect on their personal histories of racialization.[9] I begin with a discussion of the dynamics of racial silence and its implications for remembering, voicing, and locating the racialized Self. I proceed to examine how racial salience is rearticulated in ways that concurrently affirm and deny racial difference and racial hierarchies. Then, I elaborate on the relational nature of life narration to discuss how racial salience is encoded to make the Self intelligible to and integrated with others.

Roberto and the Limits of Racial Silences

Roberto, aged eighty-four, was born in Mayagüez but spent his childhood, adolescence, and most of his adult life in the Central Azucarera La Eureka, a sugar mill that operated in Hormigueros for almost a century until its gradual closing and dismantling between the late 1970s and early 1980s. He went to school in Hormigueros until the eighth grade but was unable to pursue further studies because of his family's lack of resources. He began working at Eureka "illegally" (*escondío*) at sixteen and continued working there for almost forty years until the sugar mill's closure.

The people of Hormigueros call us *los negros de la Eureka* [the black folks from Eureka]. It sounds bad, no? It's dismissive. When people are from some place they call them the residents of that place but not "the white ones" or "the pale ones." Since, as the saying goes, "the only worthy black thing is petroleum," it sounds real bad when they call us that. I know I'm black and I'm from Eureka, but I don't think I'm bad. My teacher used to say that I was *un negro blanco* [a white black]. I don't think that phrase was right because there are bad white people and bad black people, but she didn't mean any harm. I don't see why anyone's color has to be rejected or even mentioned. What is wrong with my color? What is so evil about being black? Who is to blame for one's skin color? Who's to blame for one's ugliness? Everybody would like to be as attractive as possible, to have money and health and everything in abundance. But life is not like that, you cannot change yourself. The other day I was walking in the neighborhood and some kids started looking at me weird and laughing. Maybe those kids are not used to seeing black people. There are less black people around here now; there might be more over there in San Juan, but here they've been mixing. Yeah, people are different in town now, it's like they've become more "refined," they've "refined" the race and you don't see black folks as much around here. For me what we need is not to become white, but to not focus on color, to focus on oneself and what one has. Being black has nothing to do with one's life. Yes, perhaps someone will reject you, but it's not everybody. Black is just a color; there has to be a little bit of everything in life.

One topic that surfaces in Roberto's testimony, and recurs in many of the life narratives we recorded, is his insistence that there is no need to identify oneself or others racially and, specifically, that there is no need to use the word *negro*, because it sounds "bad." He is painfully aware of the social connotations of the dichotomous racial markings of black and white; throughout his interview, he decries the negative associations attached to *los eurekeños* (constructed as homogenously black) by the dominant (constructed as homogeneously white) sectors of Hormigueros. Although Roberto recollects few personal experiences of racial discrimination, and those he recalls are minimized as unintentional and devoid of real consequences, he vividly articulates the ways in which the categorical ascription of blackness to the former residents and workers of Eureka entailed negative consequences for their social conditions and perceived moral character in Hormigueros. He wishes to disavow all racial markings as simply colors, but he is particularly wary of, and uncomfortable with, the term *negro*. Blackness is, in his narrative, something that happens, but it is neither desired nor convenient. In order to navigate the tension between inevitability and undesirability, Roberto resolves that one's life (his life?) is independent of one's (his?) blackness (race?).

In a context in which racial difference is systematically suppressed and blackness is spatially and temporally dissociated from the body of the nation, Roberto's efforts to deprecate the word *negro* and to void it of significance—if not substance—for his Self are an understandable act of self-construction. As Sidonie Smith and Julia Watson succinctly put it, "people tell the stories of their lives through the cultural scriptures available to them" (56). Roberto is neither renouncing nor rejecting his blackness; he is, however, repudiating the salience of blackness in situated discourses and practices of social organization that marked his life in and outside of Eureka.

Roberto's narrative, however, should not be cursorily read as a simple reproduction of the erasure of blackness that permeates official discourses about *la puertorriqueñidad*. The ways in which he invokes time and space to string together his story reveal that he is neither rejecting blackness nor distancing himself from it. He does wish racial markers away, but not because of a denial of racial difference; he is acutely aware that, three decades after the closing of the Eureka sugar mill, locals still erect rigid boundaries between the *hormiguereños* and the *eurekeños*. Reflecting on his life at eighty-four, Roberto does not remember exactly when he moved to Lavadero, an impoverished barrio located less than five miles from Eureka, where many *eurekeños* received land-grant plots after the closing of the mill and their forcible relocation. Yet he remembers that he was brought there against his will by relatives. His sense of estrangement in this locality is captured in the anecdote about the barrio children who pointed at him mockingly. He rationalizes their action by noting that black people are less visible "here now." Thus, he evokes the temporal and spatial dislocation of blackness iterated in official discourses, but does so in ways that shed light on how racial silencing might also have empowering and redemptive potentials for the Self.

In order to penetrate the matrix of racial silences that transpires from Roberto's story, it is useful to draw from Smith and Watson's notion of "autobiographical acts" as units of analysis for the interpretation of life narratives. One such act is the production of an autobiographical "I," which is not monolithic, but composed of multiple "I's (71). Two of them are particularly relevant to this discussion: the narrating "I," the persona of the person "who wants to tell, or is coerced into telling, a story about the self" (72), and the narrated "I," or "the version of the self that the narrating 'I' chooses to constitute through recollection for the reader" (73).[10] In Roberto's here and now—his occasional and locational site of narration (Smith and Watson 69) as an aging member of a community of memory whose referents have been decimated through dispossession and reconfigured through displacement—Roberto's narrating "I" takes recourse in the affirmation of his identity as black, as *negro*. This rhetorical maneuver allows him to clad the narrated "I" with the armor of endurance: he has survived the dislocations entailed in the passing of time; he is still standing there, neither hiding nor seeking to refine—read whiten—himself.

Irma and the Intricacies of Racial Salience

Irma, aged sixty, was born and raised in Eureka along with her six brothers. Her father was a "regular laborer" in the sugar mill, and her brothers also worked there in their youth; her mother cooked and ironed for seasonal workers who came to Eureka during the harvesting season. Irma completed some high school in Hormigueros and later, in her mid-twenties, joined the Eureka diaspora in New York City for "about five years." She eventually returned to Eureka and was among the last residents to abandon the premises in the early 1990s.

> I always remember that the first gift my father gave me on Three Kings' Day was an Indian doll. I have a lot of good memories from Eureka and I get nostalgic; you see? I'm already crying. Wherever I go, I always say, "I'm from Eureka, I was born in Eureka and I'm proud of it." It was a poor and humble place, but we distinguished ourselves because we were very close, we were always together, we were a family. We used to say that Eureka was the capital of Hormigueros because we were not intimidated by the folks from here [Hormigueros]. I used to go to school wearing fifty-cent shoes handed down by the government, but my uniform was always neatly pressed; my mom always kept us very clean. The people from Hormigueros claimed to be better than us. They would say, "Urgh, those *negros* from Eureka!" And we would say, "We are the *negros* from Eureka, but you have to respect us." We would feel bad and get angry. I always talked back to them because I fought like a *macho* with everybody, always proud to be one of the *negros* from La Eureka. When somebody would shout "The Eureka people are fighting!" we all showed up, we would all fight, even the girls, we would strike them with our high heels. That's how we demanded the respect of the people of Hormigueros. We would tell them, "Los *negros* de la Eureka, huh? Blessed be the mothers who bore us!" We never let them trample over us. I reckon that we all saw ourselves as black, even those who were a bit lighter, *claritos*, you know? We were all black in Eureka [and] we were all equal. The *blanquitos* [whites] were those who had clout: the engineers, the big ones, the bosses. They were a different world. I didn't finish high school and I used to think that when I went to an office and there were women who were trained, that they were better than me. I'd say, "Look at her in that office, look at her outfit; she is better than me." Never again! I am not better than anybody, but no one is better than me either. If I respect you, you have to respect me. Nowadays, any black person, I mean, anyone, is equal to a white person, because you can be black but have a white soul. Things have changed quite a bit and there's more respect now.

Irma's testimony contrasts with Roberto's in vital ways. Where Roberto brushes off the significance of race in (his) life while concurrently repudiating and reproducing dominant constructions of blackness, Irma embraces race in a totalizing narrative about the community that fuels her sense of identity. Where Roberto dismisses the impact of racial prejudice in his life, Irma claims it as the crucible where her identity and resilience were forged. Irma's narrative also sheds light on other issues that reveal the intricate relation between racial silence and racial salience in the telling of one's life.

By homologizing *eurekeños* and diametrically opposing them to *hormiguereños*, Irma conceives racial salience—blackness in particular—as a source of both strain and strength. Her testimony thus highlights another recurrent topic in the *eurekeños'* life narratives. When read collectively, they remind us of Pierre Nora's eloquent words: "memory is blind to all but the group it binds" (8). Infringing on the regimes of truth that have sustained the fiction of cohesion in the master narrative of the nation, the narrators orchestrate a cacophonous tune that echoes the dissonance of lives realized, remembered, and represented across racialized lines. Her recollections of *eurekeño* childhood and adolescent experiences issue a wry comment on the tenacity of the socially prescribed position for racial Others in Puerto Rican society, and are also a testimony of the mutability, in material and symbolic terms, of that place. As Irma puts it, "The *blanquitos* ... were a different world." And the frontier between their world and her world was fraught with conflict and perpetually fenced off by childhood, adolescent, and adult warfare. For Irma, who threads her life narrative through the trope of conquest, it was a feud the *eurekeños* won by taking pride in who they were, by constructing a collective sense of oppositional Self, and by rising above, individually and collectively, on moral and socio-political grounds. In the first case, as we heard from Irma, family metaphors recur to highlight the inclusionary communion that characterized the *eurekeños* and distinguished them from the exclusionary *hormiguereños*. Interestingly, in Irma's narrative, it is their alleged sameness, their equality, their identity, that elevates *eurekeños* over their counterparts. That identity is forcefully racialized in ways that subvert the distancing and dislocation of blackness.

Irma's construction of space merits attention: the discursive fissure between Eureka and Hormigueros is striking, considering that, with an area of approximately eleven square miles, Hormigueros is the fourth-smallest municipality in Puerto Rico and the smallest in the western region. Eureka was, geographically speaking, part of Hormigueros, and *eurekeños* were, grammatically speaking, also *hormiguereños*. However, it remains important for *eurekeños* like Irma to consolidate the boundaries that marked their personal histories in the dramatically transformed landscape where they now remember and reconstruct them.

The site of narration of Irma's testimony also deserves to be examined in the consideration of her life story. Smith and Watson note that sites of storytelling should be conceived not just as a physical location, but also as a socio-political space (69). In the situated context in which Irma is reconstructing the story of her life and reflecting on her journey of identity, *eurekeños* were still celebrating the first election of one of their own, "un negro de la Eureka," as mayor of Hormigueros. Across the testimonies, this is the recurrently iterated signifier of their socio-political ascendance. Irma, like other narrators, construes it as an inclusionary achievement, as evidence of *eurekeño* (and thus, in the context of her narrative, black) belongingness. Yet this construction should be read neither as a denial of racial difference nor as a negation of its salience. It is indicative of a perceived moment of rupture, perhaps even an overture—a present time when racial hierarchies might not have been resolved, but have been decently and honorably kept at bay by *eurekeños* (*negros*) like her. Thus, in Irma's progressive narrative, racial salience does harbor the potential of becoming a source of strength. Like Roberto's, Irma's testimony takes recourse to the opposition of then and now; however, Irma's figuration of the present mobilizes racial salience and blackness in ways that Roberto effaces.

Irma's testimony also allows us to examine how multiple "norms of life narration," to use Butler's term (52), might be at play, and perhaps even at odds, in the performative and interpretive act of representing the Self. She threads her life story through the collective and resistant *eurekeño* narrative of pride and prowess, but in so doing she voices an Other interpretation of racial difference in Puerto Rico, which calls into question dominant lore about national identity and, concomitantly, about race. Irma's discourse is both cognizant and critical of the localized racialization practices that marked her birth, her upbringing, and her being in the concentric but discursively opposed spheres of Eureka and Hormigueros. She also partakes in and reproduces those practices, as is most viscerally expressed in her redemptive caveat which posits that one could "be black but have a white soul." However, by casting her present and that of other *negros* in a progressive narrative of inclusion, Irma embraces the trope of racial equality. This is a significant aspect of her story because, insofar as it does not emerge from the denial of racial differences or hierarchies, it adds nuances to the lore of racial democracy. Her figuration of black people like herself in the present does not deny or submerge racial diversity, but inscribes her and them as salient participants in history and as equal partakers in its making. Irma thus conjures an image of black resilience that is at odds with dominant discourses on race in Puerto Rico.

Moreover, Irma's testimony beckons us to take stock of the significance of embodiment in explorations of racialization in Puerto Rico and the Americas.[11] As feminist scholars have persuasively argued, the body is a culturally sculpted signifier; its appearance as well as its uses accrue meanings in historically situated and power-laden dynamics. Irma's autobiographical story of redemption, her representation of her journey from self-effacement to the self-affirmation of a strident "Never again!" on the basis of her transgressively and progressively reconfigured identity, strikes a dissonant note with scriptures of race and gender. As she attempts to harmonize the episodes of her life into a rising narrative that, like Roberto's, is validating for the Self, Irma disrupts the myth of racial harmony. Needless to say, her rhetorical basis for commanding respect as a black woman, as a *eurekeña*, in this particular site of narration bespeaks her internalization of cultural memories that have historically associated whiteness and white bodies with moral rightness. What is significant, and disruptive, is that she now claims this for herself and for "any black person." Alessandro Portelli reminds us that the value of oral testimonies is not their facticity, but their ability to project the imagination, symbolisms, and desires of those who utter them (37). In light of this, Irma's narrative might be read as a transgressive expression of the salience of race and blackness in contemporary Puerto Rico, and as a progressive imagining of racial diversity and racial equality as venues for Afro-diasporic affirmation and inclusion.

Pedro and the Struggle for Community and Belongingness

Pedro, aged sixty-seven, was born in Eureka but only partly raised there. His father, who died when Pedro was seven, worked in the sugar mill during the harvest season and painted houses for "rich" people in Hormigueros during the "dead season." His mother did domestic work for unmarried mill workers but lost her vision when Pedro was still a child. Thereafter, Pedro was partly raised by a neighbor, who he regards as his *madrina* ("godmother"). Pedro completed the third grade in Hormigueros but then became sick and was diagnosed with tuberculosis, so he spent the rest of his childhood and most of his adolescence in and out of hospitals, often in the metropolitan area. At eighteen he moved to New York City with his brother and he spent over forty years there, mostly working at an extermination company.

> In Eureka there was always discrimination because discrimination has existed everywhere. Mr B., the boss, would never give the guys from Eureka a chance to advance; he'd push them aside and give the better jobs to guys he would bring in from Mayagüez. It didn't matter if they were black—he was black too—but he would humiliate guys from Eureka. The dead season was very sad. Since Mr B. preferred workers from outside who rented houses, he'd only employ *eurekeños* for a few shifts and give the full-time winter jobs to outsiders. This set off a vicious cycle for *eurekeños*; they went into debt during the dead season and then spent the *zafra* [sugar harvest] season paying installments. That's why they could never make enough to build their own shacks. Our quarters were the worst, the poorest; they were polluted and we lived in humiliating conditions... White people didn't mistreat black people in the Central, they treated everybody the same. They couldn't have discriminated because most of the bosses I met were black, except the main administrator. But in Hormigueros there has always been racism. They have always lashed at us, calling us *negritos*, *prietos*. They resented us because we commanded respect, we dressed well, we moved in

an environment where there was money. To work, they had to go to Eureka; to play baseball, they had to go to Eureka because there was no park in Hormigueros. They envied us because the *negritos* had everything and they, despite being white, had nothing. We couldn't compete with the rich kids in Hormigueros but we were unruffled by that. In New York, despite my color, I worked in places where they were all white and they accepted me so long as I did my job. [Over there] blacks are more racist than whites. They have complexes for being black, they have complexes for being ugly, they have complexes because they don't get hired. But, as my bosses would say, "They are lazy, that's why they aren't hired." Racism has always existed and will continue to exist until Jesus returns and sets it straight. Look at me, I'm black, and if I had a white daughter I wouldn't want her to marry a black man. My wife's mother didn't want her to marry me; she told her, "He's too ugly for you, look at his nose!" And I feared marrying a black woman because I didn't want my children to be black. I learned this from my grandfather: he never married black women, he only had them as mistresses. We are all racist; I'm black and I am racist. I never wanted to marry a black woman because I never wanted my children to turn out uglier than me. I wanted to *mejorar la raza*—lighten up the race. Don't get me wrong, being black is not ugly because the most beautiful people in the Bible were black. It was just a personal preference: I didn't want to marry someone like me because I didn't want my children to be lowbred. Complexes make many people suffer. I had complexes and I suffered, so I used to say, "Damn, look at me, my father is white and look how I turned out: lowbred, unrefined, ugly."

The terms of Pedro's immersion in the *eurekeño* community are starkly different from those of Roberto and Irma. He was born in Eureka but spent a significant part of his youth in hospitals outside of town. He left the Central at eighteen and never returned, except to visit. At the time of his interview, he was living in Rincón (a coastal town less than twenty miles from Hormigueros) and had spent most of his adult life in New York City. He never worked in Eureka—a rite of passage into manhood for the males of his generation. Pedro's particular site of narration thus offers a nuanced vantage point from which to appreciate self-narration as a means not just of revealing the Self, but of rendering it meaningful to oneself and to others in order to imagine community and carve out a necessary sense of belongingness.

Pedro navigates the treacherous waters of racial silencing with a prismatic compass that reveals the complexities of Afro-Puerto Rican identities, and memories, in the present. In iterating the duality between *eurekeños* and *hormiguereños*, he aligns himself with the racial Other. Like Irma, however, he codifies this Othering as a sign of his|their superiority. Unlike Irma, this balance of power is based not on moral but on material grounds: they had the sugar mill; they had the baseball field. This discursive operation adds nuance to Pedro's particular disposition to scrutinize the intersections of race, class, and, to a lesser degree, gender.

When he positions the narrated "I" in the Hormigueros of his infancy, Pedro collapses race and class differences (the rich kids from Hormigueros and the *negritos* from Eureka) but dismisses the hierarchies and inequalities that they might have implied by suggesting that what placed *eurekeños* in a privileged position was their location. Yet, when the narrated "I" is relocated to that very same location—Eureka—race and class differences accrue different and diverse undertones. Despite the fact that discrimination is, for Pedro, a universal human condition, he claims that, in the organization of labor in the mill, the white owners and administrators were egalitarian and did not exercise preferential treatment along racial lines. All of the "bosses" who he recalled were black, except for the central administrator, who lived in an estate within the premises but away from the processing and production plants, and from the *cuarteles* where the *negros* lived—the very same *cuarteles* Pedro regards as filthy, polluted, and impoverished, and blames for his perilous health conditions as a child. Despite this disparagement of the physical place assigned to him and his in Eureka, Pedro does not regard that structural organization as the result of structural racism. For Pedro, the fundamental disparities of the Central he remembers were not shored up by a history of white racism or by situated white prejudice, but were traversed by black discrimination. The recruitment and retention practices of Mr B., the black personnel manager, were what triggered the cycle that kept *los negros de la Eureka* under the press of economic dependence.

In her study of racial silencing in Puerto Rico from the 1760s to the 1910s, Rodríguez-Silva contends that "the history of harmony in Puerto Rico, anchored in the story of *mestizaje*, has successfully erased the histories of racial struggle" (10). She calls for an interrogation of the shifting nature and workings of power that enable the dynamics of inclusionary exclusion under *mestizaje*, and for an examination of the modalities of silencing that were enacted as "black and brown laboring peoples" were called to participate in the liberal-democratic sphere of the political (10). Pedro's contemporary testimony comments on these dynamics on two levels. On the one hand, it renders racial struggles as multifocal contests that are irreducible to bipolar, black-white tensions. Pedro unveils the complexities and complicities of racialization by exposing, in references to Mr B. and to himself, black racial prejudice. On the other hand, and at a higher order of analysis, Pedro's denial of white racial prejudice, his figuration of the *eurekeño* plight and his own plight as a laborer in New York City as freed from white discriminatory practices, allows him to align with his white "bosses," to establish community with them, and hence to bolster his narrative of inclusion and belongingness over the course of his life.

Perhaps the most contentious section in this narrative pertains to his professed commitment "to *mejorar la raza*"—a stock phrase that is generally translated into English as "to lighten up the race," but whose relevance in this discussion could also benefit from the more literal translation of "to improve the race." Most narrators reproduce in their speech Puerto Rican idiomatic expressions and racial valuations that confirm the supposed inferiority of blackness. Irma's figuration of a "white soul" as a superior moral condition, Roberto's and Pedro's equation of blackness with ugliness, and Pedro's description of his nose as unrefined are but a handful of the many similar utterances registered in the hundreds of transcribed pages that resulted from our Afro-Puerto Rican oral-history project. If we are to understand the vexing operations of racial silence in Puerto Rico and take stock of the complexities of Afro-Puerto Rican identities, these expressions should not be cursorily dismissed as manifestations of self-hatred, self-denial, or self-effacement. Closing off or nailing down other possible interpretations is equivalent to partaking in the silencing of race. Pedro's story calls us to elucidate other possible readings of the metaphor of "improving the race" if we approach it as a localized utterance that is deeply entwined with his search for community and belongingness.

Pedro aspired to—and did—marry a white woman, partly because, as he recalls it, it was a lesson he learned from his grandfather. His mother, whom he describes in his interview as a *negrita fea* ("an ugly little black woman"), was pursued by his white father because she was a hard-working woman. Pedro was seven when his father died, so the veracity of this tale is likely to be strengthened by its verisimilitude. From the few close family bonds he was able to sustain during his troubled childhood, Pedro learned that the best legacy to be passed on to his progeny was the possibility of bearing an appearance that was more "attractive" and socially acceptable than their own. His isolation during childhood and adolescence due to illness and the stigma of tuberculosis was compounded by his professed self-isolation as an adult because of his complexes, which had to do with his black complexion. He was in New York City at this point, where he claims he was (occasionally) discriminated against not because of his phenotypical appearance, but because of his linguistic limitations. Yet the calling to improve the race prevails in the scenario he construes, positioning and aligning himself within the narrative of legitimate inclusion and acceptance into the Puerto Rican body. He would want his hypothetical white daughter to marry a hypothetical white man so that their hypothetical white children would not have to endure the racial exclusions he tacitly acknowledges but fervently resignifies in an effort to cement his legitimate membership in his communities of reference. These communities are nation-bound and not reflective of the kind of transnational Afro-Latino|a consciousness forged in relationships with African Americans that has been observed in the analyses of other sources of public memory.[12] The fact that they are nation-bound enriches our understanding of *afropuertorriqueñidad* and nuances our figurations of the Afro-diasporic experience.

Pedro's testimony brings into sharp relief the fact that life, like our memories of it, is criss-crossed by contradiction. He acknowledges his own contradictions as a black man who aspires to eradicate the traces of that racial marking. The linguistic and conceptual forms Pedro employs to give order, meaning, significance, and a sense of belongingness to the material conditions that shaped his life bring into sharp relief the operations and complications of racial silence and racial salience in present-day Puerto Rico.

Conclusion: Self and Community in Afro–Puerto Rican Memories

Oral historians have been criticized for privileging the individual narrator, assuming that every individual's experience can be made into a purposeful story and thus failing to realize that the interview is but one form of memory-making (Hamilton and Shopes xi). As a project based fundamentally on individual inter-views, recorded under a tight funding schedule and with the artifices of micro-phones, recorders, cameras, and interview guides, ours is certainly limited in what it might be able to assert about Afro-Puerto Rican memory. Moreover, oral testimony is, admittedly, unfaithful: it can never be the same twice (Portelli 39). Nonetheless, the autobiographical narrations we elicited render a fertile landscape in which to appreciate the complex and compelling workings of mem-ory and its elusiveness.

Portelli has eloquently argued that "memory is not a passive depository of facts, but an active process of creation of meanings" (37). What most forcefully and eloquently transpires from the hundreds of pages that now represent the voices we heard—as well as the silences we filled—while conducting the research for *testimonios afropuertorriqueños* are not precise, concrete, exact histori-cal references, but a pattern of narration in which the "I" continuously finds, defines, and projects the Self in and through encounters and collisions with others. I do not mean to imply that the narrators construct their memories around a singular or simple binary logic, a static "us" versus "them." Indeed, as Pedro illustrates, there are constant and contradictory shifts in "positionings," to borrow Stuart Hall's term (395), which allude to the realignments of narrative intent that are intrinsic to any autobiographical exchange. What comes forward, however, is a committed and compelling effort to inscribe the Self as a member of a community that is neither stable nor unified, but which produces the con-texts and conditions for the narrator to become intelligible to him- or herself, and to make him- or herself explainable, narratable, to others.

The recollections of experiences that are thus woven together in these nar-ratives are ineluctably partial, both in the sense of being fragmentary and incom-plete and in the sense of being colored by particular and strategically adopted viewpoints. Let us consider, for example, Pedro's choice of evidence to justify his self-professed racism. He casts himself as just one more constituent of a racialized system that has always reigned and will prevail "until Jesus returns."

Even as this fatalistic outlook serves to naturalize and justify the racialized hierarchies in which he participates, in so doing Pedro is also able to explain his life choices and views not as the result of personal trauma, but as a testimony to his belongingness to a particular historical community. Pedro's figuration of black people in the US as racist, lazy, and with inferiority complexes, while an evident case of the scapegoating of African Americans by a first-generation immigrant, also serves to bolster an implicit claim for belongingness in a different racialized system in which he will have earned respect and acceptance for his merits. Similarly, Irma's, Pedro's, and most *eurekeños'* narratives and anecdotal evidence about the resentment, fear, and envy they inspire(d) in *hormiguereños* can be appreciated as concerted efforts to reinscribe themselves as protagonists and their disappeared home as the bastion of a centenary local history that fuels their sense of identity but has remained submerged.

It is precisely the partiality of these narratives that brings into sharp relief the deeply relational character of memory. The life narrations we collaboratively produced reveal how the act of recollecting the Self, which in autobiographical narrations also implies collecting one's Self, is bound to engage with and evoke the collectivities that the Self has recourse to, and inform it as a Self in the making. The intersubjective and partial truths that are thus registered enrich our understanding and appreciation of Afro-Puerto Rican memory as living histories. As Reyes notes, to examine the mnemonic practices of racial groups entails acknowledging that there are multiple identities that cannot be subsumed in a unitary national identity. Studies of race reveal "perhaps more starkly than any other line of research that there is no such thing as a monolithic national identity to which a unitary public memory might correspond, only practices of remembrance situated in time and enacted by discrete groups" (Reyes 2). These *testimonios afropuertorriqueños* have thus much less to do with the past and the passage than with the plural ways in which racialized subjects, such as *los negros de la Eureka*, make sense of and tell the stories of their present. Listening to them could perhaps shatter the nostalgia for that long-lost Indian doll and bring a sense of continuity to *los cuentos de la abuela* (grandma's stories)

University of Puerto Rico at Mayagüez

Disclosure Statement

No potential conflict of interest was reported by the author.

Notes

1. The project was funded by the Otros Saberes Initiative of the Latin American Studies Association and by the College of Arts and Sciences of

the University of Puerto Rico at Mayagüez. The project's objectives and collaborative methodology are discussed in Géliga Vargas (90—106).

2. For analyses of the tensions between state-led public-memory projects and vernacular manifestations of public memory, see Dávila and Marsh Kennerly. For a discussion of competing configurations of *la puertorrique-ñidad* in official and popular discourses, see Morris. For a discussion of how these tensions have been expressed in Puerto Rican literature, see Gelpí.

3. Critical discussions of the conspicuous and concerted ways in which the mythology of the three "elements" and their respective contributions to Puerto Rican identity and culture have been enacted and disseminated are elaborated by Dávila (69—79), Jiménez Román, Géliga Vargas et al., and Godreau et al. ("Lessons").

4. See, for example, Franco Ortiz, Franco Ortiz et al., Godreau et al. ("Lessons"), Goudreu et al. (*Arrancando*), and González Rivera.

5. See Suárez Findlay, Rivero, Rodríguez-Silva, Guerra, Figueroa, Díaz Quiñones, and Kinsbruner.

6. Giusti Cordero's essay, which employs the term Afro-Puerto Rican and names the field as Afro-Puerto Rican cultural studies, was published in a 1996 special issue of *Centro* devoted to race and identity. Several, though by no means all, of the contributors employ the term in their essays, but none provides a genealogy of the concept. Eleuterio Santiago-Díaz, who a decade later published a book on *escritura afropuertorriqueña* ("Afro-Puerto Rican writing"), provides other examples of early uses of Afro-Puerto Rican and variations such as Afro-Rican and Afro-Boricua (22).

7. Translated into English as "Afro-Puerto Rican Testimonies: An Oral-History Project in Western Puerto Rico," this is the title of the project proposal submitted to the Latin American Studies Association in response to its call for collaborative projects with either Afro-descendant or indigenous communities in the Americas.

8. The most influential in this process were the comparative studies across Latin America published by Andrews, Davis, and Torres and Whitten.

9. I have chosen to focus exclusively on narrators from one of the two towns where the project was conducted in an effort to make the project and my discussion of it more intelligible to readers. There is a certain cohesion in the testimonies of narrators from Hormigueros insofar as it is a community oral-history project based on individual life stories of people who shared a wide array of experiences and geographies as former residents (and most of them workers) at the Central Azucarera La Eureka in Hormigueros. After the closing and gradual dismantling of the sugar mill, most of them also shared the dislocating experience of their forcible relocation to subsidized land-grant plots in the Lavadero barrio, where the majority of the interviews took place. Engaging as well with the

parallel biographical oral-history project conducted in Aguadilla will require a more extensive discussion than is possible to elaborate in this essay. (For a comparative discussion of the methodology developed for each component of the project, see Géliga Vargas.)

10. Smith and Watson also elaborate two other dimensions of the autobiographical "I." The "real" or historical "I" is the flesh-and-blood person who lives in the material world and not in the narrative, and the ideological "I" refers to the repertoire of subject positions that is available to the narrator in the historically situated moment in which his or her story is composed (72−78).

11. For a succinct but insightful discussion of the racialization of bodies in Latin American history, see Wade ("Race"). For a profound study of the racialization of (black) female bodies in Puerto Rico from 1870−1920, see Suárez Findlay.

12. See Jiménez Román and Flores. For comparative case studies of the relationship between Latino|as and African Americans in the US, see Dzidzienyo and Oboler (157−304).

Works Cited

Andrews, George Reid. *Afro-Latin America, 1800−2000*. New York: Oxford UP, 2004. Print.

Blanco, Tomás. *El prejuicio racial en Puerto Rico*. 1942. Río Piedras: Ediciones Huracán, 2003. Print.

Butler, Judith. *Giving an Account of Oneself*. Bronx: Fordham UP, 2005. Print.

Dávila, Arlene. *Sponsored Identities*. Philadelphia: Temple UP, 1997. Print.

Davis, Darién J., ed. *Beyond Slavery: The Multilayered Legacy of Africans in Latin America and the Caribbean*. Lanham: Rowman, 2007. Print.

Díaz Quiñones, Arcadio. *La memoria rota*. Río Piedras: Ediciones Huracán, 1993. Print.

Díaz Royo, Antonio. "La historia oral en Puerto Rico: Reflexiones metodológicas." *Secuencia* 4 (1986): 123−33. Print.

Dzidzienyo, Anani, and Suzanne Oboler, eds. *Neither Enemies nor Friends: Latinos, Blacks and Afro-Latinos*. New York: Palgrave, 2005. Print.

Figueroa, Luis A. *Sugar, Slavery and Freedom in Nineteenth-Century Puerto Rico*. Chapel Hill: U of North Carolina P, 2005. Print.

Foucault, Michel. *The History of Sexuality. Volume 1: An Introduction*. 1978. New York: Vintage, 1990. Print.

Franco Ortiz, Mariluz. "Manejo de experiencias de racismo cotidiano con niñas y jóvenes: Un estudio transversal en escuelas de Loíza, Puerto Rico." Diss. U of Puerto Rico−Río Piedras, 2003. Print.

—. et al. "Violencia racista hacia niños y niñas en la escuela y propuestas hacia la transformación de su autoestigma." *Identidades* 7 (2009): 35—55. Print.

Géliga Vargas, Jocelyn A. "Afro-Puerto Rican Oral Histories: A Disruptive Collaboration." *Collaborative Anthropologies* 4 (2011): 90—118. Print.

—. et al. "*Testimonios Afropuertorriqueños*: Using Oral History to (Re)Write Race in Contemporary Puerto Rico." *Sargasso* 1 (2007—08): 115—30. Print.

Gelpí, Juan G. *Literatura y paternalismo en Puerto Rico*. 2nd ed. San Juan: Editorial UPR, 2005. Print.

Giusti Cordero, Juan. "Afro-Puerto Rican Cultural Studies: Beyond *Cultura Negroide* and *Antillanismo*." *Centro* 8.1—2 (1996): 57—77. Print.

Godreau, Isar. "Folkloric 'Others': Blanqueamiento and the Celebration of Blackness as an Exception in Puerto Rico." *Globalization and Race: Transformations in the Cultural Production of Blackness*. Ed. Kamari Maxine Clarke and Deborah Thomas. Durham: Duke UP, 2006. 171—87. Print.

—. et al. *Arrancando mitos de raíz: Guía para una enseñanza antirracista de la herencia africana en Puerto Rico*. Cayey: Instituto de Investigaciones Interdisciplinarias UPR—Cayey, 2013. Print.

—. et al. "The Lessons of Slavery: Discourses of Slavery, 'Mestizaje,' and 'Blanqueamiento' in an Elementary School in Puerto Rico." *American Ethnologist* 35.1 (2008): 115—35. Print.

González Rivera, Elena. "The Social and Educational Inequalities of Black Students Studying English in Rural Puerto Rico." *Centro* 20.1 (2008): 72—95. Print.

Guerra, Lillian. *Popular Expression and National Identity in Puerto Rico*. Gainesville: UP of Florida, 1998. Print.

Hall, Stuart. "Cultural Identity and Diaspora." *Colonial Discourse and Postcolonial Theory*. Ed. Patrick Williams and Laura Chrisman. New York: Columbia UP, 1994. 392—403. Print.

Hamilton, Paula, and Linda Shopes. Introduction. *Oral History and Public Memory*. Ed. Hamilton and Shopes. Philadelphia: Temple UP, 2008. vii—xix. Print.

Hernández Cruz, Victor. "African Things." *The Afro-Latin@ Reader: History and Culture in the United States*. Ed. Miriam Jiménez Román and Juan Flores. Durham: Duke UP, 2010. 232. Print.

Jiménez Román, Miriam. "The Indians Are Coming! The Taíno and Puerto Rican Identity." *Taíno Revival: Critical Perspectives on Puerto Rican Identity and Cultural Politics*. Ed. Gabriel Haslip-Viera. Princeton: Wiener, 2001. 101—38. Print.

—. and Juan Flores, eds. *The Afro-Latin@ Reader: History and Culture in the United States*. Durham: Duke UP, 2010. Print.

Kinsbruner, Jay. *Not of Pure Blood: The Free People of Color and Racial Prejudice in Nineteenth-Century Puerto Rico*. Durham: Duke UP, 1996. Print.

Marsh Kennerly, Catherine. *Negociaciones culturales: Los intelectuales y el proyecto pedagógico del estado muñocista*. San Juan: Ediciones Callejón, 2009. Print.

Miller, Grace. *Rise and Fall of the Cosmic Race: The Cult of Mestizaje in Latin America*. Austin: U of Texas P, 2004. Print.

Morris, Nancy. *Puerto Rico: Culture, Politics, and Identity*. Westport: Praeger, 1995. Print.

Nora, Pierre. "Between Memory and History: Les Lieux de Mémoire." *Representations* 26 (1989): 7—24. Print.

Portelli, Alessandro. "What Makes Oral History Different?" *The Oral History Reader*. Ed. Robert Perks and Alistair Thompson. 2nd ed. London: Routledge, 2006. 32—42. Print.

Rahier, Jean Muteba. Introduction. *Black Social Movements in Latin America: From Monocultural Mestizaje to Multiculturalism*. By Rahier. New York: Palgrave, 2012. 1—14. Print.

Reyes, G. Mitchell. Introduction. *Public Memory, Race, and Ethnicity*. Ed. Reyes. Newcastle: Cambridge Scholars, 2010. 1—14. Print.

Rivero, Yeidy. *Tuning Out Blackness: Race and Nation in the History of Puerto Rican Television*. Durham: Duke UP, 2005. Print.

Rodríguez-Silva, Ileana M. *Silencing Race: Disentangling Blackness, Colonialism, and National Identities in Puerto Rico*. New York: Palgrave, 2012. Print.

Santiago-Díaz, Eleuterio. *Escritura afropuertorriqueña y modernidad*. Pittsburgh: U of Pittsburgh P, 2007. Print.

Scott, Joan W. "Experience." *Feminists Theorize the Political*. Ed. Judith Butler and Scott. New York: Routledge, 1992. 22—40. Print.

Smith, Linda Tuhiwai. *Decolonizing Methodologies: Research and Indigenous Peoples*. London: Zed, 2005. Print.

Smith, Sidonie, and Julia Watson. *Reading Autobiography: A Guide for Interpreting Life Narratives*. 2nd ed. Minneapolis: U of Minnesota P, 2010. Print.

Suárez Findlay, Eileen J. *Imposing Decency: The Politics of Sexuality and Race in Puerto Rico, 1870—1920*. Durham: Duke UP, 1999. Print.

Torres, Arlene, and Norman E. Whitten, comps. and eds. *Blackness in Latin America and the Caribbean: Social Dynamics and Cultural Transformations*. 2 vols. Bloomington: Indiana UP, 1998. Print.

Wade, Peter. *Race and Ethnicity in Latin America*. 2nd ed. London: Pluto, 2010. Print.

—. "Race in Latin America." *A Companion to Latin American Anthropology*. Ed. Deborah Poole. Malden: Blackwell, 2008. 177—92. Print.

Roots and Routes: The Biographical Meshwork of Saint Josephine Bakhita

Raíces y Rutas: La Meshwork de las Biográficas de Santa Josephine Bakhita

By Maria Suely Kofes

Translated by Iracema Hilário Dulley

Josephine Margaret Mary Bakhita was born in Sudan, sold into slavery, and subsequently taken to Italy, where she converted to Christianity, was baptized, and ultimately canonized by the Vatican. This is the basic core of the several biographical narratives about Josephine that are available in books, on internet sites, and in videos. In these narratives, however, there is marked inconsistency concerning Bakhita, as each text works to situate the saint in alignment with its writer's objectives. In reading these disparate biographies through the lens of meshwork, I use the case of Bakhita to suggest theoretical reflections on the conjunctions, disjunctions, and conflicts present in biographical writing.

Josephine Margaret Mary Bakhita nació en Sudán, fue vendida como esclava, y subsecuentemente llevada a Italia donde se convirtió al Cristianismo, fue bautizada, y últimamente canonizada por el Vaticano. Es éste el punto de partida de varias de las narrativas biográficas escritas sobre Josephine que se encuentran disponibles en libros, portales de Internet y videos. Sin embargo, en estas narrativas se pueden encontrar claras inconsistencias en relación a Bakhita, ya que cada texto intenta situar a esta santa en relación con los objetivos personales de cada autor. Mediante la lectura de estas biografías incongruentes a través de un enfoque de meshwork, utilizo el ejemplo de Bahkita para sugerir reflexiones teoréticas sobre las conjunciones, disyunciones y conflictos presentados en la escritura biográfica.

In April 2013, while casually surfing the Web, I was struck by the multiple references to the name that I encountered in a search for a "brown saint." At that point, I had never heard of Josephine Bakhita. Because I was curious, I Googled the name and, as frequently occurs on the Web, I found myself following successive and connected links. These links led me to digital narratives, images, and references to books, stories, documents, and people—a multiplicity of traces and interconnections that I shall call here a biographical meshwork. The term meshwork is to be understood, according to Tim Ingold, "as a texture of interwoven threads" (xii).

From an anthropological perspective, it is useful to study the several ways in which the biographical narratives of Josephine Bakhita have been utilized to present, re-present, and represent the saint for multiple purposes: as a link between Europe, Africa, and Latin America; as a model of African Catholicism; as a critique of slavery and racism; as a mediation between Islam and Christianity; and as a successful model for Afro-diasporic and Afro-Brazilian peoples to follow in the struggle for equality. This essay will provide an overview of some of the threads of Bakhita's biographical meshwork to demonstrate the different "uses" of the life of this saint as her biography is reimagined in Europe, Africa, and Brazil. Tracing how these different threads of Bakhita's life are interwoven into a biographical meshwork suggests some of the ways in which narrated lives of saints are implicated in creating perceptions and manipulations of the saints, a concept that is made more complicated by an understanding of saints as "invisible friends" (Brown). This idea of biographical meshwork also holds further implications for the reading of multiply narrated lives.

Biographical Meshwork

When Gilles Deleuze refers to the controversial issue of the subject, the "constitution of the self," he states that singularity is to be understood not as something opposed to the universal, but as any element that might be extended until it reaches the neighborhood of another element, so as to form a junction (326–28). Let me try to establish two connections to Deleuze's statement. The first concerns his observation on the relationship that, to me, seems similar to the Möbius strip. We know that what is fundamental to the Möbius strip is that it twists in significant ways—that is, the Möbius strip is not folded from any transcendent position and there is, therefore, no possible room for absolute totalization, but only for relative distancing (Souza and Fausto).

The second connection to Deleuze's statement follows from Ingold's visual suggestion, in which he asks individuals to imagine two lines crossing each other—line A and line B—with their intersection defined as point P (83). What difference would it make to portray A and B as points and P as the line that connects them? Mathematically, these alternatives might be considered as mere reciprocal transformations; they are, thus, forms in which a relationship between A and B may be posed either as an intersection or a connection. If we do not start with an abstraction, however, but with real lines of life or movement, it makes a considerable difference. Ingold suggests that we should think not of a network of interactions, as they might conventionally appear; in the world we inhabit, he affirms, life is not a network, but a mesh of interconnected points (63). We might say, even if Ingold has not done so, that lines are composed and decomposed in their movement. I draw on these ideas to focus on the narrative of a life—that of a young African woman who was made a saint by the Catholic Church: Josephine Margaret Mary Bakhita.

This essay is an experiment. Inspired by the two aforementioned suggestions—that of Deleuze and that of Ingold—I propose here that multiple biographical narratives of a single subject can be analyzed and described as a weaving of lines. Thus, a life would be a set of moving lines, and their analytical description would show the uniqueness of a life in its connections and knots or tangles. Bakhita's life is very much appropriate for this experiment. Here, I wish to retain the concept of meshwork (as a connection of lines and not a network—a connection between points, as is clearly distinguished by Ingold), but also introduce the notion of knots or entanglements (whereas Ingold focuses only on vanishing points). I suggest this conceptual experiment to understand a life and the ways in which this biographical construction circulates and unfolds or untangles itself, as well as acts on different worlds and lives. For this experiment, I have chosen to read some of the biographical narratives of Saint Bakhita, the "brown saint" and the "patron of Sudan."

Saints as "Invisible Friends"

Using Bakhita as an example to study biographical meshwork is productively complicated by her position as a saint, because saints are believed not only to mediate between the divine and the human, heaven and earth, but also to relate people with one another.[1] This point is dependent on saints being present as images in churches, but also as following individuals in their minds, on their bodies, or in their purses and pockets—particularly in the form of pendants or other images to be worn or otherwise carried. Saints are thus imagined as "invisible friends" in intimate proximity with the individual. The process of sanctification brings about such proximity.

The process of sanctification—the invention of the saint—is carried out based on the biographical narrative, which largely includes the saint's exemplary life and recorded miracles. The image of the saint along with the biographical narrative of the saint make her or him closer to the people—an invisible, close friend and the recipient of reverence. Brown offers valuable commentary on the early stages of this process. As he writes, "new invisible companions came to crowd in around the men and women of late antiquity and the early middle ages...Mediterranean men and women, from the late fourth century onwards, turned with increasing explicitness for friendship, inspiration and protection in this life and beyond the grave, to invisible beings who were fellow humans and whom they could invest with the precise and palpable features of beloved and powerful figures in their own society" (50–51). Furthermore, he notes that "[t]he very intimacy of the emotional bond between the believer and his invisible companions...made this identification appear quite natural" (84). If, as explained from Brown's historical perspective, there is temporal difference and discontinuity between heroes and martyrs, it is also necessary to note that there is a transformed continuity between them, since narratives might attribute "heroism" to virtue. This point is suggested, for example, in the 1978 "Decree on the Heroic Character" of Josephine Bakhita's virtues by the Catholic Church. This notion of the "invisible friend," carried with the believer, impacts the biographical meshwork of Bakhita as her narrated life appears in Europe, Africa, and Brazil.

The Bakhita Meshwork

As mentioned, my search for a Catholic saint of color relevant to present-day Brazil led me to Bakhita and the links to various narratives of her life that I came to understand as a biographical meshwork. Although my idea of a biographical meshwork stems from the work of Ingold, I have departed from his theory by assigning a proper name to the strands that interweave the threads of the mesh. In the context of this essay, I build on the concept of meshwork as defined by Ingold both to analyze the life narratives of Bakhita and to describe the lines that are interwoven in these narratives.

The name of Bakhita is a reference point, a knot, a unique intersection at which moving lines stop. The biographies of Bakhita—that is, the narratives of Bakhita's life—form a tangle of lines that make up the Bakhita meshwork (see figure 1). Many of the lines intertwined in this tapestry are connected to other places, people, and even complex concepts such as race and gender. This description intends to challenge the relationship between the biographical act and social webs. My first formulation of this perspective, which purposefully intended to avoid the trap of Pierre Bourdieu's notions of field and trajectory, was that of the ethnography of an experience, which I explored in my book *Trajetórias em narrativas*. My second formulation was that of social experiences and individual interpretations. The third was ethnobiography, which I explored in my edited collection *Histórias de vida: Biografias e trajetórias*.

In the case of Bakhita, the biographical narratives available are short in length. The longest book about her life, *Bakhita Tells Her Story*, contains various images, appendices, and bibliographical references, yet amounts to only 137

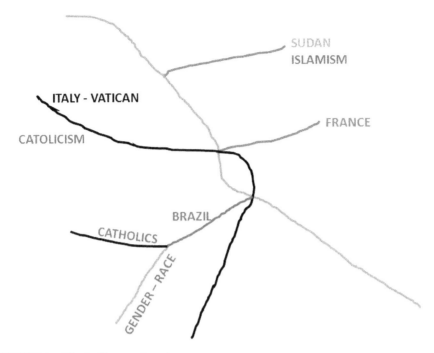

FIGURE 1. *The Bakhita meshwork.*

pages (Dagnino). It is almost a sketch in the sense that it invents a character who is liable to be unfolded or expanded on in other narratives, images, and personas. The available biographical narratives of Bakhita are not detailed ones; the narratives merely point to further potentialities. I propose to untangle some of their threads here as I test the concept of meshwork for the analysis of life narratives.

Tracing the Threads of Bakhita

The narratives that tell the life of Bakhita extend her life. These lines that make up the life of Bakhita include countries, continents, institutions, temporality, political and social relations, and individuals. Among the countries that are mentioned in these narratives, I focus on Sudan, Italy, and Brazil, and therefore three continents: Africa, Europe, and South America. Among the institutions, I pay particular attention to the Catholic Church, as well as its churches and organizations spread across continents and countries. Among the people who are mentioned, it is important to distinguish between those with whom Bakhita was directly related during her lifetime and those to whom she became an "invisible companion" after she died and was sanctified. Finally, I suggest that scholars may analyze and describe biographies as meshworks in order to understand more fully the circulation of posthumous lives. With this purpose, I will trace the threads articulated in the discourse in and surrounding Bakhita's life narratives.

The biography, *Bakhita Tells Her Story*, written by Maria Luisa Dagnino and published by the Canossian Daughters of Charity, is composed of four parts. Bakhita, Sudan, Christianity in Sudan, and slavery comprise the first part. In the second part, Bakhita tells her story as a slave on the request of a Mother Superior. In the third, the author of the book analyzes Bakhita in relation to Christianity and to her life as a Christian missionary. The final part comprises two sections, titled "Bakhita Still Talks to Us" and "What Others Say of Bakhita."

Let us focus on the second chapter: Bakhita's narrative. This retelling of her story begins with her family in "the heart of Africa," the seizure of her sister and then of herself, her suffering during slavery, how she missed her family, how she was sold to a slave merchant, the long and difficult march, the bodily marks that filled her back with scars, and her work and suffering as a domestic slave until she was bought by the Italian vice-consul in Sudan. In this second section, the biographer places importance on the changes in the treatment she was given: under the vice-consul, she no longer faces corporal punishment or other penalties and she receives affection. When the vice-counsul's family travels back to Italy, Bakhita goes with them and is given to friends of the vice-consul with the intention that she will become a nanny for their daughter.

Between this period and her admission to be educated at the Canossian Institute, one reads sentimental paragraphs on her discovery of Christianity, her baptism, and her refusal to go back to Africa, as well as her decision to dedicate her life to missionary work in Italy. The pictures included in this part of the text are divided into two sections. The first portrays a series of images depicting Africa: a daily scene in an African nation, two hands playing an African drum, and African landscapes. The final two pictures show Saint Peter's Basilica and, finally, Bakhita. Sandwiched between the pictures of Africa, those of Saint Peter's Basilica, and Bakhita is an excerpt of the Pope's discourse on the occasion of Bakhita's sanctification. This grouping of pictures is followed by additional scenes in Africa: a church in a Sudanese city, a large group of Christians in Sudan, Pope John Paul II's blessing of an African archbishop, and a smiling young African woman holding a child. Again, the biographer interweaves these images with various representations of Bahkita, and the last picture of the series displays the Canossian House in Schio where she lived.

After Sudan gained its independence from British rule in 1956, there were ongoing regional conflicts within its borders, as well as disputes between various non-Muslim ethnic groups. These conflicts are a meaningful context for understanding how Saint Bakhita is also a "political invisible companion" for the Catholic Church. In 1993, in the middle of the Sudanese conflict, Pope John Paul II preached in Khartoum, stating, "Today I give thanks to the Divine Providence that I have been granted the opportunity of fulfilling the wish of the Church in the Sudan, that Bakhita be honored on her own soil" (qtd. in Dagnino 116). He went on to express that, "[i]n the midst of so much hardship, Blessed Bakhita is your model and heavenly patron. In the terrible trials of her life, Bakhita always listened to Christ's word. She learned the mystery of His Cross and Resurrection: the saving truth about God who so loved each one of us that he gave us his only Son" (115). The Pope continued: "In her new life in Christ this sister of ours returns to Africa today. This daughter of the Christian community of Sudan returns to you today. You too are being tried in many ways, and yet life is your heritage, that life which the risen Christ has brought for all. Rejoice, all of Africa! Bakhita has come back to you: the daughter of Sudan, sold into slavery as a living piece of merchandise and still free. Free with the freedom of the saints. Blessed Josephine comes back to you with the message of God the Father's infinite mercy" (116).

After the pictures in the biography, the final item of the second chapter is titled "An Unforgettable Day." In this section of the text, the day of Bakhita's baptism is narrated, when she was given the name of Josephine Margaret Bakhita. Four years later, when she manifested the desire to be admitted to the order, she was examined by a prelate, who granted her permission to do so. The report contains the date: the year 1910. As a whole, what is narrated through images and text is not so much a problematic and tense story as a plot that creates the connection between Africa and Europe (specifically Italy and, within it, the Vatican in particular), slavery and freedom, Islam and Christianity, suffering and consecration.

One might expect Bakhita, the patron saint of Sudan, to be a mediator between Islam and Christianity, and to support the presence of Christianity in Sudan. In the book in which she "tells her story," for instance, the last chapter contains a set of quotations allegedly spoken by Bakhita herself. One of them, which she supposedly repeated several times, reads, "If our African brothers were to hear about the Lord and Our Lady, they would all be converted. They would be very good" (qtd. in Dagnino 140). Here, the biographical text invests her with an agency that manifests in words and images.

Bakhita, in "telling her story," establishes the importance of geographic, religious, and political routes to and from Africa, as well as from freedom to slavery to freedom. With these multiple routes and crossing paths, Bakhita, the "African slave girl," essentially becomes an unfolded political person, who appears either as the suffering saint, the martyr, or as neither saint nor hero but a liberating heroine. These biographical mutations comprise the Bakhita meshwork. In this case, biography contains agency; it draws lines and vanishing points: humbleness, martyrdom, the metaphor of values incorporated into Christ, and courage against inequality.

These tropes appear again in another Catholic text, "Josephine Bakhita, 1869–1947: From Slavery to the Freedom of Christ," a lecture given in March

2003 by Cardinal Paul Poupard at the Cathedral of Notre Dame in Paris. Before introducing Bakhita's biography, the Cardinal stated, "She is still hardly known in France, but the African Bakhita is like a cartoon heroine who meets Christ through slavery and finds in him the freedom to live a fully human life as a child of God. Her story might seem incredible, but it is true" (Poupard). In Poupard's twelve-page discourse, he narrates the biography of Bakhita by referencing only one source: the biography of Bakhita written by a female Canossian missionary, *Bakhita Tells Her Story*.

This speech emphasizes the different countries and continents involved in Bakhita's biographical narrative, and establishes a curious relationship between the routes of art, politics, and charity, which converge into the road of the sacred. He explains, "From a Europe looking for its soul, with Robert Schuman, to India trying to cope with misery, with Mother Teresa, Christ speaks to us through his followers and shows us how the paths of both politics and charity can converge and turn into roads to holiness" (Poupard). He goes on to cite the subjects of previous conferences and presents that day's subject by saying, "Today we are thinking of wounded humanity in Africa, and it is from that continent that the light of the Gospel is given to us to shed on our path the light of faith which opens to us the way of freedom and of holiness with Christ" (Poupard). Following this introduction, the Cardinal starts to tell Bakhita's life story.

After he begins telling the life of Saint Bakhita, he interrupts his narrative to denounce slavery, condemn the subhuman conditions to which many individuals are subjected, and critique all oppressive structures. When he resumes the narrative of Bakhita's life, he then connects it to the suffering of Catholics in Sudan. He emphasizes that Muslims and Christians once worked side by side in Sudan and points to the tolerant character of Sudanese culture, arguing that it is only the Islamic government's politics that create intolerance. Reaffirming the Catholic Church's intention to continue its work of evangelization and catechization of adults, the Cardinal then asks French bishops to pray for the return of human rights to Sudan.

Very briefly, the Cardinal states that Sudan is an African country and mentions the Muslim presence in it. He then invokes Bakhita once again and asks his audience to listen to what she had to say. He quotes her while he narrates her life, including details on how she was abducted from her family and enslaved; he then narrates her martyrdom, when she was marked with a knife, and the multiple times she was sold as a slave until she was bought by an Italian vice-consul. Finally, quoting excerpts from Bakhita's speech, he narrates her canonic biography and makes analogies. He compares her to François Xavier Nguyên Van Thuân, a Vietnamese bishop who was jailed in 1975 when the communists occupied Saigon. He affirms that "Pope John Paul II canonized our little Bakhita on 1 October 2000, thus offering her to us as a model of holiness" (Poupard). The last paragraph resumes the focus on Bakhita and her affirmation of courage and the value of freedom. In this narrative, the value assigned to Bakhita's biography is that of humility and the denial of herself to serve others. Her value is transformed into courage and brotherhood as a model to fight oppression.

These two exemplary narratives stemming from the Catholic Church emphasize Bakhita's humbleness and servitude, and hold her up as a model for successful progression through times of civil unrest in Sudan, Africa, and other parts of the world. Pope John Paul II situates Bakhita's narrative as a model for Catholics in Sudan. The Pope further situates Bakhita as a bridge between oppositions: Europe and Africa, Christian and Muslim, as well as freedom and bondage. Cardinal Poupard follows this model by reiterating the ability of Bakhita's narrative to bridge seemingly disparate binaries, advocating for a unifying model that will lead to peace and stability. Poupard, however, also seems to use the story of Bakhita to legitimize continued evangelization and catechization in Africa.

On 8 February 2013, a Brazilian Catholic website, *Portal Paulinas*, published an article titled "Saint Josefina Bakhita, the Brown Sister," which declared, on that day, "the Church celebrated the memory" of the "African saint, Sister Josefina Bakhita" ("Saint"). In order to celebrate the date in her honor, the website included a brief biographical narrative that highlighted her values—humbleness, simplicity, her constant smile—and detailed her place of birth as Sudan in 1869, her death in Venice in 1947, and her canonization, a process that started in 1959. In addition to this information, the announcement stated that Bakhita was "[a]n African flower who experienced the anguish of abduction and slavery, she opened herself admirably to the divine grace with the Daughters of Saint Magdalene of Canossa, in Italy," and that "[i]n Schio, where she lived for many years, everyone still called her our Brown Sister" ("Saint").

The narrative further states that "[t]he Divine Providence that 'cares for the flowers in the field and for the birds in the sky' has guided this Sudanese slave, through countless and unspeakable suffering, to human freedom and to the freedom of faith, to the consecration of all her life to god, for the advent of his Kingdom," and attests that "Sister Bakhita died on February 8, 1947, in Casa de Schio, surrounded by the crying and praying community. A mass of people went to the house of the Institute to see their Holy Brown Sister for the last time and asked for her protection from heaven. Many have been the graces obtained through her" ("Saint").

As evidenced by these two biographical texts—one distributed directly from the Canossian Order—the distinct and overlapping life narratives of Bakhita constantly refer to the pairs Africa and Italy, and slavery and freedom. On *Portal Paulinas*, we also find a notion that is less frequently mentioned in her biographical meshwork: that of Bakhita as a "flower." This point may be read as an association with her female gender or understood as a reference to her position as someone special in a harsh environment. In both cases, this reference connects her to nature. The term "brown," also used in this description, however, is a term that is frequently used in descriptions of Bakhita, since she is often referred to as the "brown saint." In this instance, brown may refer to a type of miscegenation, but connoting a positive connection rather than the more inflammatory interpretation of this term. It may be read as a symbolic miscegenation, implying that Bakhita successfully mediates between the continents of Africa and Europe through her migration from Sudan to Italy. This reference could also stand for the color of her skin. The statement regarding Bakhita on *Portal Paulinas* reiterates the necessary death of the body to make the saint live through those who decide to seize her image and develop a type of intimate friendship with her. This point implies that the biographical meshwork and the retelling and reimagining of the life of a saint are necessary in order to ensure the individual's belief.

On the same day and year, on a Brazilian Catholic blog, *Devoção e Fé* (Faith and Devotion), Bakhita's biography was also quoted more extensively to memorialize the date that celebrates her. The entry starts by referring to Sudan and to Saint Bakhita as the patron of Sudan. The entry goes on to provide an overview of Bakhita's abduction and life as a slave, her suffering, and her humble character. Importantly, the post also claims that her last words were, "When one loves another very much, one strongly desires to go and meet this person: Why, then, should one fear death so much? Death takes us to God," and, immediately before she died, she supposedly said, "I am very happy indeed! Our Lady, Our Lady!" (qtd. in Adriana). Following Bakhita's death, her life becomes the subject of invention. Her biography can be read as a symbol of the struggle of freedom against slavery and of antiracist struggle, but these texts may also affirm an ideal Christian: Bakhita, a servile and humble person, the holy Bakhita.

On the Geledés Instituto da Mulher Negra (Geledés Black Woman Institute) website, one finds another short biography of Josephine Bakhita.[2] This biography focuses more on her African origins and noble character. It mentions not only the country, but also the city in which she was born:

> Bakhita was born into an important family from Olgossa, a village located in the region of Darfur, in the West of Sudan. Her father was the brother of a tribal chief. Arab slave merchants abducted her when she was nine and she was sold five times in the markets of El Obeid and Khartoum during the next eight years. The trauma of being abducted led her to forget her own name, and the name by which we know her today is composed by the name given to her by the slave merchants (Bakhita, an Arab term meaning luck) and the Christian name she adopted as an adult. She was also forced to convert to Islamism. ("Josephine")

The summary of a Brazilian book on Bakhita, *Bakhita: Mulher, negra, escrava, santa. Uma fascinante história de liberdade*, included on the Geledés website, hints at why her narrative may be of such interest in Brazil. The summary states, "At the end of the 19th century, a Sudanese is made into a slave while she is still a girl. She is given to five different 'owners' and then rescued by the Italian consul. She travels to Italy, where she becomes a Canossian nun. For Africa, Bakhita is a hope for liberation. For the relationship with the Muslim world, she is a bridge through which dialogue might be established. For the black race, she is a sign of how dignity might be fully rescued. And she is a saint for all" ("Summary").

In this narrative, the proper name that is repeated is that of Bakhita, not of Saint Josephine Bakhita or Saint Bakhita. I have found this reference to Bakhita rather than Saint Bakhita only on the Geledés page, the website of a non-governmental organization for the defense of black women. On this digital platform, Bakhita stands as a name related to an action by the Afro-Brazilian movement. In this case, what matters is not necessarily the values of piety, humility, and servility, but rather that an enslaved African was released, and that an individual of African descent whose life straddles the nineteenth and twentieth centuries has been recognized in the contemporary moment.

We read that her last owners supposedly left her temporarily with the Canossian Sisters. Baptized in 1890, according to this narrative, Bakhita joined the order in 1896 and was sent to Schio, a city in the province of Vicenza in northern Italy, where she would spend the rest of her life. She left only between 1935 and 1938, when she helped train young nuns to work in Africa. In her last days, "her memories focused on her years of slavery and, in a fit of delirium, she shouted: 'Please, loosen the fetters...They are so heavy'" ("Josephine"). Therefore, in this biographical narrative, readers discover that Bakhita is venerated as "a modern African saint and a special saint relevant to slavery and oppression. She was proclaimed the patron of Sudan." This sentence displays the core of this biographical invention of Bakhita. Present in this narrative are the threads told by the Catholic Church to affirm Christianity in Muslim Africa, those told by ordinary people who see in Bakhita an "invisible friend," and those told by anti-racist movements, particularly concerning Brazil.

There have been over seventy candidates for sanctification in Brazil, but only two have been made saints: Mother Paulina, who was born in Italy, came to Brazil when she was ten, and was canonized in 2002, and Father Galvão, who was born in Guaratinguetá (São Paulo) and became a saint in 2007. There is also currently an attempt to canonize a former slave, Nhá Chica. When her beatification was announced, the life of the laywoman Francisca Paula Jesus was revealed. When she died in 1895, Nhá Chica was already thought to be a saint, but official recognition took time. The commission for her beatification was not started until almost one hundred years later, in 1989. In 1991, she was recognized as a servant of God, in 2012 she was recognized as venerable, and in 2013 she was beatified.

In the quest for Brazilian people to be recognized by the Vatican, what do sainthood and the intricacies of recognizing a former slave as a saint mean for the people of Brazil, especially for the Afro-diasporic communities? Let us consider the example of the School Quilombo of Saint Bakhita. The word *quilombo* refers to the maroon communities of Brazil, which were formed by enslaved Africans during the colonial period as resistance to the institution of slavery. Presently, activist groups in Brazil are attempting to gain recognition of and assign value to African and Afro-Brazilian culture through public policies, as well as the creation of "school quilombos" ("Cultura"). These are popular preparatory courses for the university admission examination and they attempt to "bring to present times the fierce and resistant spirit of African and diasporic people in the struggle to insert the black voice into places that were historically not reserved for it" ("Cultura").

The "First Week of the School Quilombo of Saint Bakhita—BA" was announced in 2010 on the *Portal da Cultura Afro-Brasileira* (Valverde), a news site focusing on events related to Afro-Brazilians. Several of these school quilombos, including the Quilombo do Orubu (Cajazeiras, Salvador, Bahia), draw attention to and link themselves with the Afro-diasporic struggle because of the experiences of their teachers. Those who work at the Quilombo do Orubu do not earn a salary; only their transportation costs are covered. Selecting Saint Bakhita as the name of one of the school quilombos is thus linked to educational and political struggle through the assignment of value to Afro-Brazilians in antiracist struggles.

While Bakhita's biographical narratives are used to preach patience, dutifulness, and sacrifice by the Catholic Church, alongside a legitimizing rhetoric for its continued presence in African nations, Brazilian and Afro-Brazilian organizations have placed somewhat different emphases on the same narrated life. As previously articulated, the posthumous life of a saint changes through the relationship of living, breathing human beings wishing to be "invisible friends" with that saint. In Brazil, Bakhita's life is narrated as a representation of liberation. This quest for recognition is present in the request that Brazilian and other non-European Catholic lives be considered for beatification and sainthood, thereby recognizing the value of their contributions to multiple and diverse communities. Afro-Brazilians have also expanded the posthumous life of Bakhita by adopting her as a symbol of an African and Afro-diasporic saint who successfully toppled subjugation and can be usefully employed in contemporary freedom struggles.

Conclusion: Tying the Knots

For some people, Bakhita is the slave who was set free. For the Catholic Church, she obtained her freedom through martyrdom and sanctity. For members of the Church, Bakhita came to be known as "our brown sister." For those who incorporate her into the Afro-Brazilian community, Bakhita represents the hope for the equality and recognition of individuals of African descent in the diaspora. In the struggle for equality and for the ethnic affirmation of Afro-Brazilian movements in Brazil, Bakhita is the slave who fought for her freedom and the first African to be sanctified by the Vatican. The name of Bakhita is the agent of a minimal biographical composition that is also a political metaphor—that of the liberated Africa. In one of its lines there is liberation through Christianity, while another refers to the struggle of Afro-Brazilians, to mention only the lines I have referred to in this text.

Because I am an anthropologist situated in a field of knowledge in which it is difficult to legitimate biographical and narrative research, I have proposed to explore the concept of meshwork in conjunction with that of the tangled lines of narrated lives. The experimental and exploratory character of this conjunction seems promising to me. In following a name—that of Bakhita—through writing and images, including pictures and articles on various web pages, I have found the traces that I have sketched here. I call these traces lines of the biographical meshwork. In them, names unfold into Saint Bakhita, Saint Josephine Bakhita, Sister Josephine Bakhita, the African saint, our brown sister, holy brown sister, Bakhita, and others.

The concept of meshwork and the graph that represents this concept have been modified to reflect the significant lines in the Bakhita tapestry. The graph contains two crossing lines, representing Africa and Italy, with two vanishing points standing in for other countries in Europe (France) and Latin America (Brazil). The line of Brazil folds and unfolds into two lines, which are imbued with cultural and political meaning. Thus, the line of Italy (Rome, the Vatican) is Catholic and missionary in relation to the African and American continents. The line of Africa-Sudan contains the Islamic extension and the Catholic mission. As a vanishing point, Brazil folds and unfolds into another line: Saint Bakhita and the Afro-Brazilian struggle. Thus, the initial fold develops and becomes further multiplied. Of course, this concept of biographical meshwork possesses the potential to read other instances of biographical narratives recorded by others. As we begin to unravel the knots of a biographical meshwork, we begin to understand why lives are told, retold, and told again.

Universidade Estadual de Campinas

Disclosure Statement

No potential conflict of interest was reported by the author.

Notes

1. For further elucidation, see Brown and Kleinberg.
2. The Geledés Black Woman Institute, established on 30 April 1988, is a civil society organization for the defense of black women and Afro-

diasporic peoples. *Gelede* is a Yoruba term and, among other meanings, refers to an annual festival (which occurs during the period of draught among the Yoruba from south-western Nigeria and neighboring Benin), which celebrates *awoniyawa*, or "mothers," not so much for their maternity, but as female elders.

Works Cited

Adriana. "Santa Josephina Bakhita." *Devoção e Fé: Blog Católico Apostólico Romano.* 8 Feb. 2013. Web. 23 Nov. 2014.

Brown, Peter. *The Cult of the Saints: Its Rise and Function in Latin Christianity.* Chicago: U of Chicago P, 1981. Print.

"Cultura afro-brasileira." *Faculdade Educacional de Colombo.* Web. 23 Nov. 2014.

Dagnino, Maria Luisa. *Bakhita Tells Her Story.* Rome: Canossian Daughters of Charity, 1993. Print.

Deleuze, Gilles. *Deux régimes de fous: Textes et entretiens 1975–1995.* Paris: Minuit, 2003. Print.

Ingold, Tim. *Being Alive: Essays on Movement, Knowledge and Description.* London: Routledge, 2011. Print.

"Josephine Bakhita." *Geledés Instituto da Mulher Negra.* Web. 23 Nov. 2014.

Kleinberg, Aviad M. *Prophets in Their Own Country: Living Saints and the Making of Sainthood in the Later Middle Ages.* Chicago: U of Chicago P, 1992. Print.

Kofes, Maria Suely, ed. *Histórias de vida: Biografias e trajetórias.* Cadernos do IFCH 31. Campinas: IFCH|Unicamp, 2004. Print.

—. *Trajetórias em narrativas.* Campinas: Mercado de Letras, 2001. Print.

Poupard, Cardinal Paul. "Josephine Bakhita, 1869–1947: From Slavery to the Freedom of Christ." Conférence du Quatrième Dimanche de Carême. Notre Dame de Paris. 30 Mar. 2003. *Les Missionnaires d'Afrique: Site des Pères Blancs en France.* Web. 23 Nov. 2014.

"Saint Josefina Bakhita, the Brown Sister." *Portal Paulinas.* Pia Sociedade Filhas de São Paulo—Brasil. 8 Feb. 2013. Web. 23 Nov. 2014.

Souza, Marcela Coelho de, and Carlos Fausto. "Reconquistando o campo perdido: O que Lévi-Strauss deve aos ameríndios." *Revista de Antropologia* 47.1 (2004): 87–131. Print.

"Summary of *Bakhita: mulher, negra, escrava, santa. Uma fascinante história de liberdade.*" *Geledés Instituto da Mulher Negra.* Web. 23 Nov. 2014.

Valverde, Rose. "Educação das relações étnico-raciais." *Portal da Cultura Afro-Brasileira.* Web. 23 Nov. 2014.

Tactical Lines in Three Black Women's Visual Portraits, 1773—1849

Líneas tácticas en los retratos visuales de tres mujeres negras, 1773—1849

By Joycelyn K. Moody

This essay explores power dynamics and aesthetic negotiations between artists and sitters in the production of pre-photographic portraits created as frontispiece author images for books with title pages naming a black woman as the (apparent) author. The essay traces a worried line of tradition among three black women author portraits from 1773 to 1849.

Este ensayo explora las relaciones de poder y las negociaciones estéticas entre los artistas y los modelos en la producción pre-fotográfica de retratos de imágenes autor creadas para el frontispicio de libros con páginas de título que nombran a una mujer negra como la autora aparente. El ensayo traza una preocupante line de tradición entre los retratos de tres mujeres negras datados de 1773 a 1849.

I thank God, there are no *free schools* nor *printing*, and I hope we shall not have these [for a] hundred years; for *learning* has brought disobedience, and heresy, and sects into the world, and *printing* has divulged them, and libels against the best government. God keep us from both! (William Berkeley, Governor of Virginia, 1672)

And we do well to remember, as evidenced by signed copies of her book, Wheatley's status was that most modern of things: an author on tour. (Young 71)

Even the illiterate may make literary allusions. (Wall 13)

Once, after I had lectured on *Memoirs of Elleanor Eldridge* at the University of Washington in Seattle, a colleague approached me to ask about the frontispiece image and title page I had projected (figure 1).[1] Skeptically but eagerly she asked, "Are we supposed to believe that is what Eldridge looked like?" Throughout my years of working with the biography collaboratively authored by Eldridge and Frances Whipple (Green McDougall), I had consistently assumed that the arresting woodcut intaglio engraving of a dark-skinned woman prefacing all nine editions of *Memoirs of Elleanor Eldridge* and its oft-published companion *Elleanor's Second Book*, first published the following year, in 1839, indeed was an artistic rendering of the eponymous subject of the biography. Now this insinuation that the image could not represent Eldridge propelled me anew. So, this essay asks a series of questions not only about the frontispiece portrait of *Memoirs of Elleanor Eldridge* and *Elleanor's Second Book*, but also about two other books written by women of African descent that feature frontispiece portraits of the authors: Phillis Wheatley's *Poems on Various Subjects*, Religious and Moral (1773) (figure 2) and *Religious Experience and Journal of Mrs. Jarena Lee, Giving an Account of Her Call to Preach the Gospel* (1849) (figure 3).

Author frontispiece portraits were a commonplace in books written in English by 1773, when Wheatley's *Poems on Various Subjects* was first published in London. In "The Slave Narrative and Visual Culture," Marcus Wood asserts that, "[w]ith the arrival of the press and the relatively easy integration of mass-produced wood and copper-engraved imagery within the covers of a single book, the personal portrait became irrevocably connected with authorship and ownership" (198). Contemplating each black woman's book examined here for the frontispiece of her presumed likeness, I use this essay to explore the particular artistic technique and medium used to portray each frontispiece subject.[2] Can we learn and discern why the frontispiece figure in *Memoirs of Elleanor Eldridge* is a woodcut engraving? Should we ultimately conclude that the choice reveals the unknown artist's standard work tools, or is there evidence that the engraving signals Eldridge's relative class status? Did Eldridge's woodcut engraving indicate her access to fewer financial resources in the 1830s, ironically, than

FIGURE 1. *Woodcut frontispiece depicting Elleanor Eldridge with broom from* Memoirs of Elleanor Eldridge.

FIGURE 2. *Frontispiece depicting Phillis Wheatley writing from* Poems on Various Subjects, Religious and Moral.

FIGURE 3. *Frontispiece depicting Jarena Lee writing from* Religious Experience and Journal of Mrs. Jarena Lee.

the enslaved Wheatley had had in 1773, when a painting of her likeness was commissioned by a British countess, specifically to be recast as a copper engraving for the frontispiece portrait for Wheatley's book?[3] Or do the differences in the engraving technologies and techniques more mundanely suggest developments in the tools of the trade and art of portraiture between 1773 and 1838? Are there socio-economic class implications of these various media for rendering the images of the two black women book subjects? How racialized are the choices the respective anonymous artists made in producing these portraits?[4]

In addition to these questions, I explore the power dynamics and aesthetic negotiations at work between artist and sitter in portrait production—specifically for portraits destined to evolve into frontispiece images in books with title pages naming a black woman as the (apparent) author. The relationships in these sittings would obviously have been more complicated and more complex for Phillis Wheatley in Boston before the American Revolution, for Elleanor Eldridge in Providence during the early years of Rhode Island's gradual emancipation, and for Jarena Lee in Philadelphia precisely in the middle of the nineteenth century. In an analysis of the organization of title pages in books dating back to the middle of the seventeenth century, William A. Coulter posits that, of a variety of stylistic and aesthetic options, "[t]he first and most obvious choice is that of the author-portrait" (71). Were there deliberate, class-inflected differences in the technologies an unidentified artist used *circa* 1770 to render Selena Hastings, the Countess of Huntingdon, in a way that contrasted her portrait with the painting of Phillis Wheatley, the countess's chosen charge and an object of her benefaction? The painting of Wheatley had been purposely commissioned for transcendence into a second life as the frontispiece to the title page of the poet's first book.[5] Yet the painting of the countess notably does not preface a linguistic version of her life or other verbal text of her own making. Did the artist depicting Wheatley deploy the same tools as had the artist portraying the countess—perhaps at Hastings' request? If so, can we reason as an impetus here a gesture of racialized egalitarianism, or was it because the countess might have sought to project the same quality for her charge as for herself in protection of her reputation? Or was it because those particular tools were the best and|or most readily available to the artist hired to paint Wheatley? Astrid Franke has observed a "conceptual semblance of the two portraits [that] suggests that the Countess wanted to present Wheatley as her black double, differing in color but twinned in an attitude figured by the gesture of melancholy" (227). What else can this early and complex genealogy of sitter, artist, and benefactor teach us? How and where else might we apply it to become better informed about the complexities of visual representations of women of African descent before the *de jure* abolition of slavery in the US?

Furthermore, I speculate here about negotiations between artists, sitters, and authors—especially pertinent in the case of *Memoirs of Elleanor Eldridge*, which was collaboratively authored by an interracialized writing dyad—bearing in mind what Fionnghuala Sweeney refers to as "a vocabulary of the visual" (239). Writing about Harlem Renaissance-era portraitist Archibald Motley, Sweeney argues for Motley's conscious engagement with the tradition of frontispiece portraiture in literary works by African Americans stretching back to the eighteenth century, contending that the impact of this early "literary and photographic portraiture [manifests in the ways] his paintings respond to the overlapping visual and literary dynamics that characterised responses to enslavement, drawing on the tradition of frontispiece portraiture, and translating aesthetic strategies from literature and performance into a vocabulary of the visual" (239). Moreover, Sweeney contends that "at the heart of the tradition of frontispiece portraiture" one finds "performative self-fashioning and conscious self-recognition" (240). Sweeney's claims inspire questions about collaborations and issues of control between sitter and artist over a portrait in progress. What arrangements, what contracts were possible between the black and female sitting-subject in the composition of a pre-photographic portrait intended as the frontispiece of a book bearing her name, whatever the medium of the portrait (e.g. painting, mezzotint engraving on copper, or woodcut engraving, and so on)?[6] How much control, agency, or authority could a black woman sitter exert over the rendering of her image or the design of her title page in the late eighteenth century and into the nineteenth? Reflecting on title pages in early book history, William A. Coulter cites the authors of *The Comely Frontispiece*, Margery Corbett and R. W. Lightbown, as having taken pains "to emphasize that the designs of these title pages are the work of the authors, not the engravers, and thus give us direct links to the thought processes and assumptions of those authors" (70n3). One wonders if, or how, Corbett and Lightbown's assertion fares when the title pages in question are those of published books by and|or about women of African descent.

Borrowing the trope of the "worried line" of black expressive traditions as theorized by Cheryl Wall in *Worrying the Line: Black Women Writers, Lineage, and Literary Tradition*, I analyze here the frontispiece portraits in Wheatley's *Poems*, Eldridge's *Memoirs*, and Lee's *Religious Experience and Journal*.[7] The aesthetic conventions of Lee's frontispiece in her *Religious Experience and Journal* reiterate those of Wheatley's in several ways. In 1773, an oil painting of Wheatley served as the inspiration and model for a mezzotint copper engraving of the poet, to be reprinted as her frontispiece portrait in *Poems on Various Subjects*. By 1849, despite the availability of the daguerreotype (a portrait-type choice for many ministers for their author frontispieces), Lee chose instead a lithograph based on an oil painting for her text.[8] Indeed, the introduction of the daguerreotype process had coincided with a jump in the number of slave narratives "from nine in the 1830s to twenty-five in the 1840s and continued rising until the end of the 1860s," according to Sarah Blackwood (97). Nonetheless, between Wheatley's *Poems* and Lee's spiritual autobiography, a pre-photographic image deploying a very different aesthetic and invoking a different tradition of African womanhood served as the frontispiece to *Memoirs of Elleanor Eldridge*, for, in virtually every year between 1838 and 1847, the same intaglio woodcut was reprinted without alteration or modernization in each edition and printing of *Memoirs of Elleanor Eldridge* and *Elleanor's Second Book.*[9] Whereas the renderings of Wheatley and Lee adapt the high, Anglo-American style of colonial Boston portraitists such as John Singleton Copley, the imagistic woodcut preceding Eldridge's narrative is reminiscent of seventeenth-century broadsides advertising the sale of African captives, in that, like the earlier broadsides, the Eldridge portrait trusts (or, alternatively, exploits) the textures and qualities a woodcut can produce not only to suggest the color of the subject's skin, but also to present the lines of her body and clothing—and, significantly, her work instrument—in sharp contrast to her skin.

Wheatley and Lee are better-known early US black women than Elleanor Eldridge because literary, social, and religious historians engaged in recovery studies have often privileged (black) women writers and intellectuals over women without traditional literacy. This essay discusses the frontispiece to *Memoirs of Elleanor Eldridge* in order to reintroduce an important but little-known biography, and also to argue for the significance of its visual narrative of the ways that women of African and indigenous descent could not only survive, but also succeed, if unhindered in the early American North. *Memoirs* reveals Eldridge's socio-economic class ascendancy, her rise to wealth, and her accumulation of real-estate property in Providence, Rhode Island. Eldridge was born into African and indigenous family lines—and cultural contexts—that esteemed landowner-ship as a precious source of political, social, and economic power. The work tool in the hands of the figure in Eldridge's frontispiece challenges the quill pen held by the subjects in Wheatley's and Lee's portraits as an archetypal trope of black liberation; it tacitly suggests an alternative way a black woman could enter the early national workforce with influence and dignity, and ultimately also enter African American letters, while simultaneously making an indisputable case for black people's right to citizenship. It is no coincidence that Eldridge's singular image appears prominently in virtually every text—lengthy and brief, bound and virtual—that even merely mentions *Memoirs of Elleanor Eldridge.*[10]

One prominent intervention of *Worrying the Line* is Wall's cogent claim "that nonliterary texts, such as blues, sermons, and recipes for conjure, insert themselves in African American tradition and worry this literary line" (11).[11] Wall breaks free from literary criticism that focuses exclusively on written literature. First, though, she reconstructs a history of mid to late twentieth-century African Americanists such as Robert Stepto and Henry Louis Gates, Jr., who theorized the concept of an African American literary tradition (11−12)—and the various critiques of some of those theorizations by black feminist critics, especially in the 1970s through the 1990s, including Hazel Carby, Deborah McDowell, Barbara Smith, Wall herself, and Mary Helen Washington. Rather than a black literary tradition without women, they theorized and thematized black women writers as blues symbols of "commercial, cultural, and historical potency," and as symbols of "female creativity and autonomy whose art informs and empowers their own" (Wall 7). In a lineage of visual representations formed by the frontispieces to the books by and about Wheatley, Eldridge, and Lee, the portrait in Eldridge's book breaks, worries, or "cuts."[12] In that black literary traditions typically manifest improvisation and invention, the three author portraits studied here demonstrate each sitter's imaginative inventiveness.

In "Slave Narratives and the Rhetoric of Author Portraiture," Lynn A. Casmier-Paz reminds us that the earliest portraits of black authors served the pedagogical function of teaching readers how to resolve a putative puzzle—"the ideological contradiction of the writing slave" (93).[13] She asserts that the frontispiece performed a "strategic, and political," role—one that diluted the inherent ironies of presumed oxymorons such as *slave author* and *slave portrait* (91–93). That black authors would seek to provide a visual counternarrative is easily understood in light of European caricatures of dark-skinned Africans wearing powdered wigs and white waistcoats, such as the infamous portrait *Francis Williams, the Negro Scholar of Jamaica* (*circa* 1745).[14] Apparently, a frontispiece portrait for a (literary) work by an author of African descent presented an enigma to Anglo- and European-American readers because it violated the stereotype of people of African descent as unlettered and uneducable, barbaric and soulless. From the earliest renderings of the human image, however, a portrait was believed to depict its subject's "character" as interpreted by the artist, in addition to representing a person's outer appearance. A national obsession with representing one's inner essence, or soul, indeed played a key role in the inclusion of author images in narratives by or about a good many formerly enslaved and other free(d) black people.

Throughout "Reading the Runaways: Self-Fashioning, Print Culture, and Confidence in Slavery in the Eighteenth-Century Mid-Atlantic," David Waldstreicher documents the extensive uses of the instability and theatricality of appearance and disguise—clothing; accent; voice; language; hair texture, length, style, or color; complexion; comportment; posture; aptitude; skills; personality traits; and so on—as generative resources that enslaved black people adapted to pursue freedom from the very beginning of print-culture traditions in colonial North America.[15] Advertisements for fugitive slaves might alert community members to material goods that out-of-place black people might have in their possession: besides the familiar slave pass—once genuine but now counterfeit(ed)—or a mother escaped with her children, they might mention or image a black figure carrying a pole weighed down with what appears to be personal items tied into a knapsack and thrown over one shoulder. Not unlike the icons in these coarse colonial-era slave bills, the refined author portraits of Wheatley, Eldridge, and Lee can also be said to depict each woman handling her own reconfiguration of the liberty-pole trope: writing tool or work tool, each woman fingers a liberating pole, conveying a semiotics of both whiteness and Africanity arguing for self-authored African-descended womanhood.[16]

Moreover, the particular pre-photographic portraiture technologies of the frontispieces in the books by or about Wheatley, Eldridge, and Lee subvert the print and aesthetic modalities generally deployed before the advent of the daguerreotype to depict savage racializations of black women, and they antici-pate some of the complex identity and authenticity issues that would emerge during the antebellum period when African American authors turned to photog-raphy to defy racist stereotypes.[17] Each woman's verbal and visual authorial self-portrait constitutes a collaboration with at least one visual artist or arti-san—painter, engraver, bookmaker, printer—to vanquish what Patricia Hill Collins calls "controlling images" of black women (76). Similarly, Hazel Carby has noted that "the objective of stereotypes is not to reflect or represent a reality but to function as a disguise, or a mystification, of objective social relations" (qtd. in Collins 76)—that is, stereotypes control perceptions of reality so as to make them seem natural, normal, and incontestable. In defiance of pejorative stereotypes about women of African descent circulating in 1773, 1838, and 1849, each of the three frontispieces reveals self-conscious signifying as their respective subjects manipulate visual- and print-culture media to determine how the black female body is depicted as a symbol and icon; each image ulti-mately authorizes black female subjectivity and interiority. The three portraits examined demonstrate black women's rejection of the controlling images of African womanhood and their work to replace them with images that black women control.

Wheatley and Lee: "Doing Phillis"

While, in visual and print culture, graphic images of women of African descent pre-date Wheatley's 1773 portrait, Gwendolyn DuBois Shaw argues that, regarding the author frontispiece prefacing *Poems on Various Subjects*, "there is no direct precedent for this image… [thus rendering Wheatley] the first colonial American woman of any race to have her portrait printed alongside her writings" (27).[18] Shaw situates the frontispiece of Wheatley's book in a tradition of author images of eighteenth-century British and Anglo-American authors, including Hannah More and Alexander Pope, and contends further that one aim of situat-ing Wheatley's imagistic identity amid this company would be to defy ideologi-cally controlled visual codes "of black bodies in the Americas" (39). Remarkably, the frontispiece lithograph of Jarena Lee revises her predecessor's even as it, too, draws on traditions of formal European painting, portraiture, and lithography.

The frontispiece portrait prefacing Wheatley's *Poems* reproduces (or is similar to?) a portrait painting of Selina Hastings, the Countess of

Huntingdon, to whom *Poems* is dedicated.[19] Hastings consented to the inclusion of this dedication in *Poems*; in January 1773, Captain Robert Calef, an agent of Hastings, wrote to Phillis Wheatley's mistress, Susanna Wheatley, that the countess "is fond of having the Book dedicated to her; but one thing She desir'd which She said She hardly tho't would be denied to her, that was to have Phillis' picture in the frontispiece. So that, if you can would [*sic*] get it done it can be Engrav'd here" (qtd. in Carretta, *Phillis* 93). Suggesting, too, that a frontispiece portrait of the poet would increase sales of the volume, Hastings lent prestige to the enslaved poet and problematized her status as chattel property, since portrait painting was theoretically reserved for the rich and prominent, those whose visages were deemed worthy of preservation for posterity—ironically, those faces already well known, such as politicians and monarchs, and persons with the leisure to sit throughout the slow and painstaking process of completion.[20]

Regarding Wheatley's portrait, Vincent Carretta remarks that "[a] frontispiece depicting an eighteenth-century black woman capable of writing poetry had revolutionary implications" (*Phillis* 101).[21] In "Revolutionary Women," Betsy Erkkila locates the radical stances and multivalent discourses of women, both black and white, in Wheatley's post-revolutionary Boston, as "they learned to speak with a double tongue, manipulating the language of republicanism in a manner that challenged while it appeared to enforce traditional female bounds" (219). Moreover, Erkkila remarks that the frontispiece of the first issue of the *Lady's Magazine* of 1792, titled *The Genius of the Ladies Magazine*, features "a petition for the Rights of Woman to American Liberty; and passages from Mary Wollstonecraft's *A Vindication of the Rights of Woman* (1792) are excerpted within it" (219).[22] For Barbara Lacey, too, Wheatley's portrait is "revolutionary" (175). Lacey comments on some of the more radical aspects of the frontispiece when she observes that, although "the inscription on the portrait's border identifies her as 'Phillis Wheatley, Negro Servant to Mr. John Wheatley, of Boston'... [s]he is presented to English readers as a woman of refinement, a poet, and a servant—an improbable, thought-provoking combination of roles" (172). In addition to the provocative image of an African woman depicted writing with a European-style pen to challenge, if not also revise, issues of race, caste, and class, many scholars have noted the engraver's subversive use of light and shadows, depth and profile, and tropes of domesticity and literacy.[23] Among these, Wood has written, "This is a vision of a young poet making art:... her lips are pursed in concentration, her one visible eye stares into the middle distance, and she is lost in the process of creation. So deep is her focus on the work that the reader is not acknowledged at all" ("Slave" 204).

Let us grant for a moment a conscious design to limit the revolutionary implications of her portrait, following Carretta's suggestion that a number of elements in Wheatley's frontispiece "seem designed to limit those [revolutionary] implications" (*Phillis* 101) discussed above. We might read Wheatley as having deployed what Karlyn Kohrs Campbell has identified as "feminine rhetoric," which is fundamentally defined by expressions of mistrust or misgiving, especially on the part of women, with respect to masculinist and patriarchal claims to authority, and usually made using tentative, seductive, self-effacing, or personal claims (qtd. in Foster 327). In "Resisting *Incidents*," Frances Smith Foster applies Campbell's speech theories to Harriet Jacobs' *Incidents in the Life of a Slave Girl*, written nearly one hundred years after Wheatley's *Poems*. Foster scrutinizes Jacobs' antebellum slave narrative for feminine rhetoric because its first-person narrator often appeals directly to readers using a "discourse of distrust" that is akin to signifying strategies consistent with a great deal of African American literature. Foster concludes, however, that Jacobs' race status as an enslaved "mulatto" abrogates the power usually obtaining in feminine rhetoric, since "Racism exacerbates distrust" (327). Significantly, when Jacobs published her autobiography in 1861, years after the life events it narrates, she tactically omitted an author frontispiece, even though such images were de rigueur in slave narratives, as Michael Chaney has suggested (27).[24] Jacobs even used a pseudonym—Linda Brent—for her eponymous enslaved girl-self. In order to get feminine rhetoric to work for her to the extent that it does, however, Jacobs had to augment her manuscript with the authority of established white woman abolitionist Lydia Maria Child. In 1861, success ensued.

Generations before Jacobs, Wheatley faced a similar predicament, and she seems to have utilized a variant of Campbell's feminine rhetoric of visual and print culture to solicit the favor of prospective readers of *Poems on Various Subjects*, specifically engaging them as collaborators in the construction of Wheatley as a deserving portrait sitter. In other words, we might read the frontispiece as depicting Wheatley in what Sweeney describes (regarding a painting of a much later black woman) as "a gesture of performative kinship" (241)—hence, to achieve that resonance, the repetition of Hastings' portrait in Wheatley's own: the reiteration of costumes (bonnets, blouses, collars, shawls), body gestures, books and other props, and signs of domesticity, if not also the two women's gazes, poses, and positionalities.[25] Both Hastings and Wheatley are depicted with neutral mouth and facial expressions, as is customary in portraits of the late eighteenth century, with the sitter's personality and emotional state being insinuated through the artistic representation of her eyes, brows, and gaze. The countess is rendered in full face, and her gaze is focused directly into the eyes of the artist and the viewer. By contrast, Wheatley (and later Jarena Lee, emulating her) is imaged in partial profile, three-quarter view, and looks slightly away from those gazing on her, with the slight tilt and introspective look of the intellectual in a conventional posture of contemplation. Lacey notably reads Wheatley as figured in a gesture of self-protection: "Wheatley's portrait shows her as more pensive than Equiano, with an upraised arm to put distance between herself and the spectator. She is protecting herself, as well as meditating, while she writes" (175). Read this way, Wheatley could be understood to have solicited the attention of persons she disdained—people in her milieu from whom she reasonably sought to distance herself.

Wheatley's incisive arrangement of her affairs as she sailed to London in June 1773, just as the Mansfield decision made possible her self-emancipation, provides sufficient evidence that she was capable of astute negotiation for the production of her portrait.[26] As Carretta wryly notes of both the poet and the scholars who have studied her, "We have come to appreciate Wheatley as a manipulator of words; perhaps we should have more respect for her as a manipulator of people as well" (*Phillis* 137). Inseparable from the visual representation offered by the author portrait, Wheatley's literary achievement, her book, was "still in demand more than five years after first being published" (174).[27]

The Preacher and the Poet

In 1849, seventy-odd years after Wheatley published *Poems*, Jarena Lee would reimagine the poet's portrait, updating it by removing its confining oval frame.[28] The lithographic portrait of the author in *Religious Experience and Journal of Mrs. Jarena Lee, Giving an Account of Her Call to Preach the Gospel* (1849) is, its caption states, "drawn from life by A. Huffy," and her title page states that the text has been "written by [Lee] herself."[29] Indeed, an isolated line near the foot of Lee's title page reads in full: "Revised and corrected from the Original Manuscript, written by [Lee] herself." (*The Life and Religious Experience of Jarena Lee, a Coloured Lady* had been published without an author image in 1836.) Foster comments on a similar—and generic—designation in Jacobs' *Incidents*: "Reading the words 'Written by Herself' that follow the subtitle and words 'Published for the author' that come at the bottom of that page, a reader confronts not only the exercise of literary prerogative, of claiming authorial responsibility for the text's selection and arrangement, but also an assumption of self-worth, of meaning and interest in her personal experiences that exceed the specific or personal" (326).

It is this antebellum tradition of self-naming and self-making that, Sweeney contends, proved to be so influential on Harlem Renaissance portraitists such as Archibald Motley. Significantly, Lee's 1849 printer and publisher are not identified by their names, where the title page notes the spiritual autobiography was "Printed and Published for the Author" (*Religious* 1). As in other texts by nineteenth-century black women writers, with the clauses "published for the author" and "written by herself," and the additional declarations that she "revised and corrected" her own narratives, Lee establishes her authority over the material reality of the book as a print-culture artifact, as well as over the intellectual property it contains and the life experiences it chronicles.

Lee's portrait expresses the sitter's desire to emulate Wheatley's in some ways, and thereby to establish, or continue, a worried line of black women's resistant and self-determined transgenerational imagery. Lee's image pays homage to Wheatley's portrait with its visual cues of imagination and intelligence paradoxically alongside servitude and confinement. It suggests perhaps a greater access to literacy in its relative excess of key tropes borrowed from its predecessor: where Wheatley is featured with a single feather pen and two small bound volumes beside her inkwell and several sheets of paper, Lee is depicted with two quill pens, an inkwell, numerous already inscribed manuscript pages, and two oversized books, the spines of which clearly designate them as *Bible* and *Dictionary*. Furthermore, seated with an arm resting on the large Bible, Lee is "doing Phillis," as Shaw dubs the pose: the critical work of "fashion[ing] an identity" to compete with commonplace caricatures of black women as incompatible with tropes of pious and elite white womanhood (Shaw 39).

Wheatley and Lee each appear alone in the image, as is typical of author portraits, and their solitude accentuates the power each assumes as an iconic intellectual, thinker, and visionary. The intersection of visual and verbal representations—again, what Sweeney calls the "vocabulary of the visual" (239)—honors each woman's singleness within the "frame" of her portrait. Moreover, a black woman imaged alone registers in a particular way, for it suggests her detachment from the heteronormative family, from normative (white) women's traditional spheres. How shall we read a black woman depicted alone on a canvas? P. Gabrielle Foreman cogently argues that one reading of the absent black male partner at the side of an antebellum black woman of marriageable age is the latter's banishment from the institution of marriage (524). Also, from one angle, a woman alone depicted wearing the costumes that Wheatley, Eldridge, and Lee wear visually implies disinterest in men and marriage—a putatively non-normative but reassuring rejection of sexual desire, contrary to myths about aberrant African female lust and savage hypersexuality. As Lacey contends, "In eighteenth-century America, as blacks gained literacy and set out to redefine who and what a black person was in opposition to already solidified stereotypes, they chose to be visually presented in portraits that show introspection and self-mastery, which were the hallmarks of black self-construction" (175). Astute articulations of power, and also subjection, formed from the sitters' eyes as much as the artists'.

Significantly, the Bible on which Lee's right arm rests recalls not only the genealogy of Wheatley's black woman author portrait, but also that of the African Christian author portrait represented by the frontispiece of the spiritual autobiography—slave narrative hybrid *The Interesting Narrative of the Life of Olaudah Equiano, or Gustavus Vassa, the African* (1793). Equiano had arranged to have himself depicted in formal dress and posture, piously holding open a Bible at Acts 4.12 and gazing into viewers' eyes as if reading aloud or exhorting us.[30] His portrait offers visual assurance that he is a reader, and the same image provides textual assurance that the book in which his face appears was "written by himself." Over half a century later, Lee's frontispiece tropes her as both a reader and a writer by depicting her beside two large books and two quill pens. The self-composed portrait positions her elbow such that viewers' eyes are guided to the quill pen in her right hand. In addition, the contents of her autobiography articulate her self-efficacy as an itinerant minister—that is, as a self-reliant woman literally and freely working outside of domestic and maternal spheres. Though in her *Journal* Lee identifies herself as a "poor coloured female instrument" of God (Lee 12), she offers an almost direct gaze out to viewers from where she sits, tall and resolute, in an upholstered high-backed chair.

In other words, while Lee's frontispiece portrait draws a connective line to Wheatley's, there are nonetheless noteworthy differences between the two images. For one, the ring that Lee wears on her right hand—the one prominently holding a quill pen—reminds us of her status as once a wife, now a widow: her license to itinerant ministry without social censure. Lee's legal marriage heavily underlines Wheatley's enslaved status at the publication of *Poems on Various Subjects*, when she had no possibility of a free, legal marriage in Boston. Whereas Lee writes of her freeborn sons, had Wheatley become a mother before her manumission in 1773, her children would have suffered her condition of involuntary servitude under colonial Massachusetts law. Lee is further depicted as a matron by the white bonnet and shawl she wears, reminiscent of Revolutionary-era middle-aged and elderly women of New England rendered iconic by John Singleton Copley. The white bow under the chin in the Lee portrait especially contrasts with the black string around the subject's neck in the *Poems* frontispiece. Carretta writes, "The dark string around Wheatley's neck subtly reminded viewers of her enslaved colonial status"; he likens the collar, too, to images of enslaved people in earlier paintings who were depicted collared to specify ownership, as were pet animals (*Phillis* 101).[31]

Lee's *Religious Experience* was her second spiritual autobiography. The first, *The Life and Religious Experience of Jarena Lee, a Coloured Lady*, was published two years before Eldridge's *Memoirs* appeared in 1838; it had not included an author frontispiece, perhaps because, as a traveling minister dependent on the churches she visited for sustenance, Lee lacked the resources to illustrate her twenty-four-page autobiographical tract. By 1849, however, not only was her itinerant ministry more established and secure, but arguably she was also by then a wiser, shrewder autobiographer, and knew the collateral advantages a frontispiece author portrait could provide. For what Erkkila observes about Wheatley in 1773 was no less true for Lee in 1849: "Within the discourse of racial inequality... the fact of a black woman reading, writing, and publishing was in itself enough to splinter the categories of white and black, and explode a social order grounded in notions of racial difference" (202). Years before, Elleanor Eldridge and her collaborators had also seemed to understand that merely to associate a black woman in affirmative ways with literacy, visual, and print cultures was a revolutionary act.

Eldridge: Outlier in a Worried Line

The 1838 frontispiece to *Memoirs of Elleanor Eldridge* contests all the same stereotypes that Wheatley's portrait rejected in 1773 and those even more egregious images of African womanhood—the "blacklash" of vicious Bobalition broadsides and the like—perhaps not coincidentally appearing shortly after Wheatley's revolutionary frontispiece.[32] On the one hand, the *Memoirs of Elleanor Eldridge* frontispiece joins the tradition of visual representations of black women of "good character," and works with the frontispiece portraits in the books by both Wheatley and Lee to establish a temporal, as well as traditional, line of black women using visual self-representation to accentuate and proclaim their resolve to effect self-determination. On the other hand, the frontispiece portrait of Eldridge deviates from those of Lee and Wheatley as images of black women who inscribed their own texts and whose intellectual and mental subversions differed from Eldridge's more physical, but no less mentally challenging, signifying labors. The portrait of Eldridge includes an emblem of her handicraft and aptitude, her labor voluntary and paid, and her status as a free woman—a sign different from the quill pens of the enslaved poet and the minister, and simultaneously different from other tools wielded by enslaved and free(d) black (and indigenous) womanhood of the 1830s and 1840s.[33] Indeed, the contrast between Eldridge's image and Wheatley's portrait illustrates how the latter obscures the poet's accomplishments as, in fact, enslaved labor. Partly because of the limitations of the woodcut as aesthetic methodology and apparatus, there is little resonance between the imagistic portrait of Eldridge in the frontispiece and the textual portrait that follows under Whipple's hand. This is all the more reason, then, to consider Eldridge's agency and her access to power in the visual depiction preceding her *Memoirs*.

Eldridge could have chosen the lithograph, too: lithographic sketches used to illustrate books reach back before William Blake's "Job in Prosperity," dated 1807 (Twyman, *Lithography* 30). Michael Twyman locates "the first English lithographic press outside London at the fashionable city of Bath" in 1813 (34−35), and continues, "The success of lithography was confirmed in 1817 from two very different standpoints: in that year the artistic possibilities of the process were first brought before the public when Lasteyrie sent a selection of lithographs to the Salon, and on 8 October 1817 the potential threat of lithography to the security of the state (and incidentally, therefore, to that of the printing trade) was acknowledged when it was subjected to the regulations already in force for letterpress and copper-plate printing" (56). Thus, by the time Eldridge and Whipple approached B. T. Albro to print the first edition of

Memoirs of Elleanor Eldridge in Providence, Rhode Island, a lithographic portrait was an open option. Cost seems a likely reason they chose a woodcut engraving instead.

About representations of black women that comment "ironically on gender and that indeed subvert male traditions of representation," Wood has provocatively suggested, "[i]t could be argued that this process in fact pre-dated the male infiltration of the [enslaved] author portrait genre" ("Slave" 203—04), for most of the earliest extant images of enslaved or free(d) black women depict them at labor, literally or figuratively with their hands full. Concurrent with the painting and engraving of Wheatley are colonial paintings, engravings, and other artworks depicting black women as (in)voluntary sexual partners of white men, such as *Joanna*, a scantily clad woman drawn for engraving by the late eighteenth-century British explorer John Stedman for his *Narrative, of a Five Years' Expedition*.[34] A superabundance of images of US black women appearing after Wheatley's image was circulated, especially during the antebellum era, imagine or envision black women as objects of subordination, in dumb domestic service to whites—as nursemaids for white youth and as cooks or kitchen help and odalisques for white women. In 1811, a legendarily gifted black nurse named Elizabeth Freeman (*circa* 1742—1829) became another of the earliest black women portrayed in a miniature portrait painted "in watercolor on ivory" (Public Broadcasting Service).[35] Freeman, also known as Maum Bett, Mumbet, and Mum Bett, was nearly seventy years old when she became a portrait sitter for Susan Ridley Sedgewick (b. 1788), whose father-in-law had led Freeman through a successful freedom suit in Massachusetts' courts on 21 August 1781.[36] Formerly enslaved and also presumed to be an ancestor of W. E. B. Du Bois, Freeman became the subject of a portrait that joins the line of extant black women portraits with Wheatley's, Eldridge's, and Lee's.

Given the images of women of African descent circulating before the advent of the earliest photographs, even today one might assume Eldridge rather than Wheatley to have been the enslaved woman. Eldridge's frontispiece portrait differs from both Wheatley's and Lee's, and Freeman's as well, since Eldridge was freeborn to African and indigenous parents in 1785, since she was not conventionally literate, and since she was a skilled artisan and an entrepreneur who was affluent enough to purchase land and yet not classed apart among elite black people, as was Wheatley. Her posture in the portrait differs from the two more book-learned black women's in their respective portraits. Significantly, Eldridge is depicted standing, not sitting like Wheatley and Lee. Moreover, she faces forward and stands upright, on her own two feet, as it were, underscoring the portrait's signifying emphasis on Eldridge's self-actualization and autonomy, despite her dependence on an amanuensis for the literary inscription of her *Memoirs*. Her gaze and the orientation of her unframed figure on the page convey what Sweeney calls a "comfortable intimacy" with both her artist and her viewer (241). The anonymous artist suggests Eldridge's stature through her hips, which are outlined beneath a long, loose white shawl. The intimation of her portrait, like Wheatley's and Lee's, is that the black woman writer subject appears in print as she "naturally" is in life and, in Eldridge's case, her contentment as a craftsperson is symbolized by the broom or brush she holds.

In "Visual Images of Blacks in Early American Imprints," Lacey regards portraits as offering "the most positive, complex, and individualistic representations of blacks" (167). Lacey reports that, in the eighteenth century, "[p]ortraits were usually undertaken after sitter and artist had determined how the individual wished to be represented with respect to expression, pose, and accompanying goods. Thus, when analyzed, frontispieces can reveal important elements of black self-construction" (169). The proceeds from the sale of Eldridge's biography would ultimately determine whether she could afford legal counsel to regain extensive real-estate property that had effectively been stolen away from her in the early 1830s.

A visual portrait of Eldridge prefaces each of the nine editions of *Memoirs of Elleanor Eldridge*. Arguably, the extent to which Eldridge is known at all correlates to an awareness and reproduction of this portrait, which is revolutionary in part because it forms one of a very few extant positive, "fully realized," respectful images of early nineteenth-century women of color—for Eldridge came of age just after the South African Sarah Baartman, staged in Paris as the freakish Hottentot Venus, and other black and indigenous women the world over were viciously mocked and lampooned as a matter of course, partly to exalt (and contain) European womanhood.[37] Purposely unlike Baartman's, and like Wheatley's and Lee's, Eldridge's body is rendered as fully clothed, in contrast to sexualized, generally caricatured images of enslaved black women of the period, such as the Joanna depicted in Stedman's travel narratives. Indeed, Maum Bett, cited above, is rendered in layers of clothing commensurate with the cold climate of New England, where she, too, lived. Furthermore, Maum Bett is also depicted in fashionable, albeit modest, matronly clothing; her well-dressed appearance suggests she dressed specifically for the sake of having her portrait crafted. Conversely, Eldridge's more commonplace dress artfully insinuates that her portrait was unplanned or perhaps that her likeness was taken on any ordinary day[38]—perhaps even that any day and any dress formed routine workdays for Eldridge, whose narrative atypically makes no mention of her religious beliefs. The broom she holds, too, underscores Eldridge's role as a laborer rather than a lady.

Regarding Lacey's observation of sitter—artist collaboration, and drawing also on Alan Trachtenberg's research on necessary collaborations between photographers and their sitters, I want to consider the carefully managed negotiation between Eldridge as portrait subject, the unknown artist who drew and engraved her image (perhaps Whipple as coauthor), and certainly the printer of *Memoirs of Elleanor Eldridge*. While the narrative that follows the portrait does detail how the girl-child Elleanor came as an adult to develop skills as a cheese and a mattress maker, an oft-sought laundress, a seamstress, and a nurse, Whipple seizes the verbal space of *Memoirs* to narrate her own (unsigned) version of Eldridge's life. Significantly, the white woman recounts the black and indigenous woman's life through the conventions of a sentimental and romantic biography—even to the inclusion of love letters—rather than as an autobiography. Thus, Whipple transparently manipulates how readers read her experience as a white woman responding to both Eldridge's material success and the injustices threatening it. Accordingly, our contemplation of the control Eldridge could exert over her image is crucial. As the sitting (or, rather, standing) subject, Eldridge collaborated on the orchestration of an (auto)biographical portrait, just as she collaborated with Whipple on the textual narrative: she worked with the artist, the printer, and perhaps her interlocutor, too, to represent herself as a complex social figure depicting several interlocking identities, none of which were akin to the abundant degrading stereotypes of black women circulating among the folks she hoped would buy her book, but rather all of her intersectional identities that would be pleasing to white and other readers of her biography. Mutual responsibility for the final product lay in all parties' arrangement of the angle of the sitter's body, the light(ing) and shadow, the backdrop, the furniture, the positions of the sitter's limbs and gaze, "the posture and deportment of [her] countenance," to take a phrase from Casmier-Paz (92), what clothing she wore, how she was positioned, and so on—as in daguerreotypes after 1839, so too in Eldridge's intaglio woodcut of 1838. Ultimately, then, Eldridge exerted a measure of power over the image of herself that preceded the narrative of her life—and the very fact of the image arguably also discloses her resolve to show herself to be an agent in the arrangement of the portrait.

The portrait racializes Eldridge as a woman of African descent.[39] To a degree, "race" is depicted in this portrait through the representation of an "African" phenotype, and uncovered curly "African" hair. She has a pleasant round face and a long neck; in the woodcut, shaded areas insistently accentuate a variety of textures on her shawl and skirt, on her exposed skin, and on the brush she holds. The poet M. Nourbese Philip speaks to the virtual impossibility of accurately describing (African) skin tones: "She! with the eyes of a tiger. And a skin so fine. I have no words for its color: a genealogy of silences. The language helpless to describe our usness. To say her skin was 'tawny' is to stray into the Frank Yerby world of mulattos, octoroons, and quadroons. To say it is brown is to leave as much unsaid: it was also yellow and black and even red" (12). Nonetheless, the artist's choice of a woodcut proves strategic in texturizing the portrait in a way to suggest the subject of the Eldridge portrait has relatively dark skin. Moreover, her cheekbones have been shaded to highlight fullness and to emphasize her slight smile. Her uncovered, close-cropped curly hair is symmetrical and orderly.[40] Significantly, the figure in the image returns a gaze to the artist and the spectator without challenge, hostility, or umbrage, and neither subjugation nor defiance. Instead, the direct and confident gaze conveys moral self-assurance.[41] The figure is not a naif, nor is the style primitivistic. Her eyes are pleasingly wide and open, evenly situated in the face; her brows are even and drawn carefully, thickly across the forehead. The figure stands alone, insinuating perhaps that Eldridge is not a member of a mutinous community of color, and she apparently has no male spouse and no dependent children. This putatively heartening aspect of her character is highlighted by the empty space of the background behind her: she appears as an isolated "colored" figure suspended in a vacuum—decontextualized, androgynous or sexless, tranquil, safe.[42]

Eldridge is gendered female in subtle ways that repudiate interlocking white, patriarchal, supremacist stereotypes of mammy, wench, Sambo, squaw, warrior, and insurrectionist. A purifying light-colored shawl modestly draped around her neck and broad shoulders feminizes her; she wears no apron or turban or bandana.[43] The shawl Eldridge wears anticipates the biography's recurrent reference to her exceptional skill as a handloom weaver—a major source of her income and wealth. Likewise, her garments convey respectability and dignity. Departing from images of iconic middling-class white womanhood, Eldridge here holds a work tool symbolic of work that is gender-neutral or gender-ambiguous, for both men and women performed work as house painters and wallpaper hangers around the turn of the nineteenth century.[44] The effect is a gender-ambiguous portrait of Eldridge and her labors—that is, Eldridge, Whipple, and the artist decided on a costume that was gendered less conventionally female and feminine than Wheatley's and Lee's. Significantly, over the next several decades, the formerly enslaved Sojourner Truth would wrap herself in lace shawls and bonnets alongside knitting needles, rather than harken back to the aesthetics of Eldridge's portrait. And White House modiste Elizabeth Keckley would show off her dressmaking talent in postbellum photographs depicting her lavishly bedecked in the fruits of her sewing-entrepreneur and fashion-designer enterprises. To be sure, the narrator of *Memoirs of Elleanor Eldridge* proclaims that Eldridge owned fashionable outfits: "Elleanor stood among her people, in the very highest niche of the aristocracy. She always accompanied her brother to these [black election] festivals, dressed in such style as became the sister of 'His Excellency.' On some of these occasions she wore a lilac silk; on others a nice worked cambric; then again a rich silk, of a delicate sky blue color; and always with a proper garniture of ribbons, ornaments, laces, &c." (Whipple and Eldridge 111). Yet, for the frontispiece of her biography, simple work clothes assert meticulous claims against prosperity and leisure to argue instead for prudence, agency, modesty, and honor.

Eldridge was approximately fifty-three years old when the first edition of *Memoirs* was published in 1838. At whatever age the portrait is intended to represent her, she is illustrated as a robust, vigorous worker. Eldridge appears satisfied and capable, too, with the artist emphasizing her physical strength by foreshortening and exaggerating her right arm and foregrounding it, to lead the spectator's gaze directly to it. Conversely, the portrait abnegates the actual challenges Eldridge likely faced in her daily work—from sexual molestation to environmental hazards to cheating clients.[45] Without any obvious symbol of displeasure, Eldridge flourishes a sign of her trade—perhaps a wallpapering brush.

Remarkably, an ornate, elegant signature appears beneath the portrait image on the *Memoirs of Elleanor Eldridge* frontispiece. Whose textual signifier is this? The signature regally suggests that Eldridge is not an ethnographic subject, not an anthropological study, in the way that other black women of the era such as Joanna and Sarah Baartman are reduced to when whites write about them and|or about images of them.[46] The size of the portrait of Eldridge in relation to the size of the signature substantiates her body and subjectivity as more significant than the lavish signature, which she may or may not have written.[47] The visual image and impact of her corporeality carry the idea of the truth of her person more than this appended, subordinate textual signifier—even though the two work in tandem to establish the biography and the biographical subject as both credible and creditable. Put another way, some combination of the authors, artist, printer, and publisher of *Memoirs of Elleanor Eldridge* has carefully crafted and designed the frontispiece to confront any reader's "resistant incident" with the text's own powerful iconographic resistance.[48] Joseph Rezek's recent claim about the impact of Wheatley in 1773 as an author seems to have been proved on *Memoirs of Elleanor Eldridge* in 1838: "Later responses to Wheatley and [Ignatius] Sancho suggest they became representative figures after book publication. When readers could hold an object in their hand, one that required a few hours to read and cost a few shillings, they generalized from the particular to the rule. These were objects that, given the frontispieces that depict authors of African descent, could by their material existence claim to *embody* the black body and reveal the black mind" (29–30).

Eldridge's frontispiece can be read as conforming to the late eighteenth-century broadside print culture that Lacey discusses in "Visual Images of Blacks in Early American Imprints." A woodcut that Lacey includes depicts two nearly nude "Africans," each with a small figure at the side—"probably representing a mother and child," Lacey theorizes (141). "The small figure may have been included to signal the fertility purchasable with a female slave" (139). She suggests also that the smaller figure might have depicted some West Africans' religious notion of the "little man" within—the soul or human interiority. Overall, Lacey cogently claims that the creator of these broadsides was familiar with diverse African spiritual traditions. In each broadside, an "adult African" carries a spear or scepter—one not unlike the work implement in Eldridge's frontispiece. Can we conceptualize Eldridge's tool as an African retention, a kind of lingering shadow text to signify her black ancestry and her agency? For Eldridge was freeborn in Rhode Island, where neither her labor nor her person nor her fertility were for sale. Definitively, the textual narrative that follows the frontispiece names a subject and narrates her life as a black and indigenous woman who chooses to remain unmarried and without children, in order to grow a business rather than a family.

Conclusion: Legacies of Resistance and Awareness

More critical and theoretical attention is needed to the technologies and visual media available to Wheatley, Eldridge, and Lee as portrait sitters, especially since we are sometimes fooled by the author portrait of Wheatley that prefaces *Poems on Various Subjects*; we mistake some reproductions of the portrait of the poet for the genuine article, even though they mock Wheatley's image and prominence, even though they mock us. Shaw astutely asks whether we are paying enough attention to portraits of black women in early America (36–40). Are we aware of the subtle and sometimes overt manipulations to which we are subjected? Have we realized the large number of reproductions of Wheatley's portrait? Why have we so easily accepted Scipio Moorhead as Wheatley's portraitist and engraver without any more material evidence than that the poet, who was famous for her elegies, addressed a poem to him?

In the worried line consisting of author portraits of Wheatley, Eldridge, and Lee, all created and published before 1850, we can read what Philip calls "legacies of resistance," "genealogies of resistance," and a tradition of resistance to injurious iconography and imagery, black women stereotypes, and myths about Africans. There exists a tradition and genealogy of awareness of black women who were determined to insinuate their own and each other's heterogeneous humanity and diverse ways of living black womanhood. We are not white women, the images taken together assert; nor are we the same as black men and, as black women, we are not and need not be the same as one another. They facilitate such later self-representations as those of Harriet Tubman and Sojourner Truth, two black women who famously invested in photographic iconography, illustrating, demonstrating, and shaping how black women could imagine themselves beyond bondage—for after the first publication of *Memoirs of Elleanor Eldridge* in 1838, during the second half of the nineteenth century, "printing and book production had changed even more substantially in response to the demand for faster, cheaper and greater quantities of printed products, and also for more strongly graphic and pictorial work" (Twyman, "Two Centuries" 104), among them author frontispiece portraits of formerly enslaved Americans in now classic slave narratives.

Ultimately, one might ask about the efficacy of pre-photographic representations of black women such as the woodcut-engraving frontispiece in *Memoirs of Elleanor Eldridge*. Does Eldridge's frontispiece advocate for the sitter's subjectivity? Was there a sitter at all, or did the artist, rather, rely on stereotypes and icons of black women of the era? Is it even possible for the technology of the woodcut engraving to capture human subjectivity? Could one convincingly argue, rather, that an engraving such as the alleged rendering of Eldridge in the frontispiece to *Memoirs of Elleanor Eldridge* cannot but flatten out human subjectivity, rather than capture and condense it—that a woodcut engraving, by definition, cannot cast or reprint such fine details in the ways of, say, an etching in copper? I have demonstrated in this essay tropes and functionality in the *Memoirs of Elleanor Eldridge* frontispiece that exceed these conventional limitations. The portrait rendering of Eldridge depicts her autonomy, agency, and subjectivity in ways that sustained its reprinting over the years between 1838 and 1847. Elleanor Eldridge's collaboration with her coauthor Frances Whipple and with the visual artist who created her image left us with both a literary and a pictographic record that correspond to the historical and tax records in her name. In each of these, Eldridge appears as an arresting woman of substance and mettle, indomitable and independent. From the frontispiece to the appendix, the subjectivity at the center of *Memoirs of Elleanor Eldridge* emerges with distinctive character and interiority as a woman who impressed everyone she met.

The University of Texas at San Antonio

Acknowledgements

Special thanks to Jasmine M. Cobb, Kathryn Gines, Eric D. Lamore, and Scott Sherer. I am deeply grateful to Ricia Chansky and Emily Hipchen for their patience and generosity. Thank you to all participants in the 2013 "Auto|Biography across the Americas" conference in Puerto Rico, as well as to Shanna Benjamin, Elizabeth Cali, Allegra Castro, Erin Ranft, Kent Rush, Tara Schmidt, and Vincent J. Schleitwiler.

Disclosure Statement

No potential conflict of interest was reported by the author.

Notes

1. I wish to thank Sandra Silberstein for this question in May 2009, after my lecture.
2. There is conflicting scholarship on the prevalence of author portraits in print culture before 1800. Establishing the uncommonness of Wheatley's portrait, Carretta writes in *Phillis Wheatley*, "Eighteenth-century books rarely included frontispiece-portraits of the author, especially not during the author's lifetime. Frontispieces were in effect status claims for

authors as well as for the readers who could afford them" (99). Conversely, in "'Conceited Portraiture before His Book... to Catch Fools and Silly Gazers': Some Reflections on *Paradise Lost* and the Tradition of the Engraved Frontispiece," William A. Coulter proclaims the inclusion of a frontispiece in print culture as so conventional by 1650 that its "deliberate absence" could be read as a commentary on previous texts within the same tradition. Coulter also directs readers to Helgerson's *Self-Crowned Laureates* for more on author-portrait frontispieces. On the history of frontispieces featuring (enslaved) black author portraits, see Casmier-Paz.

3. Cf. Pohl's discussion of the evolution of a portrait of George Washington and his family surrounded by servants.

4. Shaw writes, "While it [the original painting of Phillis Wheatley] has often been attributed to another enslaved African American, Scipio Moorhead, there is little concrete evidence to support this attribution" (58). For more of Shaw's rejection of Moorhead as the artist who painted Wheatley, see Shaw 26–28.

5. I follow Franke's dating of the painting of Hastings' portrait.

6. Many excellent critical and theoretical studies of African American photography from its earliest years to the present are emerging today (see, especially, Chaney; Foreman; Wallace and Smith; Willis and Krauthamer; Wood, *Blind Memory* and "The Slave Narrative and Visual Culture"). However, I am especially interested in studying pre-photographic portraits of black people in the North American colonies and later the US. On Wheatley's portrait in particular, see Balkun and Franke.

7. Although no author is named in any edition of *Memoirs of Elleanor Eldridge*, Whipple is usually identified as the single author under the name Frances H. Green or Frances H. McDougal. For a discussion of the collaborative authorship of this biography, see Moody.

8. According to Twyman, "By 1820 lithography was being widely used in Germany for a variety of jobbing work such as circular letters, diagrams, and statistical tables, and for map and music printing; it was used occasionally too for items such as visiting cards and book covers and for producing facsimiles of both texts and illustrations from old books. Lithography had also become firmly established as a suitable medium for the draughtsman—for original drawing and for making illustrations for books, topographical and portrait prints, and copies of paintings and drawings of the old masters" (*Lithography* 24). He continues by noting that lithographic techniques soon became "the stock-in-trade of professional lithographers in England and France" (24).

9. No edition of either Eldridge biography appears to have been printed in 1844.

10. The frontispiece portrait is reproduced, for example, in books ranging from Gates and Higginbotham's *African American National Biography* to Santamarina's *Belabored Professions*, and to the website featuring Rachel Kranz's *African-American Business Leaders and Entrepreneurs*.

11. On black women writers' challenges with respect to constructing or conforming to existing literary traditions, see Foster ("Resisting," *passim*).

12. Wall writes, "'Cuts' or 'breaks' in the line of literary tradition allow for the discontinuities and the 'cross-currents' that, as [Hortense] Spillers asserts, are characteristic of black women's writing" (16).

13. On formerly enslaved authors' use of visual self-representations, see Chaney.

14. Scholars disagree about the earnestness and quality of the portrait of Francis Williams, which he himself apparently did commission. Cf., for example, Carretta ("Who" 213, 225) and Shaw (14).

15. See also "The Slave Narrative" on the incongruity of runaway slave advertisements. Also see Blackwood's discussion of Wood (100−04).

16. For Wall's discussion of Stepto and literacy as the "pregeneric myth" of African American literature theory, see *Worrying* (248n18). In Eldridge's case, also deployed is a semiotics of indigeneity that it is beyond the scope of this essay to explore. For more on this topic, see Moody. Also, I thank Kathryn Gines for her observation that (mis)reading the quill pen as a trope of whiteness can be mistaken as an erasure of Lee's and Wheatley's affiliation with Africanity; that is not my intention here.

17. Cf. Senchyne's analysis of stereotype as a liberating technology in the early 1800s as compared to leaden type, and also his analysis of the multiple meanings of "stereotype" as both a plate for printing and a figure of representation.

18. Among early nineteenth-century portraits of black women in the US, cf. the putative engraving of an enslaved woman in Philadelphia known as Alice, "black Alice," and "Alice of Dunk's Ferry," who reportedly lived for 116 years. According to Kim Coulter, her image appeared in Isaiah Thomas's now lost *Memoirs of Remarkable Female Characters, Ancient and Modern* (1804).

19. Cf. Shaw: "Wheatley's interest in ecphrasis indicates not only did she wish to see with words, but that she herself may have wanted to be seen beyond words. And because the world in which she was raised, the world within which her sight-filled words operated, was one that had a set of objectifying tropes associated with the bodies of women of African descent, Wheatley and her portraitist had to employ a strategy to manipulate and defy the visual rhetoric associated with these conventions in order to assert control over them and to present the poet as a creative, intellectual, black woman whose self was connected to her text" (35−36).

20. See Casmier-Paz (93), Shaw (27–30), and Carretta (*Phillis* 100–02). For a discussion of the first advertisements of Wheatley's *Poems*, see Rezek (23–25).

21. Franke asserts that "[p]resent-day critics have argued that the engraving that prefaces Wheatley's poems represented a significant public, even political, act" (225).

22. Erkkila goes on to note, however, that the revolutionary spirit of the frontispiece is undercut by the contents of the magazine, "in which the ladies avow their intent to 'inspire the Female Mind with a love of religion, of patience, prudence, and fortitude—In short, whatever tends to form the ACCOMPLISHED WOMAN, the COMPLETE ECONOMIST, and the greatest of all treasures—a GOOD WIFE'" (219).

23. For a summary of critical assessments of Wheatley's portraits, see Franke (225–26).

24. By contrast, Wood asserts that "[t]he majority of published slave narratives did not carry any imagery, and of those that did, the vast majority carried only one image, the author's portrait" ("The Slave Narrative" 198).

25. Wood, among others, observes that "Phillis is dressed in her servant's attire, including an apron just visible below her right elbow" ("The Slave Narrative" 204).

26. On Wheatley and the Mansfield decision, see Carretta (*Phillis* 129, *passim*); on Wheatley's business acumen, see Carretta (*Phillis* 96, 137, 147).

27. On the inseparability of African American literal and visual histories, see Sweeney (243).

28. William A. Coulter references the common use of the oval frame for ornamentation on a title page or frontispiece in Milton's day (71).

29. For a history of lithographic sketches and the challenges early English artists faced as they attempted, *circa* 1807, to draw in traditional methods, primarily etching on copper, engraving on wood, working on stone, and drawing with quill pens, see Twyman (*Lithography* esp. 74). Lee's printer and artist were Peter S. Duval (*circa* 1804–86) and Alfred M. Hoffy (*circa* 1790–?), a French-born lithographer and an English immigrant artist, respectively, who worked together to produce many now iconic mid nineteenth-century American images, ranging from the *Battle of New Orleans—January 8, 1815* (1840) to *American Fashions, Fall and Winter 1849–50, by John R. Shankland* (*circa* 1849), and including portraits of US presidents and statesmen. Their lithograph portraits included one of Lee's black women contemporaries and colleagues, *Mrs. Juliann Jane Tillman, Preacher of the A. M. E. Church*, painted and printed in 1844. Tillman's portrait and Lee's share several stylistic and aesthetic traits in common, including the subject's formulaic dress, posture, props, light, shadow, and gaze. Thus, they illustrate each portrait's functionality as a subversion of the conventional or archetypal minister portrait, as well as

a repudiation of myths of African American women, free(d) or enslaved, as either wildly zealous in their religious fervor or altogether barbaric and savage, beyond Christian redemption.

30. For a brilliant discussion of the New Testament passage in Equiano's portrait, see Casmier-Paz (93–97). For a discussion of Equiano's frontispiece and his arrangement with portrait miniaturist William Denton to paint him, see Carretta ("'Property'" 134).

31. One thinks also of the iron collar used to punish enslaved people and others when judged to be recalcitrant.

32. See, for example, such broadsides as *Reply to Bobalition of Slavery* (1819), *Grand Bobalition, or "Great Anniversary Fussible"* (1821), and *Dreadful Riot on Negro Hill!* (1827).

33. For a discussion of the ways that the earliest daguerreotypes of enslaved black women in the US represented their exposed bodies as tools for "the pornography of forced labor," see Willis and Williams (21).

34. Lydia Maria Child featured Stedman's "Joanna" as a distinct, illustrated narrative her abolitionist collection *The Oasis* (1834). The key to the image of Joanna in the "List of Engravings" (p. v) in the fore matter of Child's Oasis lists the image as "Joanna. Reduced from a likeness drawn by Captain Stedman. Engraved on copper, by G. G. Smith. Printed by Andrews." See also an infamous anonymously produced and undated painting known as *Virginian Luxuries*, housed today at the Abby Aldrich Rockefeller Folk Art Museum in Williamsburg, Virginia. Although this painting apparently condemns slavery, I use it here to illustrate the pervasiveness of early national visual images of black women as sexual prey for white men, especially elite white men.

35. For a related discussion of the frontispiece portrait in *Memoirs of Elleanor Eldridge* and its relationship to early images of African American women such as Maum Bett, see also Moody. For more on Bett and Sedgewick, see Public Broadcasting Service.

36. According to Dumas, her case was listed as *Brom and Bett* v. *J. Ashley, Esq.* (716).

37. Among numerous black feminist scholarly analyses of Baartman's life and captivity, see Hobson and Sharpley-Whiting.

38. Thanks to Jasmine Cobb for this insight.

39. Evidence of Eldridge's indigenous background seems to be also insinuated in the portrait, but I am less qualified to comment on this in detail.

40. The direct gaze in Eldridge's frontispiece sharply contrasts with that of Delia and Drana, two black women infamously photographed by Joseph T. Zealy for the Swiss zoologist Louis Agassiz. As Willis and Krauthamer theorize, the enslaved women "were required to stare directly at the camera and thus at Zealy, as well as subsequent viewers, to facilitate their presentation as scientific specimens" (7).

41. On images of people of African descent from the seventeenth century to the present, see Willis and Williams.

42. On the technologies used for visual and graphic representations of people of color in nineteenth-century print texts, see Senchyne.

43. Note that Eldridge is depicted wearing her shawl draped—that is, in a style typically used in depictions of both Native American men and women. Interestingly, a few years before the first edition of *Memoirs of Elleanor Eldridge* was published, Swiss artist Karl Bodmer painted *Chan-Cha-Uia-Teuin, Teton Sioux Woman* (1833—34), a portrait of an indigenous Nebraska woman wearing a shawl loosely draped around her shoulders in precisely the same way as the figure in the *Memoirs of Elleanor Eldridge* frontispiece. For a discussion of early nineteenth-century portraits of Native Americans, see Pohl (170—73).

44. For a discussion of early antebellum laborers and labor unions, see Pasley.

45. Compare accounts in *The Life of William J. Brown* of William J. Brown's documentation of his repeated wrangling with white employers in Providence, Rhode Island, to receive the full amount of pay negotiated for his services (Brown seems to have been Eldridge's distant kinsman). For the dangers faced by free(d) and enslaved women of color with respect to labor and employment, see Hunter, Jones, and White. For the specific case of Addie Brown as a skilled, working-class black woman in domestic service in mid nineteenth-century Connecticut, see Hansen and Griffin.

46. For my discussion of the signature on the Eldridge biography frontispiece, I am borrowing from Foreman (517).

47. One of the women endorsing *Memoirs of Elleanor Eldridge* writes that "if she had received an early education, her mind might have soared above a laborious life, and her useful labors lost to the world" (Moody 150). In other places throughout the biography, the narrator indicates that Eldridge received no formal academic education.

48. On "resistant incidents," see Foster.

Works Cited

Balkun, Mary McAleer. "To 'Pursue th' Unbodied Mind': Phillis Wheatley and the Raced Body in Early America." *New Essays on Phillis Wheatley*. Ed. John C. Shields and Eric D. Lamore. Knoxville: U of Tennessee P, 2011. 371—96. Print.

Blackwood, Sarah. "Fugitive Obscura: Runaway Slave Portraiture and Early Photographic Technology." *American Literature* 81.1 (2009): 93—125. Print.

Bodmer, Karl. *Chan-Cha-Uia-Teuin, Teton Sioux Woman*. 1833–34. Watercolor and pencil. Joslyn Art Museum, Omaha.

Brown, William J. *The Life of William J. Brown of Providence, R.I.: With Personal Recollections of Incidents in Rhode Island*. Durham: U of New Hampshire P, 2006. Print.

Carretta, Vincent. *Phillis Wheatley: Biography of a Genius in Bondage*. Athens: U of Georgia P, 2011. Print.

—. "'Property of Author': Olaudah Equiano's Place in the History of the Book." *Genius in Bondage: Literature of the Early Black Atlantic*. Ed. Carretta and Philip Gould. Lexington: UP of Kentucky, 2001. 130–50. Print.

—. "Who Was Francis Williams?" *Early American Literature* 38.2 (2003): 213–37. *Project MUSE*. Web. 5 Mar. 2014.

Casmier-Paz, Lynn A. "Slave Narratives and the Rhetoric of Author Portraiture." *New Literary History* 34.1 (2003): 91–116. Print.

Chaney, Michael A. *Fugitive Vision: Slave Image and Black Identity in Antebellum Narrative*. Bloomington: Indiana UP, 2008. Print.

Cohen, Lara Langer, and Jordan Alexander Stein, eds. *Early African American Print Culture*. Philadelphia: U of Pennsylvania P, 2012. Print.

Collins, Patricia Hill. *Black Feminist Thought: Knowledge, Consciousness, and the Politics of Empowerment*. Boston: Unwin Hyman, 1990. Print.

Coulter, Kim. "Alice of Dunk's Ferry." Sidebar, "Slavery and the Slave Trade," by James Gigatino. *The Encyclopedia of Greater Philadelphia*. Web. 10 Dec. 2014.

Coulter, William A. "'Conceited Portraiture before His Book... to Catch Fools and Silly Gazers': Some Reflections on *Paradise Lost* and the Tradition of the Engraved Frontispiece." *Renaissance Papers* 2007: 69–81. Print.

Dreadful Riot on Negro Hill! 1827. Broadside. *Prints and Photographs Online Catalog*. Lib. of Cong. Web. 10 Dec. 2014.

Dumas, Bethany K. "Elizabeth Freeman (Mumbet, Mum Bett)." *Africana: The Encyclopedia of the African and African American Experience*. Ed. Kwame Anthony Appiah and Henry Louis Gates, Jr. 2nd ed. Vol. 2. New York: Oxford UP, 2005. 715–17. Print.

Equiano, Olaudah. *The Interesting Narrative of the Life of Olaudah Equiano*. 8th ed. Norwich: The author, 1794. Print.

Erkkila, Betsy. "Revolutionary Women." *Tulsa Studies in Women's Literature* 6.2 (1987): 189–223. Print.

Foreman, P. Gabrielle. "'Who's Your Mama?' 'White' Mulatta Genealogies, Early Photography, and Anti-Passing Narratives of Slavery and Freedom." *American Literary History* 14.3 (2002): 505–39. Print.

Foster, Frances Smith. "Resisting *Incidents*." *Incidents in the Life of a Slave Girl: Contexts, Criticism*. By Harriet A. Jacobs. Ed. Nellie Y. McKay and Foster. New York: Norton, 2001. 312–29. Print.

Franke, Astrid. "Phillis Wheatley, Melancholy Muse." *New England Quarterly* 77.2 (2004): 224–51. Print.

Gates, Henry Louis, Jr., and Evelyn Brooks Higginbotham, eds. *The African American National Biography.* 8 vols. New York: Oxford UP, 2008. Print.

Grand Bobalition, or "Great Anniversary Fussible." 1821. Broadside. *Prints and Photographs Online Catalog.* Lib. of Cong. Web. 10 Dec. 2014.

Griffin, Farah Jasmine, ed. *Beloved Sisters and Loving Friends: Letters from Rebecca Primus of Royal Oak, Maryland, and Addie Brown of Hartford, Connecticut, 1854–1868.* New York: Ballantine, 2001. Print.

Hansen, Karen V. "'No Kisses Is Like Youres': An Erotic Friendship between Two African-American Women during the Mid-Nineteenth Century." *Gender and History* 7.2 (1995): 153–82. Print.

Helgerson, Richard. *Self-Crowned Laureates: Spenser, Jonson, Milton, and the Literary System.* Berkeley: U of California P, 1983. Print.

Hening, William Waller, ed. *The Statutes at Large; Being a Collection of All the Laws of Virginia, from the First Session of the Legislature in the Year 1619.* Vol. 2. New York, 1810. Print.

Hobson, Janell. *Venus in the Dark: Blackness and Beauty in Popular Culture.* New York: Routledge, 2005. Print.

Hoffy, Alfred M., and Peter S. Duval. *Mrs. Juliann Jane Tillman, Preacher of the A.M.E. Church.* 1844. Lithograph. P. S. Duval, Philadelphia.

Hunter, Tera W. *To 'Joy My Freedom: Southern Black Women's Lives and Labors after the Civil War.* Cambridge: Harvard UP, 1997. Print.

Joanna, or the Female Slave. A West Indian Tale. Founded on Stedman's Narrative of an Expedition against the Revolted Negroes of Surinam. London: Printed for L. Relfe et al., 1824. Print.

Jones, Jacqueline. *Labor of Love, Labor of Sorrow: Black Women, Work and the Family, from Slavery to the Present.* 2nd ed. New York: Basic, 2010. Print.

Joyce, William Leonard, and American Antiquarian Society. *Printing and Society in Early America.* Worcester: American Antiquarian Soc., 1983. Print.

Kranz, Rachel. *African-American Business Leaders and Entrepreneurs.* New York: Facts on File, 2004. Print.

Lacey, Barbara. "Visual Images of Blacks in Early American Imprints." *William and Mary Quarterly* 3rd ser. 53.1 (1996): 137–80. Print.

Lee, Jarena. *Religious Experience and Journal of Mrs. Jarena Lee, Giving an Account of Her Call to Preach the Gospel.* Philadelphia, 1849. Print.

—. *The Life and Religious Experience of Jarena Lee, a Coloured Lady, Giving an Account of Her Call to Preach the Gospel.* Philadelphia, 1836. Print.

Moody, Joycelyn K. Introduction. Whipple and Eldridge 1–80.

Pasley, Jeffrey L. "The Cheese and the Words: Popular Political Culture and Participatory Democracy in the Early American Republic." *Beyond the Founders: New Approaches to the Political History of the Early American Republic.*

Ed. Pasley, Andrew W. Robertson, and David Waldstreicher. Chapel Hill: U of North Carolina P, 2004. 31–56. Print.

Philip, M. [Arlene] Nourbese. *A Genealogy of Resistance: And Other Essays*. Toronto: Mercury, 1997. Print.

Pohl, Frances K. *Framing America: A Social History of American Art*. New York: Thames, 2002. Print.

Public Broadcasting Service. "Portrait of Elizabeth Freeman (Mum Bett)." *Africans in America*. Public Broadcasting Service, n.d. Web. 10 Dec. 2014.

Reply to Bobalition of Slavery. 1819. Broadside. *Prints and Photographs Online Catalog*. Lib. of Cong. Web. 10 Dec. 2014.

Rezek, Joseph. "The Print Atlantic: Phillis Wheatley, Ignatius Sancho, and the Cultural Significance of the Book." Cohen and Stein 19–39.

Santamarina, Xiomara. *Belabored Professions: Narratives of African American Working Womanhood*. Chapel Hill: U of North Carolina P, 2005. Print.

Senchyne, Jonathan. "Bottles of Ink and Reams of Paper: *Clotel*, Racialization, and the Material Culture of Print." Cohen and Stein 140–58.

Sharpley-Whiting, T. Denean. *Black Venus: Sexualized Savages, Primal Fears, and Primitive Narratives in French*. Durham: Duke UP, 1999. Print.

Shaw, Gwendolyn DuBois. *Portraits of a People: Picturing African Americans in the Nineteenth Century*. Seattle: Addison Gallery of American Art and U of Washington P, 2006. Print.

Stedman, John Gabriel. *Narrative, of a Five Years' Expedition, against the Revolted Negroes of Surinam, in Guiana, on the Wild Coast of South America, from the Year 1772, to 1777: Elucidating the History of That Country, and Describing Its Productions, Viz. Quadrupedes, Birds, Fishes, Reptiles, Trees, Shrubs, Fruits, & Roots; with an Account of the Indians of Guiana, & Negroes of Guinea*. 2 vols. London, 1796. Print.

Sweeney, Fionnghuala. "Memory, Mobility, Modernity: Archibald Motley's Portraits and the Art of 'Serious Painting.'" *Slavery & Abolition* 34.2 (2013): 236–51. Print.

Trachtenberg, Alan. *Reading American Photographs: Images as History, Mathew Brady to Walker Evans*. New York: Hill, 1989. Print.

Twyman, Michael. *Lithography, 1800–1850: The Techniques of Drawing on Stone in England and France and Their Application in Works of Topography*. London: Oxford UP, 1970. Print.

—. "Two Centuries of Printing: Book Production History Diagrams." *Publishing History* 36 (1994): 103–14. Print.

Virginian Luxuries. N.d. Painting. Abby Aldrich Rockefeller Folk Art Museum, Williamsburg.

Waldstreicher, David. "Reading the Runaways: Self-Fashioning, Print Culture, and Confidence in Slavery in the Eighteenth-Century Mid-Atlantic." *William and Mary Quarterly* 3rd ser. 61.2 (1999): 243–72. Print.

Wall, Cheryl A. *Worrying the Line: Black Women Writers, Lineage, and Literary Tradition*. Chapel Hill: U of North Carolina P, 2005. Print.

Wallace, Maurice O., and Shawn Michelle Smith. *Pictures and Progress: Early Photography and the Making of African American Identity*. Durham: Duke UP, 2012. Print.

Whipple, Frances Harriet, and Elleanor Eldridge. *Memoirs of Elleanor Eldridge*. 1838. Ed. Joycelyn K. Moody. Morgantown: West Virginia UP, 2014. Print.

White, Deborah G. *Ar'n't I a Woman?: Female Slaves in the Plantation South*. Rev. ed. New York: Norton, 1999. Print.

Willis, Deborah, and Barbara Krauthamer. *Envisioning Emancipation: Black Americans and the End of Slavery*. Philadelphia: Temple UP, 2013. Print.

—, and Carla Williams. *The Black Female Body: A Photographic History*. Philadelphia: Temple UP, 2002. Print.

Wood, Marcus. *Blind Memory: Visual Representations of Slavery in England and America*. New York: Routledge, 2000. Print.

—. "The Slave Narrative and Visual Culture." *The Oxford Handbook of the African American Slave Narrative*. Ed. John Ernest. New York: Oxford UP, 2014. 196–218. Print.

Young, Kevin. *The Grey Album: On the Blackness of Blackness*. Minneapolis: Graywolf, 2012. Print.

(Un)Translatability and the Autobiographical Subject in Maryse Condé's *La vie sans fards*

(In)Traducibilidad y el sujeto autobiográfico en *La vie sans fards* de Maryse Condé

By Bella Brodzki

Maryse Condé's second autobiographical narrative, *La vie sans fards*, depicts the author's experience living in West Africa as a "doomed affair," a story of dashed expectations. The text, however, can also be read as an example of untranslatability, of a self-definition finding no dynamic equivalence in a different cultural context or linguistic framework.

La segunda narrativa autobiográfica de Maryse Condé, *La vie sans fards*, describe la experiencia del autora de vivir en el oeste de Africa como una "aventura condenada," y expectativas descontinuadas. De todas formas, el texto puede ser tomado como un ejemplo de "intraducibilidad," de una auto-definición al no encontrar una dinámica equivalente en un contexto cultural o marco lingüístico diferente.

In her introduction to *La vie sans fards* (2012), Maryse Condé's second autobiographical volume, which is dedicated primarily to the years she spent in West Africa, the Guadeloupean author (b. 1937) distinguishes her motivations for writing from the idealizing ones most often attributed to the conventional enterprise of recounting a life. That Africa "occupied a considerable place in my life and in my imagination" was certain (16).[1] Though she cannot explain exactly what it was she was looking for there, over the course of the narrative she does relate what she found. In preparing the reader, she proclaims her passion for "unvarnished" truth-telling, as she stakes a claim for her singularity while also invoking a more abstract, albeit gendered, universality. This is a tall order. Generally, autobiography is the space where models of exemplarity (the best of a group) and exceptionalism (different from the rest) cancel each other out. Eliding|eluding any political or social markers of racial or ethnic identity in favor of other modes of identification, Condé explicitly aligns herself with the first modern declaration of selfhood, Jean-Jacques Rousseau's *Les confessions*, and thus inscribes herself squarely into the French Enlightenment and Romantic traditions: "I want to display to my kind a woman in every way true to nature, and the woman I portray shall be myself" (12).[2]

The intertextual implications of such an overture are not unitary in effect: to a francophone (here I mean those of the French hexagon and those of the French Caribbean) audience, they signal the Cartesian intellectual formation that shapes this project and the cultural capital it represents; and to every reader of autobiography familiar with Rousseau's famous address, this secular, transnational confessional and testimonial model rings loud and clear as a defiant refusal to allow one's heart to be judged by others. Indeed, Condé's Rousseauian stance is not merely rhetorical: there are repeated echoes in this text of a Romantic sensibility, one that is predicated on passion and sentiment as much as on will and intellect. Cumulatively, Condé suggests that she is an autobiographical subject who, in mining her "painful" memories, is seeking to set the record straight—on her own terms—from the entitled vantage point of old age. In response to having been previously criticized for her early novelistic depictions of unhappy young Caribbean heroines in Africa, especially in *Heremakhonon* (1976) and later in *A Season in Rihata* (1988), which were too often read as straightforward reproductions of her own experience, she offers in this life narrative a more nuanced vision|version of that difficult engagement. In this vision|version, the events and experiences that almost overcame the autobiographer in life are eventually recuperated and relegated to the material of fiction; for that act of mastery, Condé commands recognition from her readers across a spectrum of differences. In this autobiographical sequel, in which France, the Caribbean, and Africa are not reduced to the points they occupy in a colonial constellation, but are explored through a variety of interpersonal and intercultural transfers|transactions—some more successful for her than others—Condé represents herself as untranslatable. This paradoxical sense of her own untranslatability, as I hope to show, drives the narrative in *La vie sans fards* as the autobiographer struggles against forces and structures that threaten her integrity, as literally and metaphorically understood.

Condé recounts having made very few visible attempts in Africa to adapt or accommodate to her new surroundings, which turn out, repeatedly in each changing context, to be more foreign than she ever imagined. Instead, in terms of dress, social mores, and even language, she presents a woman who expects to be taken as she is and understood within her own frames of reference. Displaced and frustrated by her lack of agency, she is only vaguely curious about how certain signifiers travel across time and space, or what possibilities exist for mediating their reception otherwise. Strangely enough, Condé's parents' formerly described class-based sense of alienation in Guadeloupe in *Tales from the Heart: True Stories from My Childhood* is mirrored back to her in Africa, where her inability to find herself represented there reinforces her sense of isolation and exclusion. Halfway through the narrative, Condé describes feeling wounded, enraged, and mystified by the mixture of contempt and envy reflected in such epithets as *toubabesse* ("white woman"), which are directed at her as an Antillaise (perhaps implied as French, as well), even as she, resisting facile and conflated formulations of racial identity, can only presume what it is that, for example, her Malinke-speaking, Muslim, Guinean mother-in-law holds against her: "I sensed that it went deeper than this. It wasn't simply a matter of deportation and Middle Passage that separated us from each other, that dispossessed me of my land, my traditions. It had to do with an ontological order of difference. I didn't belong to the same ethnicity, that sacrosanct ethnicity. No matter what I did, I would always remain excluded from the human species" (*La vie* 114).

What grounds this certitude is a question worth posing. Whether, or in what ways, she may be categorically different from the mother-in-law with whom she cannot converse comprises the stuff of this life narrative; whether it is diasporic otherness or a more essentialist disidentification, Condé presents this and many other instances of untranslatability, rather than mistranslation, as givens. According to Condé, she has been sharpening her critical tools since childhood. An example of the tension between a life lived and a life written about, between a merely self-serving account and one which produces more profound self-gratification, is voiced in her reprise of a vignette from *Tales from the Heart*. The earlier book of recollections of her bourgeois upbringing in Guadeloupe in the 1950s (made more piquant by her parents' self-description as "*Les Grands Nègres*") closes with the launching of her independence as a student in Paris, and is dedicated to her mother, who died while she was abroad. A story of unresolved and unreconciled maternal guilt and loss runs through this life narrative. In *Tales from the Heart*, Condé planted the source event whose belated significance she sharply distills in *La vie sans fards*: the moment, at the age of ten, when she discovered her vocation as a writer. If the full psychoanalytic punch of this episode in Condé's narrative was yet to be revealed in the earlier account, it nonetheless already contained something critically ambiguous, given the vignette's provocative title: ("Bonne fête, Maman!") ("Happy Birthday, Mummy!" 67).

The occasion was, indeed, her mother's birthday, when the young Maryse offers the gift of an elaborate poetic|theatrical composition depicting "the many facets" of her adored mother's complex personality (73). In the earlier, more extended vignette, Condé represents herself as mystified and sobered by what she had produced (in every sense of that word), based on her mother's distressed reaction and response—"So that's how you see me?" (75). The emotional lesson the child drew from it then—that one must never tell the truth to those one loves, but rather paint an embellished and admirable portrait for them to believe in—is later rejected in favor of another kind of artistic credo promulgated in *La vie sans fards*.

In the latter, when the autobiographer uses the same event, she makes the experience emblematic of "a feeling of power that I have sought to relive, book after book" (13). It is the linking of the writer's vocation as a truth-teller—even, or especially, if it comes at her own expense—with the attendant realization of her capacity (and desire) to shock her readers by undermining illusions, exposing hypocrisy, and not dissimulating—by, as she puts it, piercing or "popping a blister" (13)—that defines this autobiography. It is followed by a more modulated acknowledgement of the broader pleasures that writing both affords and signifies, and an explanation of why, despite her early promise, she came so late to publishing her first novel: life itself was exigent and urgent, while it is a luxury to be able to recast imaginatively or sublimate through art the events that caused so much pain. She could only do the former when she was released from the latter.

Among their many differences, Condé's first autobiography is devoted to the role of the Antilles in shaping a woman who, by the time she left Guadeloupe at the age of sixteen, had never learned Creole, while the second, to repeat, is all about Africa: Africa in the politically promising days of decolonization and then the corruption, hypocrisy, and repression of the post-independent regimes. Or, more precisely, it is about a continent that did not understand Condé and her not being able to accommodate herself to its subordinating demands—despite long and varied opportunities living in Guinea, Ghana, Ivory Coast, and Senegal—to learn to speak Malinke, Fulani, Peulh, or Wolof. If establishing affinities with Rousseau's autobiographical project at the opening of her own is an imperious and intriguing gesture that sets the stage for the aesthetic strategy and intertwining themes of identity and affiliation, eros and literature, and memory and translation that will characterize this text, the close is no less rhetorically remarkable. If it is impossible for Condé to account for the ill-fated affair she had with Africa, she locates a parallel in Proust's meditation on lost time, in Swann's final commentary on the saga of Odette: "To think that I wasted years of my life, that I wanted to die, that I felt my deepest love, for a woman who did not appeal to me, who was not my type!" (396).

Eros and politics, alliances and betrayals are easily muddied in the challenging years of decolonization, when the autobiographer focuses on a different kind of sentimental education during the rise of promising African nationalist movements, especially under Sékou Touré's regime in Guinea, and the impact of pan-Africanism à la Senghor. As informative an exposé from the inside as Condé provides of the challenges of assimilating as a woman *tout court*, her refusal to understand the terms of engagement is read as acts of either political or personal resistance by others. Though they are, in a sense, I would argue as well that a resolute individualism governs those choices. Romantic projection, whose contours Proust delineated with such finesse, is a psychodynamic in which the subject's desire precedes and exceeds its particular object. For Condé, Africa offered her a set of joyful, open-ended possibilities that had been previously evoked only in literature. She had no idea what to expect on her arrival in 1959 as a single mother with a baby in Bingerville, Ivory Coast, assuming her new job as a teaching assistant in French.

Her consistent use of amatory language to express her relationship with Africa—"My first contact with Africa was not a matter of love at first sight" (40)—suggests, of course, that even within an erotic|political dynamic, the erotic was dominant. Indeed, the narrative is punctuated, and often determined, by her many actual romantic liaisons and relationships, though she admits that it was the birth of three more children that created the greatest challenges and constraints, and prevented her from fulfilling her potential and rising above the "mediocrity" in which she was mired (243). Thus, for all of her attestations and evidence of feisty independence and political risk-taking, the autobiographer's story is imbricated in a dense network of amorous and filial associations. Condé's lively and sometimes harrowing narrative is framed, on its first and last pages, by her two husbands: the Guinean Mamadou Condé and the Englishman Richard Philcox, whom she met in Senegal. Mamadou Condé, whose resumé as an actor and dramaturge Maryse Condé reports as inflated by comparison to his actual achievements, turns out to be a surprisingly responsible and caring father of her four children (despite her first child being the product of an earlier affair with Haitian journalist Jean Dominique). Her marriage to Philcox will take place outside the narrative, but she pays homage to their first meeting and telegraphs what is to follow: "He was the one who would change my life. He would take me to Europe and then to Guadeloupe. We would discover America together. He would help me gently separate from my children and resume my studies. Above all, thanks to him, I would begin my career as a writer" (334).

It is quite fitting that Philcox, who is credited with having rescued Condé from her struggling existence in Africa, became her English translator. Being translated, especially into English, has meant that her work has exceeded its linguistic and cultural bounds, and lived beyond its own temporal and spatial borders, however they have been originally defined and constituted. To cast it in less metaphysical terms, Condé's pre-eminent status as a global Caribbean writer—in the company of Derek Walcott, Caryl Phillips, Édouard Glissant, Patrick Chamoiseau, Raphaël Confiant, and Edwidge Danticat—is the result of translation and its role in bringing her to the widest possible audience. And yet Condé, who taught for many years at Columbia and other esteemed US universities, refers to translation at best as a mechanistic exercise or practical necessity, not a creative practice worthy of her serious attention. In *La vie sans fards*, she recounts how, in order to fight the deadly boredom of having to translate as a part of teaching—reduced to what she calls "the manipulating of texts" (244)—she rose above it to find inspiration in the beauty of her own perceptions about the readings.

Condé's stance toward translation is provocative, especially since she lives on such intimate and privileged terms with her own translator. Their arrangement is clearly a matter of trust and based on mutual indebtedness in the Derridean sense (see Derrida). As is evidenced from a fascinating 1996 interview that Doris Kadish and Françoise Massardier, the authors of *Translating Slavery*, conducted with Philcox (with Condé present), in which he describes his training, strategy, and evolution as a translator, he sees his role as critically important, and valorizes the complex process of "recreating" a text and bringing the writer to a different cultural audience (751). Whereas the translator, invested in transmission and reception, considers his work to be coextensive with the original author's, Condé sees them as distinct. She has stated her position on numerous occasions, and in her many interviews, that translation—being a transforming principle—does not regard her. It is her way of saying that, fundamentally, she and her work do not carry over—they are untranslatable. In a conversation with Emily Apter, which was conducted in French and then "transposed," not "transcribed" (Apter's words), and translated into English, and appeared in 2001, Condé elaborated, "I have never read any of my books in translation.... In translation, the play of languages is destroyed. Of course, I recognize that my works have to be translated, but they are really not me. Only the original really counts for me. Some people say that translation adds to the original. For me, it is another work, perhaps an interesting one, but very distant from the original" (92). When asked about the use of Creole as a political and cultural instrument for Caribbean writers, she explained that, for her, formal, narrative, and linguistic issues are paramount. When Apter suggested that critics have drawn parallels between her work and that of James Joyce and Virginia Woolf, she concurred: "I am interested in the polyphony of voice.... I'm still looking for the right form of the novel, the right voice. I'd like to create a Maryse Condé language" (96).

Sarah Lawrence College

Disclosure Statement

No potential conflict of interest was reported by the author.

Notes

1. All translations from *La vie sans fards* are my own.
2. *Les confessions*, a French classic and often considered to be the first modern autobiography, was written in two parts and published in 1782 and 1789.

Works Cited

Apter, Emily. "Crossover Texts|Creole Tongues: A Conversation with Maryse Condé." *Public Culture* 13.1 (2001): 89–96. Print.

Condé, Maryse. *La vie sans fards*. Paris: J. C. Lattes, 2012. Print.

—. *Tales from the Heart: True Stories from My Childhood*. Trans. Richard Philcox. New York: Washington Square, 2004. Print.

Derrida, Jacques. "Des tours de Babel." *Difference in Translation*. Trans. and Ed. Joseph F. Graham. Ithaca: Cornell UP, 1985. 165–248. Print.

Kadish, Doris, and Françoise Massardier. "Traduire Maryse Condé, entretien avec Richard Philcox." *French Review* 69.5 (1996): 749–61. Print.

Proust, Marcel. *Swann's Way*. Trans. Lydia Davis. New York: Viking, 2003. Print.

Exploring Narratives of Contested Gender Identities in Jamaican Dancehall

Explorando las narrativas de identidad de genero impugnadas en el dancehall jamaiquino

By Donna P. Hope

This article focuses on the male body in dancehall culture as a site of contested discourses of gender identity that emanate from and are impacted by the wider terrain of gendered and social discourses in Jamaican society. These discourses are debated in dancehall culture's lyrics, as well as in its other popular cultural manifestations—music videos, stage-show presentations, fashion and style, and dancehall slang, among others. This essay draws on contemporary dancehall lyrics, and other discursive tools, to highlight dancehall culture's selective positioning of the male body and its simultaneous play with and against manifestations of Jamaican hegemonic masculinity.

Este escrito se enfoca en el cuerpo masculino dentro de la cultura del dancehall como un escenario para discursos impugnados de identidad de genero que emanan de y son impactadas por un terreno mas amplio de discursos sociales y de genero dentro de la sociedad Jamaiquina. Estos discursos son debatidos por las liricas de la cultura de dancehall, en adicion a otras de sus manifestaciones culturales populares, como lo son los videos musicales, presentaciones en el escenario, moda y estilo y jerga utilizada en el dancehall, entre otros. Este ensayo utiliza liricas contemporaneas del dancehall y otros discursos para llevar la atencion de los lectores hacia la posicion selectiva de la cultura de dancehall en relacion con el cuerpo masculino y su posicion a favor y en contra de las manifestaciones de hegemonia de la masculinidad Jamaiquina.

Since its rise to dominance in Jamaica in the 1980s, dancehall culture has developed into and remains a critical site of popular sociocultural engagement with a variety of discourses that emanate particularly from within Jamaican society. Many of these discourses are tackled in dancehall culture's lyrics, as well as its other manifestations, such as music videos, stage-show presentations, fashion and style, and dancehall slang. The male body in dancehall culture remains a central site of contested discourses of gender identity, and these discourses emanate from and are impacted by the wider terrain of gendered and social discourses in Jamaican society. Dancehall's gendered narratives arguably function as a form of life writing or self-narration that engages a variety of auto-biographical acts to bring the artists|authors and audience|readers into a sphere of mutual creation and interpretation of artistic and social identities. I draw on my earlier research on contemporary dancehall lyrics and audience responses to examine the mutual creation of meanings on dancehall's male body, and its simultaneous play with and against manifestations of Jamaican hegemonic masculinity.

Narrating Male Identity

Here, it is critical to interrogate the role of dancehall's lyrics, performance, and audience interaction as critical caches of autobiographical life narratives. Self-narration occurs in multiple historical definitions of autobiography as self-life writing that privileges primarily written methods of self-reflection. However, Sidonie Smith and Julia Watson suggest an understanding of the term "*life narrative*...as a general term for acts of self-presentation of all kinds and in diverse media that take the producer's life as their subject, whether written, performative, visual, filmic, or digital" (4).

In this regard, it is critical to examine popular-music lyrics, performances, images, and audience response (where possible) as forms of self-narration that expand the range of texts beyond the purely written. For example, the strategies employed in the creation and performance of dancehall's narratives about the male body reflect a critical range of activities, including performativity, which are crucial to the process of self-construction that layers self-narration with multiple and complex meanings. Identities are not fixed attributes of subjects, but rather productions of and reiterations through cultural norms that result in their often unstable and provisional natures. The dancehall audience and the wider cultural and gendered community of Jamaica|ns who form the outer layer of dancehall's core audience all participate as contributors to the construction of dancehall's male body in a communal process of narrating the various male selves that are part and parcel of dancehall culture's offerings. This narrative process occurs in conversation with the existing ideas and meanings that coalesce around Jamaica's framing of its hegemonic masculinities.

Jamaica's Hegemonic Masculinities

Tim Carrigan, Bob Connell, and John Lee argue that hegemonic masculinity should not be understood as the "male role," but as one particular variety of masculinity to which women and other young effeminate, or homosexual, men are subordinated. Carrigan, Connell, and Lee argue that this hegemonic masculinity is a question of "how particular men inhabit positions of power and wealth and how they legitimate and reproduce social relationships that generate dominance" (179). Discourses of Caribbean male identity utilize different factors, including "biological difference and specificity, in behavioral terms and in terms that objectify their masculinity—that is, cars, boats, houses, dogs, guns may become extensions of one's masculinity" (Lewis 97)—to narrate conceptions of the masculine self into being. Notwithstanding this, the core issues that underscore Caribbean masculinity are those of power and control, and historical shifts in Afro-Caribbean masculinities are informed by the concept of hegemony.

As one popular example of Caribbean masculinity, Jamaica's hegemonic masculine ideal was, and purportedly is, an extremely conservative one, defined as wealthy, educated, employed, and definitely heterosexual. Expensive cars, liaisons with multiple attractive women, and absolute control over domestic arrangements were among the traits of idealized Jamaican manhood during and since the 1980s. Dancehall culture's prominent place as a dominant, popular, and musical force in Jamaica since the early 1980s suggests that it provides an ideal stage from which to narrate and project fantasies, experiences, and perspectives that tackle gender relations and reflect on notions of hegemonic masculinity in Jamaica. Dancehall culture's most prominent incarnations of masculinity arguably feed into and off of the traditionally accepted definitions of Jamaica's hegemonic masculinity, and manifest themselves in the dialogic creative process that is a component of dancehall's on- and offstage narratives. At the same time, dancehall culture's masculine fantasies are projected as extreme and often threatening variations of these hegemonic roles, and therefore breach the traditionally accepted modes of "decent" behavior in "polite," middle-class Jamaica—as, for example, with dancehall's persistent outing and rendering visible of the male homosexual, who has historically been cast as invisible and powerless in traditional hegemonic engagement with male homosexuality in Jamaica. In this regard, even while they are brokered on hegemonic cues, dancehall's narratives construct masculine exemplars that continue to feed the deepening hegemonic dissolution in their continued clash with the socially accepted models of masculinity in Jamaica.

Lyric Narratives of the Contested Male Body in Dancehall Culture

The concept of life narratives is critical to the framing of this work, since the artist—audience nexus in dancehall culture creates a rich platform for the projection of highly ritualistic and often communal representations of various identity discourses. The lyrics of popular dancehall songs narrate multiple ways of being, and arguably function as repositories of diverse images, imaginings, and acts of self- and communal representation that are played out and incarnated on, within, and beyond dancehall's performative stages. Thus, while drawing on earlier work with dancehall audiences, I utilize the conceptual term "lyric narratives" throughout this article to capture and highlight the role that dancehall lyrics play in providing a critical repository of personhood, everyday life, and gendered fantasies, imagings, and imaginings.

As discussed in my earlier work *Man Vibes*, dancehall culture's fantasies of masculinity are interwoven with multiple identity debates that flit across the stages of dancehall culture. In this regard, dancehall's ritual performances of heterosexual masculinity are very prominent and often feature graphic and explicit lyrics. Dancehall's lyrics arguably function as communal life narratives of the artist-audience that usher particular variants of masculinity into being. At the same time, these life narratives or lyric narratives also construct a highly contested terrain of masculine being, which is riven through with multiple paradoxes and consistently challenges the veracity and legitimacy of particular forms of this male body. In this vein, my earlier work highlights and critiques several strands in the debate on the male body in dancehall culture: a hyper-heterosexuality that stresses promiscuity and sexual prowess (the "Ole Dawg" construction); the aggression articulated through gun talk and lyrics, as exemplified in the "Badman" or "Shotta" representations of guns and violence (the "Badman" construction); and the vigorous policing of the hegemonic heterosexual consensus in Jamaica, which condemns male homosexuality (the "Chi Chi Man") through an extreme, graphic, and violence-laden discourse. Additionally, conspicuous consumption and excessive posing articulate another sphere of expression for male identity in dancehall (the "Bling Bling" construction). The foregoing are significantly problematized by the softened and feminized masculinity evident in the growing post-millennial "refined aesthetic" physicality and in the choreographic impulses and colorful and flamboyant styles exhibited by some male artists and dancers in dancehall (the "Fashion Ova Style" construction). This article focuses specifically on narratives that surround the communal construction of two masculine exemplars in dancehall—the Badman and the Fashion Ova Style. Here, the work draws on the auto|biographical propensity of artists' lyrics and dancehall's necessary cultural consensus as critical facets of the meaning-making that characterizes this sphere of creativity. As a part of popular culture's discursive lyric narratives of masculine being, dancehall's overarching Badman is positioned at the highest point of its masculinity continuum. Other masculine exemplars, such as the Gyallis or promiscuous male, are located close to the highest point of this continuum, while the Chi Chi Man, or homosexual male, is located at its lowest point, as the antithesis of the heterosexual

Badman. What I label the Fashion Ova Style variant is raised in the spaces of dancehall as a more contemporary and hybridized form of masculinity, which marries elements from multiple points on dancehall's masculinity continuum to problematize the exemplars raised within this framework.

The Badman: Hardcore Articulations

Dancehall culture's Badman is incarnated through lyric narratives that identify his key features and simultaneously reject corrupting influences. Many of these lyric narratives indirectly articulate the Badman's identity. Nonetheless, they identify him as the epitome of dancehall's heterosexual machismo culture, with violent tendencies. For example, in the lyrics for "Bad Man Nuh Flee," dancehall artists Beenie Man and Mr. Vegas narrate the violent and nihilistic Badman into being:

> Badman nuh flee
> (Eh!)
> After di bwoy dem nuh tough like we
> Some only bad thru dem a walk inna posse dem a fool
> Lord dem nuh see how we lock di city
> And dem a nuh tough like we
> [Badmen do not flee
> After all, those boys are not as tough as we are
> Some of them are only behaving as if they are bad because they are
> walking in a posse, they are fools
> Lord, haven't they seen how we lock (down) the city?
> And none of them are as tough as we are] (lines 7–11)

In this regard, Beenie Man and Mr. Vegas highlight some of the violent tendencies of a real Badman, one who is unafraid and does not flee from any antagonist. The Badman is narrated as a singular being who does not need the support or backing of a group or posse to engage in violent activities. The song's chorus also imputes a warning to antagonists who may not have seen (or heard about) the violent activities of the|this Badman|Badmen who have locked (down) the city (taken it over by force and violence). The reiteration of the point that no one is as tough as they (the Badmen) are is important in projecting this aura of ruthlessness and nihilism, which remains an important plank on which this Badman is incarnated.

This song further describes additional characteristics of this cold-blooded Badman:

> Badman nuh wait
> Pon night fi come down
> Anything fi happen

Mek it happen and done
Naw catch me inna
No bar ah drink rum
Naw left me yard careless
Fi get bun

[A Badman does not wait
For the cover of nightfall
Anything (violent) that should happen
Let it happen
You will not find me in a
Bar drinking alcohol
I will not leave my head carelessly
Exposed to get burned] (lines 18—25)

Here, Mr. Vegas notes that a Badman is fearless and does not need to wait to be covered by the dark of nightfall to carry out violent (and criminal) activities; therefore, "Anything fi happen | Mek it happen and done." However, a Badman is also careful about protecting his persona and so does not ingest alcohol (publicly), which may lead to vulnerability and careless exposure to rivals, or could result in his getting "burned" or killed.

In another Badman treatise, "Real Badman," Vybz Kartel defines several key markers of the Badman:

Cah mi nuh inna chattin', no yappin', no flippin', no floppin'
Mi strappin' fi clappin', mi lass dem fi choppin'
Mi trick him, mi trap him, di riffle dem whop him
Him run but dem drop him, him choking, him gappin'
People ah run out bout "what happen, what happen?"
Dem run back inside when more shots start attackin'
Di K long like wicket and when dat start battin'
Dem ah bawl Jesus Christ, Holy Ghost could not block him (awoh)

[Because I am not involved with chatting, yapping, flipping, or flopping
I am strapping up with my gun to shoot, my cutlasses are to be used for chopping
I tricked him, trapped him and my rifles whopped (shot) him
He ran but they dropped him to the ground, he is choking and gasping
People ran out asking, "What happened, what happened?"
They ran back inside when more shots started attacking
The AK-47 is as long as a cricket wicket and when that starts batting
They bawled out Jesus Christ but the Holy Ghost could not block him] (lines 15—22)

The lyric narratives of "Real Badman" delineate a highly aggressive and violent masculinity that clearly vocalizes the retaliatory actions to be taken if faced with intimidation. Here, Kartel claims a legacy of violence by claiming that his violent tendencies existed from the time he was a youngster, and from that early age he had never been in fear of any man: "Cah fram me a likkle bwoy me nuh fear man" ("Because ever since I was a small boy I have not been in fear of any man") (line 4). Throughout the song, Kartel consistently displays violence toward his intimidators—for example, noting that "Mi strappin' fi clappin', mi lass dem fi choppin' | Mi trick him, mi trap him, di riffle dem whop him."

Kartel underscores the value of similar violent tendencies in another set of lyrics, similarly titled "Real Bad Man" (labeled as "Real BadMan 2"): "Real Bad Man never afraid | We got bombs and guns and hand grenades" (lines 18—19). Here, he communicates another key anti-Badman propensity that is critical to the maintenance of the artist—audience consensus which spawns and incarnates dancehall's Badman, noting that "Di chatty chatty business mi lef dat to Ragga" ("I leave the gossipy behavior to Ragga") (line 13). Ragga, also known as Ragashanti, or Dr. Kingsley Stewart was a university lecturer, popular talk-show host and comedian, known particularly for his vocal and "talkative" approach to many issues. This included Ragga's leaning toward what many Jamaicans perceived as a feminine trait, in his propensity to gossip and expose vulgar and sexual topics on the radio or onstage. Kartel's reference to "chatty business" and leaving that to "Ragga" in this lyric narrative articulates a wider Jamaican social and cultural consensus about male identity—that chatting|arguing|reasoning is left to a (lesser) man of this sort, who dabbles in feminine practices and behaviors. Kartel reiterates this notion, stating "Cah mi nuh inna chattin', no yappin', no flippin', no floppin'" ("Because I am not involved with chatting, any yapping, no flipping and no flopping [of the tongue]") (line 15).

Additionally, in negating the feminine, Kartel posits that "me nuh soft like cherry," which can be interpreted as having a tough persona that is in line with the ideals of a real Badman. As noted in Kartel's "Real Badman," dancehall's narratives of Badmanism negate all lesser male forms, such as the gossipy or "chatty chatty" male. They also reject social and cultural contaminants that can weaken the aura and taint the image of a Badman, and strengthen the artist—audience consensus for this lyric narrative. For example, in the lyrics for his "Badman," Elephant Man narrates several acceptable and unacceptable behaviors of a Badman:

Badman don't bade wid him baby modda rag…
Badman dweet hard…so shi go road go brag…
Shotta clothes don't wash…wid gyal underwear
Shotta youths don't play…certain games round here

[A Badman does not bathe with his babymother's washcloth
A Badman engages in rough sex so his woman will brag in the streets

A Badman's clothes are never washed with female underwear
Badmen don't play certain types of games here] (lines 9—16)

These lyrics highlight an important Jamaican taboo against female contamination of masculinity, which is critical to the communal construction of dancehall's masculine exemplars. In Jamaican inner-city and dancehall culture, a babymother (especially the mother of a man's first child) holds significant regard and pride of place in a man's life. According to popular narrative, she is the woman who "turns a boy into a man" by producing visible and verifiable signs of his ascendancy into manhood, defined as fathering a child. Yet, even with this culturally central positioning as a positive form of femininity in his ascendancy to manhood, the strong female taboos at work in Jamaica also contravene this positive placement of a babymother in the life of a man. Popular myths suggest that, since a babymother is also a woman, she can simultaneously weaken a man by exposing his male body|identity to a variety of contaminating substances that are routinely excreted from the female body. Thus, as the lyric narrative suggests, a Badman should not use the same washcloth as his babymother. In a related theme, at no time should a Badman's clothing be washed in the same tub or washing machine as female underwear because, as the myths and narratives in dancehall and wider Jamaican culture strongly suggest, this too is a site of purported contamination that can weaken and damage the male body|masculine identity. This lyric narrative is founded on a critical and very strong cultural taboo around the incarnation of male identity that is rooted in both Jamaican folk culture and the society's strong religious fundamentalism, where women are simultaneously objects of desire and fear.[1] Indeed, since 2007, this issue has been raised every semester in one of my most popular courses.[2] As a part of the in-course discussion, I pose a question to the male students: if, in an instance of her debilitation due to a critical illness, he would wash (by hand or in the washing machine) his woman's (wife's, girlfriend's, or babymother's) underwear once her stock of clean underwear was depleted. Every single male student to date has responded in the negative. More recent responses indicate that, beyond the usual, "I will call their mother, sister, or a female friend" to undertake this task, or these men might "go shopping for new ones." My queries regarding the presumably less contaminating task of removing his woman's underwear from the clothes line in the case of imminent rain, or clean from the washing machine, also continue to receive the same negative responses. Dancehall's lyric-narrative articulation of this phenomenon around and upon the body of its privileged Badman exemplar responds to and reflects the wider dancehall and Jamaican audience's communal constructions of autobiographical narratives and meanings around the Jamaican male body. It is also reflected in my male students' responses and behaviors.

The issue of heterosexual virility and sexual prowess is a dominant discourse of hardcore male identity in Jamaica, and is also critical for the identity of a Badman. Thus, Elephant Man narrates that the "Badman dweet hard…so shi go road go brag…" ("A Badman engages in rough sex so his woman will brag [about his prowess] in the streets"). The ability to perform as a sexual superstar must also be validated by publicizing this prowess to others in a ritualistic cycle of private performance, public posturing, public accolade, and public performance, which is critical for the public sociocultural maintenance of meaning-creation and validation of a private act that empowers and incarnates true masculinity. And, as Elephant Man opines, in the final analysis, there are other things, "certain games," in which the Badman or Shotta does not engage—a catch-all phrase that imputes multiple deviant activities, including a slide into "freaky" or homosexual activities. In a related vein, Spragga Benz's "Badman Nuh Switch" (Badmen do not switch their sexual codes—i.e. engage in homosexuality) stridently denounces any thought or possibility of homosexual or related sexual engagement by a Badman, and foregrounds the centrality of heterosexual activity as a core narrative in the incarnation of dancehall's Badman.

The fashion and style of a Badman are also important to this image of masculinity in dancehall, as Kartel notes in his hit dancehall song "Clarks":

Real Badman nuh model inna shorts
Straight jeans, cut off foot parts
Everybody haffi ask wheh mi get mi Clarks

[A real Badman does not model and pose around in shorts
He wears straight (not tight) jeans and pants that have been cut
Everyone has to ask me where I got my Clarks shoes from] (lines 5−7)

Here, Kartel distinguishes between "shorts" and "[s]traight" (not tight-fitting) pants or "jeans" as an acceptable mode of clothing for a real Badman. This discussion about the closeness of male pants recurs in multiple sociocultural locations,[3] but more so in dancehall's lyric narratives, raising multiple questions about the relationship between this costume choice and problematic or deviant forms of masculinity. For example, in "Caan Believe Mi Eyes," Bounty Killer notes that "mi cann believe say tight pants come in again" (line 9), declaring his disbelief that these so-called Shottas or Badmen are dressing in garb that is deemed culturally inappropriate for the male body because it suggests a slide into femininity and|or homosexuality.

Kartel suggests that short pants as a costume choice are appropriate only if the pants have been deliberately altered by cutting (or hacking) the bottoms short, usually in a fashion that is unrefined and thus results in a hardcore and edgy style that is far removed from the refined aesthetics of custom-made shorts or short pants. This hacked|cut or chopped style maintains the unrefined, hardcore masculine ethos that is critical to this image. The pairing with Clarks shoes also imputes the hardcore, gangster, or Badman image because Clarks shoes have long been associated with hardcore masculinity in Jamaica, with styles such as Desert Clarks, Bank Robber, and Wallabees (suede or leather) being the variants of choice. Indeed, Kartel highlights this in his foregoing song "Real Badman," wherein, chastising an unnamed rival or competitor, he notes, "Feel seh yuh bad tep pon mi Bank Robber" ("You feel as if you are so bad you stepped on my Bank Robber") (line 8). This highlights the importance of particular modes of dress like the popular Clarks brand to the designation of a (real) Badman in both dancehall's narratives and popular Jamaican culture.

Another dancehall narrative that ties into the post-millennial discussions about the incarnation of the Badman is Ding Dong's "Badman Forward Badman Pull Up," which forms part of this era's move into the creation of multiple dance moves backed by titled songs. Ding Dong notes at the introduction of this song, "You know how long di real Badman wahn dance and cyan dance—how come? | Yeah ah Ding Dong always seh everything a work and nutten nuh pluc out" ("Do you know how long it has been that real Badmen want to dance and cannot dance—Why? | Yes I, Ding Dong, always said that everything is fine, and nothing is out of place") (lines 1–2).

Ding Dong articulates a rhetorical question about the role of dance as a gendered activity that has problematized the identification of dancehall's ideal male body—the Badman. In my book *Man Vibes*, I have argued that the image of "dancing men in tights" (*Man* 137) has been anathema to the hardcore heterosexuality that is privileged in dancehall culture. This was so, based on Jamaican culture's identification of choreographed male dancing as a marker of homosexuality or reduced masculinity. Notwithstanding the visibility of renowned male dancers in Jamaican creative sectors over the decades, engagement in choreographed and explosive male dancing, particularly in groups, stood as a gendered and classed borderline that hardcore dancehall and working-class men refused to cross for fear of losing their masculinity.[4] This changed at the turn of the millennium with the explosion in choreographed male dancing at the center of dancehall culture. Ding Dong's lyric narrative from within dancehall culture captures this broader cultural movement. He articulates the multiple possibilities for real Badmen to engage now in stylistic dance:

> All Duff from Nannyville ah do di Badman Pull Up
> You ting it scratch, no it nuh scratch up
> Badman foward Badman pull up
> Pressi and di Click ah do di Badman Pull Up
> Badman foward Badman pull up
> Watch Jungle and di crew ah do di badman pull up
> Badman foward badman pull up
> [Even Duff from Nannyville is doing the Badman Pull Up dance
> Your thing is spoiled, no it is not spoiled

Badman move forward, Badman stop
Prezi and the Click are doing the Badman Pull Up dance
Badman move forward, Badman stop
Look at the crew from Jungle doing the Badman Pull Up dance
Badman move forward, Badman stop] (lines 22—28)

Several real and known Badmen are identified by name (or alias) and their territory of control, including "Duff from Nannyville," "Pressi and di Click" (from West Kingston|Tivoli Gardens), and "Jungle and di crew." In this naming and identifying, Ding Dong suggests renewed opportunities for hardcore and other forms of male identity. Indeed, if these powerfully figured men in dancehall and inner-city culture are publicly engaging in this new dance, then others of a lesser identity are empowered to engage with this positioning of the male body without damage to hardcore masculinity or other male identities in dancehall. This narrative of empowerment symbolizes the emergence of new mechanisms for the construction of male identity from old, restrictive gendered paradigms. It articulates a critical component of what I see as the auto|biographical narratives that signal transformation in Jamaica's gendered paradigms and point the way toward renewed constructions of identity.

Based on the foregoing, dancehall's lyric narratives first call the Badman into being as a paradoxical figure, who is nihilistically violent, involved with guns and other weapons, is heterosexual, antihomosexual, and inherently macho, but also has a flair for fashion and leans toward fashionable dance and posing. As a critical part of this highly debated and contested incarnation, the Badman is also narrated into being via the not-Badman lyric narratives that are always in conversation with the wider dancehall and Jamaican audiences. These lyric narratives include exhortations against multiple "deviant" practices and behaviors by hardcore male actors. They include exhortations against wearing female clothing or dabbling in other female aesthetics, such as skin bleaching and fashionable hairstyles, and engaging in feminized behaviors, such as being "chatty chatty" or gossiping, and being soft and submissive. Yet this Badman is also encouraged to traverse into once-forbidden and formerly feminized spaces, such as choreographed male group-dancing. In this regard, dancehall's Badman is also figured in its lyric narratives of a refined and renewed male physicality, which I have labeled "Fashion Ova Style" masculinity in my book *Man Vibes*.

Fashion Ova Style: Renewed Incarnations

The incarnations of the Fashion Ova Style variant of masculinity, brokered on earlier forms of masculine engagement in Jamaica, popular music, and dancehall culture,[5] have exploded in dancehall culture's public post-millennial spaces in a way that was denied in all preceding eras. In my work, I have argued that this figure in dancehall culture highlights the development of transitional and trans-gressive sites of male identity formation and signals a form of borderline identity (see Hope, *Man*; *"Pon"*). It is also critical that, in narrating what is "not-Badman," dancehall simultaneously highlights the facets that incarnate this Fashion Ova Style masculine body. For example, lyric narratives such as Harry Toddler's "Bad Man Nuh Dress Like Girl" and Bounty Killer's "Caan Believe Mi Eyes" of the late 1990s set the trend for a growing category of popular dancehall songs that directly identify, question, and chastise a range of female aesthetics, includ-ing refashioned modes of dress, choreographed dancing, and skin bleaching, which have become increasingly appropriated by men in dancehall and beyond since the late 1990s. These were followed by post-millennial narratives such as Mavado's "Nuh Bleach wid Cream," Ce'Cile's "Woman Ting," and Macka Diamond et al.'s "Too Much Bull," which engaged with what they saw as the questionable patterns of male behavior. Dancehall's lyric narratives around the Fashion Ova Style variant of masculinity emerge from an ongoing process of engagement within and beyond dancehall. At this sociocultural juncture, dancehall artists, dancehall audiences, and others in Jamaican society engage in a multilayered series of autobiographical conversations with Jamaica's gen-dered structures and the multiple transformations in male behavior patterns and aesthetic choices that are unfolding before their eyes.

For example, in "Bad Man Nuh Dress Like Girl," Elephant Man (a member of the then Scare Dem Crew with Harry Toddler, Nitty Kutchie, and Boom Dandimite) insists

Badman nuh dress like girl
Wi nuh bore nose an we nuh bleach face
An we nuh wear drops curls
An some freaky freaky bwoy nuh stop dress like girl

[Badmen do not dress like girls
We do not pierce our noses and we do not lighten the skin of our faces
And we do not wear long curly hairstyles
And some freaky boys will not stop dressing like girls] (lines 8—11)

As noted in my earlier work, "Elephant Man lyrically distances the Badman from the early re-imaging of dancehall's hardcore male identity and...documents several practices that are considered precipitously close to the gendered border-line...such as the piercing of the nose, bleaching (lightening) of the face, wearing drop curls or elaborate hairstyles and dressing in styles that closely resemble those chosen by women" (Hope, *Man* 127—28).

In a related vein, Bounty Killer's song "Caan Believe Mi Eyes" comments on the forging of relationships between heterosexual and homosexual males—

formerly a taboo activity. At the same time, he highlights his growing consterna-
tion at the aesthetic transformations in the Shottas|Badmen:

Mi nuh know how dem man yah fi talk bout dem a run di place an how dem
a badman
A bleach dem face an a cream dem hair an inna tight pants
Bun out dem bumboc—! laat!

[I cannot understand how these men are able to state that they have control
over this place and that they are Badmen
When they are bleaching their faces and processing|straightening their hair
and are wearing skintight pants
Burn them out   ! (expletive)!] (lines 1—3)

The chorus signals his disbelief ("caan believe mi eyes") and dismay about
male skin bleaching and other fashion choices such as tight pants, which suggest
the feminization of the Badman (here referred to as the Shotta):

Mi caan believe some man wheh mi hear say ah men
Mi caan believe say tight pants come in again
Mi caan believe say gunman an battyman a fren
Mi caan believe mi eyes, mi caan believe mi eyes…
Mi caan believe di Shotta dem a bleach out dem face

[I cannot believe the identity of some men whom I hear are homosexual
I cannot believe that tight pants have made a comeback
I cannot believe that gunmen are friends with male homosexuals
I cannot believe my eyes, I cannot believe my eyes…
I cannot believe that Shottas are bleaching out their faces] (lines 8—11, 13)

Bounty Killer's consternation is backed up by Mavado's post-millennial lyric
narrative "Nuh Bleach wid Cream," which functions explicitly as a component of
his ongoing lyrical clash with arch-rival Kartel, but simultaneously reads as a thematic sibling of multiple other songs that cast scathing denunciation at perceived
slippages in hardcore male identity:

Mi nuh bleach wid cream, mi bleach wid mi M16
Wid extra magazine, mi alone create mi crime scene…
You a disgrace, bleaching yuh face
Tru yuh fuckin face yuh marrow drop…

Yuh bleach wid cream, but mi bleach wid mi M16
An mi nuh bleach wid team, mi alone step pon mi crime scene
Shotta nuh bleach wid cream, wi bleach wid wi M16

[I do not use bleaching creams, I use my M16
With extra magazines, I create my crime scenes all by myself...
You are a disgrace, bleaching your face
Through your fucking face your marrow falls...
You use creams to bleach, but I bleach with my M16
And I do not bleach in a team, I step onto my crime scene all alone
Shottas do not use bleaching creams, we bleach with our M16s] (lines 5—6, 15—16, 31—33)

This lyric narrative rejects particular "disgraceful" activities such as "bleach [ing] wid cream"—a feminized activity. It simultaneously positions engagement in activities such as bleaching with M16 guns, enduring the long hours of dark (ness) into (day)light with M16s without any visible physical deterioration, as appropriate and accepted behaviors for a Shotta|Badman.

Dancehall's lyric narratives around the ideal (and not ideal) male body provide critical moments of debate and discussion for both male and female artists. For example, dancehall artist Ce'Cile's "Woman Ting"[6] and Macka Diamond's collaboration with a range of female dancers "Too Much Bull" reflect the feminine dismay at the apparent conflict in male identity negotiation. Ce'Cile's treatise speaks explicitly to problematic male fashion choices that lean toward the feminine by exhorting men to leave women's things alone: "Mek me tell u something | Low woman things, low woman things let me tell u something" ("Let me tell you something | Leave women's things alone, leave women's things alone, let me tell you something") (lines 1—2). Additionally, Ce'Cile suggests that the practice of men buying women's clothing has resulted in women not being able to be as fashionable anymore:

We cant hot again cause a di man dem
Dem a buy off we blouse and we pants dem
Them thief we pink color my God then
Dem nu soon start want wear wi thong then

[We cannot be fashionable anymore because of the men
They are buying out our blouses and pants
They have stolen our color pink, my God
Then won't they soon begin to want to wear our panties too] (lines 8—11)

Ce'Cile's reference to the wearing of tight pants by men reflects a similar narrative that struck a chord of disbelief in Bounty Killer's "Caan Believe Mi

Eyes," and she continually queries the need or desire for male clothing styles to rival or challenge those of their female counterparts. This lyric narrative is brokered on multiple discussions around the issue of tight pants, which, as mentioned, has been a hotly debated issue in dancehall culture, in which "pants like tights" (Hope, *Man* 137) are seen as homosexual or feminine garb. Yet, while being ardently contested, this issue of tight pants has also reflected the paradoxical responses that color both Jamaica's and dancehall's concerns.

In its entirety, this lyric narrative explicitly highlights and chastises Rastafari's "fire burn" ethos, suggesting that not every taboo item should be burned or purified. For example, in one of his earlier treatises, Beenie Man insisted that "pants fi have room", however, he contradicts this notion in a later song, Better Learn (Fire Burn), stating: "....Put on yuh Versace cause a tight pants a wear/Yuh come out yuh hear a Rastaman say Bun dung a queer/Yuh feel like yuh want disappear" (15—17). (You put on your Versace (pants) because tight pants are in fashion/You step out and you hear a Rastaman say burn down a homosexual/You feel as if you want to disappear). Beenie Man's statement that tight pants by Versace are fashionable and should not be burned clearly suggests that fashionable brand-name tight pants are acceptable garb for heterosexual men (in dancehall?). In an earlier period in the 1990s, from his position as the then-dominant dancehall deejay, his articulation of the term "pants fi have room" resonated throughout dancehall culture and beyond as a lyrical directive and cultural norm subscribed to by men from multiple social and cultural locations in Jamaica, and, within that historical moment, a man considered a real gangster would avoid wearing tight pants because doing so could work to delegitimize his hardcore|violent identity.

Other fashion codes narrated in dancehall culture include Kartel's "Straight Jeans and Fitted," which is loaded with contemporary dictates for the fashionable dancehall male and reinforces the same as the accepted fashion code for hardcore post-millennial dancehall men, stating, for example, that "Straight jeans and fitted (baseball caps) | Inna white t shirt we did it" (line 3—4). It is noteworthy that what is represented as "straight jeans" in this era would have been referred to as "tight pants" in the 1990s; however, transformations in fashion codes from one era to the next are celebrated in dancehall's lyric narratives as a component of its autobiographical documentation of cultural movements. Indeed, this transformation has faced its own critique, and the apparent lack of any clear differentiation between "tight pants," "tapered pants," and "fitted pants" has figured in multiple formal and informal discussions within dancehall and in the media. I have participated in several of these discussions both within and outside dancehall, and, as the cultural narrative about pants and sexuality goes: "tight, tapered pants are for women and homosexual men, while fitted pants are for real men." Another point of debate has been a direct backlash against what Beenie Man legitimized in his earlier "pants fi have room" exhortation—to wit, that if "pants have room," then another man can "rent a room" in your pants (engage you in homosexual activity). Thus, fitted pants are now more appropriate, and current Jamaican and dancehall fashion codes suggest that tight pants have transcended their former taboo status to become regarded as "swag." Here, a dancer or other dancehall male showcasing an extremely tight pair of pants in the videolight[7] is not seen as homosexual, but as "swagging," or expressing style and fashion.

In problematizing the discourse around the contested male body, Ce'Cile's "Woman Ting" highlights the paradox of gangsters, or Badmen, who are decked out in feminine garb. She insists that they should not look like "Sally" (a woman), nor should they be "pretty" like dolls, but rather they should look and dress like men (as in "Ken" and not "Barbie"):

> Gangster youth u nuffi look like Sally
> And u nuffi pretty pretty and favor dolly
> U fi be Ken u nuffi be di Barbie
> From u look feminine boy you can't chat to me
> Man all a make mistake call u Shorty
> Cause di style a u clothes make u favor Shari
> Stop buy di gyal dem clothes nuh Marky
> And gi u hipsters dem to u sister Shari

> [Gangster youth, you should not look like Sally (a woman)
> And you should not be pretty and resemble a doll
> You should be Ken, you should not be the Barbie
> Once you look feminine boy, you cannot speak to me
> Men are even making the mistake of calling you Shorty
> Because the style of your clothing causes you to resemble Shari (a woman)
> Marky, stop buying the girls'|women's clothing
> And give your hipsters (jeans) to your sister Shari] (lines 32—39)

In the final verse, Ce'Cile identifies additional aesthetic markers of femininity, such as pierced noses and shaved eyebrows, which have been appropriated by hardcore Badmen:

> Lollypop and tight pants a fi di gyal dem
> Pink clothes, bore u nose boy u wrong den
> A shave u eyebrow like Sharon dem
> And nu see say something wrong boy u condemn
> Left di wining to Keiva and Michelle dem
> And di crawl up pan di box to Stacey dem
> And di bruk out bruk out to Junkoo dem
> Who nu like when mi talk try something then

[Lollypop and tight pants belong to the girls|women
Pink clothing, pierced nose, boy you are very wrong
Shaved eyebrows like Sharon and the others
And you don't see that something is wrong, boy you are condemned
Leave the "wining up" (erotic dancing) to Keiva and Michelle
And the crawl up onto sound boxes to Stacey and others
And the frenzied dance styles to Junkoo and others
Anyone who does not like what I am saying should try to do something about it] (lines 48–55)

As I note in *Man Vibes*, "Cecile pinpoints what she sees as inconsistencies in the presentation of hardcore masculinity as it has been historically defined in popular culture and in dancehall. In verse three of her song she notes that for her (and others), women's clothing, the color pink, tight pants and 'di wining and di bruk out bruk out' dance styles all constitute markers of femininity that have been selectively appropriated by men in a highly transgressive move… Cecile ridicules men who engage in these practices, comparing them to women and denouncing their slippage into femininity as regressive" (129–30).

The predominance of dancing men in tight pants in the center of dancehall (perhaps in response to Ding Dong's call to Badmen to "forward" and "pull up") resulted in Macka Diamond et al.'s "Too Much Bull" of 2010. This dancehall narrative, delivered by an all-female cast, added to the contentious debates and discussions around the gendering of the male body and expressed female displeasure with the predominance of male dance groups at dancehall events doing choreographed acrobatic dances in the preferred space of the videolight,[7] while many women were forced to stay on the fringes:

A bag a thick man inna di video like Spartacus
Nuh waan wine wid nuh gyal dem waan war wid us
Hey bwoy nuh push me nuh mek mi cuss
Stop elbow Mumzell she have a dance fi buss
Too much bull inna di videolight…don't
Too much bull inna di videolight…unu weh
Let out the gyal dem
Wine pon di gyal dem

[A lot of thick-bodied men are in the video as if they are Spartacus
They do not want to wine with any women, they want to (make) war with us
Hey boy, do not push me and cause me to quarrel
Stop elbowing Mumzell, she has a (new) dance to display.
Too many bulls (men) are in the videolight, isn't it true?
Too many bulls are in the videolight…you all go away
Let out the girls|women
Wine on the girls|women] (chorus)

The song features dancehall artist Macka Diamond and popular female dancers Mystic, Mad Michelle, Mumzell, and Queen Latisha, along with popular female disc jockey ZJ Sparks. It highlights the aggression with which the male dancers compete with the females for the spot in the videolight ("Hey bwoy nuh push me...Stop elbow Mumzell") and asserts that women should reclaim their space in dancehall and the videolight, both of which have been stolen from them by the dancing men. This all-female engagement in a ritualistically male discourse suggests the powerful communal and gendered processes at work both within and beyond dancehall culture's narrative spaces.

The multiple lyrical contestations over transformations in the male body and incursions into historically delineated female aesthetic processes and dance arenas reflected dancehall's post-millennial dis-ease with the continued manifestations of a renewed Badman, whose hegemonic placement as idealized masculinity becomes seemingly tarnished (or updated?) by these incursions. As a component of this debate, a selection of dancehall artist Kartel's lyric narratives is brokered on public dis-|unease with his aesthetic transformations that paralleled the Fashion Ova Style variant of masculinity. This is articulated, for example, in his song "Cake Soap,"[8] which counters the Jamaican and dancehall notion that male dalliance with feminine aesthetics is reflective of a slide toward or into homosexuality. In an effort to nullify such notions, Kartel self-narrates and promotes notions of his desirability as a heterosexual to members of the opposite sex. He also promotes his virility, highlighting his lack of any need for sexual enhancements or aphrodisiacs like Viagra and horse tonic.[9] In addition, Kartel rejoins his hardcore male counterparts, within and beyond dancehall, by displaying the accepted narrative pointer—explicitly rejecting male homosexuality with the statement, "Mi nuh love man so tek you yeye offa mi" ("I am not attracted to men, so take your eyes off me") (line 9). Here, Kartel's self-narration calls this renewed male body into being, while simultaneously identifying this renewed incarnation as virile, sexually potent, heterosexual, and non-feminized, even with his obvious incursions into what has been historically delineated in dancehall and Jamaican culture as feminized territory (e.g. skin bleaching).

Beenie Man also engaged in a similar lyric-narrative conversation with members of an unnamed audience in "Nuttin Dat." This song explicitly responds to and chastises those who are commenting on his and other dancehall men's (like Kartel's) renewed aesthetic, and expresses his firm grip on heterosexuality:

Chat bout
Everyday
Bout mi pants tight, how mi shirt tight
My youth everything is all right
Everyday dem a talk bout how mi bleach out
While to me a girlfriend a reach out

Mi pants tight ah nuh nuttn dat
Coo gyal inna di dance and ah man yuh ah watch Fassy
Mi bleach out ah nuh nuttn dat
Wi only brown outside but inside we still black Fassy
A bwoy nuh like mi ah nuh nuttn dat
Wi ah hot bwoy ah road an a gyal wi a jack Fassy
Ah man love you ah suppm dat
Wi ah go wipe off yuh name and kick you offa di map

[Chatting about
Every day
About how tight my pants are, how tight my shirt is
Everything is all right my youth
Every day they are commenting about how my face is bleached
While women are reaching out to me (i.e. desiring me)
My pants are tight and that means nothing
Look at women in the dance and you are watching the men, Fassy
(derogatory term)
My skin is bleached out and that means nothing
We are only brown on the outside but on the inside we are still black
A boy does not like me and that means nothing
We are hot (desirable) boys in the public and we have sex with women,
Fassy
If a man loves you, then that means something
We are going to wipe out your name and kick you off the map (get rid of
you)] (lines 1—14)

The images and imaginings projected through dancehall's lyric narratives articulate the paradox of dancehall's male body. The Badman continues to renew itself, even as it simultaneously contests its own renewal. The role of dominant male and female dancehall actors in this process is key because they set the stage and narrate the manifestation of this contested gendered body into being—what was not-Badman becomes recast as a new variant of Badman. Consequently, this new dancehall man is a softened variant who engages in female aesthetic practices: he wears tight pants or tight shirts, bleaches or lightens his skin, sports intricate hairstyles, engages in energetic choreographed dancing, is aggressive and can defend himself, criticizes or rejects male homosexuality, and is desired by and desires women—and is thus heterosexual.

Inconclusive Conclusions

Dancehall culture's lyric narratives around a highly contested male body reveal much about the autobiographical acts of dancehall artists and the communal processes of creation that underlie dancehall's masculine exemplars. For this work, the discursive narratives and challenges to Badman, real Badman, not-Badman, and Fashion Ova Style all incarnate the Jamaican male body within and without dancehall as a site of contested, gendered articulations that grapple for dominance in a changing sociocultural and gendered context. The movements in local, national, and global imperatives underpin dancehall's hegemonic ideals of the true masculine body in its ongoing contestation with and challenge to post-millennial impetuses. Thus, even as dancehall's Badman is reified as the primary and dominant mode of masculine being in dancehall culture, multiple narrative debates and conflict around the problematic Fashion Ova Style male body in dancehall articulate a renewed variant of masculinity that is at once feminized, heterosexual, hardcore, assertive, and in focused struggle with multiple heterosexual codes—a transient and transitory being. As such, direct conclusions are not signaled in these transitory moments. Rather, moments are created for critical and analytical reflection on these transitional processes as they unfold via multiple creative images and imaginings, and spark communal autobiographical discourses that are articulated through dancehall's lyric narratives.

Disclosure Statement

No potential conflict of interest was reported by the author.

Notes

1. See, for instance, the story of Samson and Delilah in the Bible at Judg. 16; also Douglas (154) and Hope (*Man* 62).
2. I developed this undergraduate course, which is offered in the Institute of Caribbean Studies at the University of the West Indies at Mona, Jamaica, and titled "CLTR3507—Culture, Gender, and Sexuality in Jamaican Popular Music." It interrogates the production and consumption of Jamaican popular music, and critically examines the intersections of gender and sexuality within this framework. It also explores, among other things, how the creation, consumption, and understanding of culture are dependent on often unconscious assumptions regarding gender and sexuality.
3. For example, in print and electronic media discussions, and also during in-depth interviews and group discussions as part of my research over an extended period (2004–13), my participant-observation sessions at several barbershops, and ongoing discussions with my students at the University of the West Indies, Mona, since 2007.

4. William "Willie Haggart" Moore's popular group|crew|gang the Black Roses Crew—whose activities cut across multiple stages, including dancehall dance, fashion, and posing—remained the sole example of any such activity, and their forays across the dancehall stage remained secondary to their identification as a hardcore inner-city crew, headed by an area leader with reputed links to the narco-culture and gun culture that formed a part of Kingston's inner-city activity.
5. For example, the plurality of Jamaican masculinities in the 1960s, which included face-men, sweetboys, Rasta, and Rudeboys.
6. Dancehall artist Ce'Cile (Cecile Charlton) was originally known as Cecile. Her name appears in several variations, including Cecile, Ce'Cile, Ce'cille, and Cecille, among others.
7. In other work, I have labeled the dancehall propensity to orient activities around the light of video cameras as the "Videolight Syndrome" and define it as "the insatiable desire of many dancehall patrons to have their presence duly documented at the dances, stage shows and other dancehall events that they attend," where "many of these individuals will go to great lengths to ensure that their images are captured on camera. This includes the wearing of elaborate and expensive jewellery and regalia, conspicuous purchase and consumption of expensive, brand-name beverages like Moet & Chandon and Alize, together with the wearing of erotic, revealing clothes and performance of erotic, x-rated dances by women" (Hope, *Inna* 127–28).
8. The term "cake soap" has become synonymous with the most recent wave of skin bleaching|lightening by many Jamaicans, particularly by fans and not-so-fans of dancehall. In the current era, this was engineered particularly by Kartel's public referencing to cake soap as a part of his theatrics onstage and in his music videos. However, as I note in "From *Browning* to *Cake Soap*," despite Kartel's apparent ownership of the cake-soap debate, the use and value of cake soap as a component of Jamaican cultural and aesthetic practice pre-dated his superstar status, his entry to dancehall, and even his year of birth. I was introduced to the apparent dermatological wonders of cake soap as a teenager at high school in the late 1970s|early 1980s. For many working-class and inner-city individuals, the cheap and easily accessible cake soap was more than just a cheaper version of the laundry soap that many preferred to use because it made your clothes cleaner and your whites whiter; it was also a dermatological wonder. If one's face was washed only with cake soap, it had the capacity to reduce the dreaded "shiny and greasy" look, leaving your face "cool" and free of pimples—or so the story went. Assertions by Kartel that the blue version of "cake soap" (often referred to by the name of the popular Blue Bomber brand) is his cosmetic of choice, backed by the appropriate dancehall

lyrics, were brokered on this culturally approved and decades-old relationship with cake soap of ordinary Jamaicans.

9. Jamaican folklore identifies "horse tonic" as a viable aphrodisiac that enhances male sexual stamina and sexual performance. The term usually refers
to a popular plant—medina—which is also known as horse tonic. The
leaves of this plant are often boiled as a tea. The leaves may also be boiled
in water along with those of several other plants and mixed with other
condiments to produce a tonic. According to Jamaican folklore, the term
also refers to a special concoction which is prepared and fed to horses and
has a similar positive value for men, as outlined above.

Works Cited

Carrigan, Tim, Bob Connell, and John Lee. "Hard and Heavy: Toward a New
Sociology of Masculinity." *Beyond Patriarchy: Essays by Men on Pleasure, Power
and Change.* Ed. Michael Kaufman. New York: Oxford UP, 1987.
139—92. Print.

Douglas, Mary. *Purity and Danger: An Analysis of Concepts of Pollution and Taboo.*
London: Routledge and Kegan Paul, 1966. Print.

Hope, Donna P. Inna di Dancehall: Popular Culture and the Politics of Identity
in Jamaica. Kingston: University of the West Indies Press, 2006. Print.

Hope, Donna P. "From *Browning* to *Cake Soap*: Popular Debates on Skin Bleaching in the Jamaican Dancehall." *Journal of Pan African Studies* 4.4 (2011):
165—94. Print.

—. *Man Vibes: Masculinities in the Jamaican Dancehall.* Kingston: Ian Randle,
2010. Print.

—. *"Pon di Borderline*: Exploring Constructions of Jamaican Masculinity in Dancehall and Roots Theatre." *Journal of West Indian Literature* 21.1—2
(2012—13): 105—28. Print.

Lewis, Linden. "Caribbean Masculinity: Unpacking the Narrative." *The Culture of
Gender and Sexuality in the Caribbean.* Ed. Lewis. Gainesville: UP of Florida,
2003. 94—125. Print.

Smith, Sidonie, and Julia Watson. *Reading Autobiography: A Guide for Interpreting
Life Narratives.* 2nd ed. Minneapolis: U of Minnesota P, 2010. Print.

Discography
Beenie Man. "Better Learn (Fire Burn)." *The Doctor.* VP Records, 1999. CD.

—. "Nuttin Dat." *Various Artists—Steel Frog Riddim.* Truckback Records, 2010.
CD.

— and Mr. Vegas. "Bad Man Nuh Flee." *The Doctor.* VP Records, 1999. CD.

Bounty Killer. "Caan Believe Mi Eyes." *Next Millenium.* VP Records|TVT
Records, 1998. CD.

Ce'Cile. "Woman Ting." B-Rich Records, 2005. DSR|Vinyl.

Ding Dong. "Badman Forward Badman Pull Up." *Reggae Gold 2006*. Universal Records, 2007. CD.

Elephant Man. "Badman." Fiesta Riddim, 2003. *Youtube.com*. Web. 23 Nov. 2013. Uploaded by Massaganaa, April 7, 2011.

Harry Toddler. "Bad Man Nuh Dress Like Girl." *Reggae Gold 1998*. VP Records, 1999. CD.

Macka Diamond (feat. Mystic, Mad Michelle, Mumzell, Queen Latisha and ZJ Sparks). Too much Bull. Loud Disturbance Records, 2010. Youtube.com. Uploaded by Blaqk Sheep, June 23, 2010.

Mavado. "Nuh Bleach wid Cream." Big Ship Productions, 2008. CD.

Spragga Benz. "Badman Nuh Switch." Revenge Label, 2002. CD.

Vybz Kartel. "Cake Soap." *Dancehall Hero Raw*. Tad's Records, 2011. CD.

—. "Real Badman." *More Up 2 Di Time*. Greensleeves Records, 2003. CD.

Vybz Kartel, Real Badman Nuh Fraid, Blackout Riddim, 2004. Youtube.com. Web. Uploaded by ganjablunta, Dec. 6, 2008.

—. "Straight Jeans and Fitted." *Dancehall Hero Raw*. Tad's Records, 2011. CD.

Vybz Kartel and Gaza Slim (feat. Popcaan). Clarks. Stronger We Get, 2012. CD.

Patti Smith Kicks In the Walls of Memoir: Relational Lives and "the Right Voice" in *Just Kids*

Patti Smith patea las paredes del memoir: Relacionales vive y "la voz derecho" en Solo niños

By Julia Watson

In *Just Kids*, Patti Smith's relational narration "kicks in the wall" separating autobiography from biography. It alternately takes up the voices of a tender fairy tale of two young artists' quest for fame, an autoethnographic portrait of their cultural moment, and an autothanatographic tale of loss that seeks to "awake the dead." Smith's performance makes clear that voice in memoir need not be monologic, as she moves between two subjectivities, narrating both personal and collective stories. In joining Robert Mapplethorpe's and her own stories, Smith generates a "third" intersubjective voice linked to photographs of the couple, their artifacts, and documents that resonates in the "memory museum" of the epilogue and the photograph album added to the paperback edition of *Just Kids*.

Patti Smith patea las paredes del memoir: Relacionales vive y "la voz derecho" en Solo niños En Solo niños, la narracion sobre la relacion de Patti Smith rompe las paredes que separan la autobiografia de la biografia. Alterna entre las voces que relatan un cuento de hadas sobre dos jovenes artistas y su busqueda de fama, un retrato auto-etnografico de su momento cultural y un relato auto-tanatologr afico sobre perdida que busca "revivir los muertos." La ejecucion de Smith hace claro que la voz dentro de un memoir no necesita ser un mon-ologo, mientras se mueve entre dos subjetividades, narrando historias tanto personales como colectivas. Al unir sus historias con las de Robert Mapplethorpe, Smith genera una tercera voz intersubjetiva que se entrelaza con las fotografias, artefactos y documentos de la pareja que resuenan en el "museo de memorias" del epilogo y del album de fotos añadido a la edicion de bolsillo de Solo niños.

In *Just Kids*, Patti Smith refers to American avant-garde artists as the "new guard," those who overthrow stale convention in pursuit of personal vision and formal innovation. As a "kid" in Lower Manhattan in the early 1970s, Smith learned that artists are necessarily also revolutionaries when a man she knew at the time only as Slim Shadow (later revealed as the young playwright Sam Shepard) tells her, "When you hit a wall, just kick it in" (170). *Just Kids*, despite its beautifully crafted language and literary connoisseurship, does kick in a wall— that is, it blurs the retaining wall between distinct genres of memoir and undercuts the boundary separating autobiographical and biographical modes. To do so, it mobilizes several genres of life writing in telling a relational story—what Paul John Eakin has insightfully defined as not only "the autobiography of the self but the biography *and* the autobiography of the other" (58).[1] Smith's writing—tender, precise, and fierce—crafts an intimate, lyrical prose that calls on readers to think about the centrality of voice, her own and those of others, particularly Robert Mapplethorpe, as the trace of embodied memory.

As a memoir of entwined lives, *Just Kids* gives new meaning to the often fuzzy notion of "relationality" in life writing. It exemplifies what Susanna Egan, in her concept of relational intersubjectivity, terms "mirror talk"—a reciprocal communication between partners or collaborators at moments when their voices merge, which erodes the boundaries of discrete personhood. In this world of mutual partnership, where the flow of speech back and forth conjoins subjects, the separate practices of autobiography and biography become blurred. Smith tells her story as the intertwining of two lives: her own and that of the famous—and notorious—photographer and artist Robert Mapplethorpe, who died of AIDS in 1989 (both were born in 1946). She crafts a narrative voice for navigating seemingly incompatible autobiographical genres—the artist's coming-of-age tale (*Künstlerroman*), the story of grief and mourning (autothanatography), and the socially oriented account of a cultural moment (autoethnography)—in a meditative narrative on how memoir writing might defy the pastness of the past. To do so, she takes up voices associated with separate genres and orchestrates a polyphony as complex as any in her music.

For nearly four decades Patti Smith has, of course, had a long and varied artistic career as a celebrity lauded for her voice as a rock singer, poet, performer in theater and film, and, recently, photographer.[2] Her voice and image as a protopunk stylist have merged ever since her breakthrough album, *Horses*,[3] brought her national attention. There was the combination of defiance, menace, and pounding rhythm in its first cut, "Jesus died for somebody's sins, but not mine." There was the album cover: Robert Mapplethorpe's iconic half-body photograph of her in a man's white shirt, tie, and pants, jacket tossed over her shoulder, hair ratted à la Keith Richards (Smith, *Just* 140), which encapsulated what Mapplethorpe called "the magic" of his best shots.[4] At a moment when cross-dressing was emerging as a way to experiment with the "androgyny" of alternative gender identities, Smith appears as an ambivalently sexual figure directing a steady, unsmiling gaze at the viewer. Since then, Smith has reigned as an icon of cool,[5] despite her retreat from stardom in 1978 to marry Fred "Sonic" Smith, the leader of MC5 (of "Kick Out the Jams" fame), and live for nearly two decades outside Detroit, raising their children, Jesse and Jackson. Her remarkable career continues, with her eleventh album, *Banga*, issued in 2012. Patti Smith is still celebrated as a rock goddess. On the cover of the *New York Times Style Magazine* in October 2011, she appeared, in her mid sixties, behind a vintage Polaroid camera, as if shooting the viewer, embodying the self-reflexively confrontational style of her lyrics.[6] As the politically committed artist of such songs as "People Have the Power" (1988), she evokes Shelley's legacy of poets as the legislators of the world. Notably, her autobiographical writing has been ongoing, from her childhood diaries and *Woolgathering*, a small-press book of memoir sketches, to her autodocumentary film, *Dream of Life*. It was, however, *Just Kids*, a partnership memoir, which brought Patti Smith wide national and international prominence.

Despite its understated title, *Just Kids* is a serious literary work, which received the American National Book Award as the best nonfiction book of 2010.[7] Including numerous photographs by Mapplethorpe, Smith, and others, and a selection of her poems, it has been widely embraced as the chronicle of a musical and artistic moment at the start of what Andy Warhol called the postmodern era of "15 minutes of fame."[8] But *Just Kids* also deserves attention as a groundbreaking—and "kicked-in"—relational auto|biography, tracking the Smith−Mapplethorpe collaboration in life and art. In addition to blending many voices, *Just Kids* exposes some conundrums of narrating one's own subjectivity in relation to that of another as it breaks new ground in writing outside the walls. Its "personal voice," as a fractured polyphony of voices, creates a textured performance that is different from the utterances of a historical "I" who tells its story according to the conventions of biography.[9]

Finding "the Right Voice"

I turn first to the question of voice because the voices that populate life narratives are usually mediated by an overriding authorial voice; in contrast, *Just Kids* multiplies voices in words and images. It includes Mapplethorpe's voice not just in dialogue, but as a co-presence, and it creates a shared "third" voice that resonates verbally and visually. One might assume that Smith's narrative voice in *Just Kids* is taken from her musical voice, given the extraordinary range of what Barry Shank calls Smith's "vocalese," which can assault listeners with the abrasive in-your-face energy of "Gloria," the scathingly hip dissing of "Rock 'n' Roll Nigger," the fierce passion of "Power to the People," the polyglot rush of "Babelogue," or the tender mournfulness of "Maria" (153).[10] (She has, however, remarked that the music she now listens to most is opera.)[11] But, strikingly, *Just*

Kids's narrative voice is not an echo of her rock lyrics, nor does it appear to be a transcript of the diaries she kept as a young woman (fragments of which are photographed in the memoir) or of her earlier memoir sketches. From where did Smith draw her inspiration for the voices of *Just Kids*?

We have to turn to materials not included in the original hardback edition to situate *Just Kids*: the paratexts of some of Smith's comments about it and "A note to the reader" (henceforth referred to as the "note"), a section with a two-page postscript and eighteen pages of photographs that was added for the late 2010 paperback edition. The "note" instructs readers how to understand the memoir and situates it within a collection of photographs and documents that form a kind of memory museum. It is clear that Smith sought to avoid writing simply a chronicle. As she told interviewer Kevin Berger after *Just Kids* was published, "People have written about us in that period but never with the accurate voice, the accurate atmosphere, the accurate magic." *Just Kids* strives to create an authorial voice that is not just a style of telling, but *is* the story—a fusion of tone and tale that conjures up the commingling of two lives. Before exploring the voices that Smith found, I want to situate the text further in relation to this "postscript" material and link it to the brief introductory "Foreword" that prefaces the narrative, because these "bookends" shape its ultimate purpose, audience, and ambience.

Bookends: Framing "the Right Voice"

Underlying Smith's innovative, "kicked-in" memoir is another desire, which emerges in *Just Kids's* brief initial and closing paratexts: the "Foreword" and the epilogue, the "note," which is followed by eighteen unpaged pages of photographs and poems. In fact, the "note," dated 22 May 2010, and the final photographs were not part of the original hardback edition published in early 2010, but were added for the paperback version.[12] As "bookends," they frame the five chapters that focus on moments in the story, situating the "kids'" past within Smith's account of Mapplethorpe's death and her reflections on his enduring significance to her.[13] The addition of the "note" changes the ending of the memoir—and the reader's experience.[14]

I turn first to the brief "Foreword," which chronicles the night of 9 March 1989, when Smith, in Detroit, received news that Mapplethorpe had died in New York. She recounts details of Patti's moment of realization that she has lost Robert's voice (he had been too sedated to respond to her call): "I held the receiver and listened to his labored breathing through the phone, knowing I would never hear him again" (*Just* xi).[15] In her wordless sorrow the next morning, she hears on the radio the beautiful aria from *Tosca* in which Tosca sings, "I have lived for love, I have lived for Art," which becomes her voice of farewell (xii).

In the narrative's arc of discovery, arrival, and realization, the memoir's fifth and originally final chapter also returns to Robert's illness, as first his partner, Sam Wagstaff, and then he succumbs to the ravages of AIDS. In poignant vignettes, Patti recounts her last visits with him and the anguish not just of his suffering, but of her own letting go, far from him. She vows to remake her grief into a memorial song (278), which anticipates the memoir. And yet the memoir's last paragraph, meditating on memories of Robert, asks plaintively, "Why can't I write something that would awake the dead?" (279). This would seem to mark the limit of grief writing because it acknowledges letting go of the beloved who has irrevocably passed on. Both the "Foreword" and chapter five register Patti's initial shock about the loss of a loved one in a way similar to that of grief memoirs such as Joan Didion's *The Year of Magical Thinking* and Edwidge Danticat's *Brother, I'm Dying*. They frame the memoir as an act of saying "goodbye" (xii), an "autothanatography," as studies by Nancy K. Miller and Susanna Egan have explored.[16] Like those narrators, Smith's own grief stirs her to make in writing a memorial to a beloved other, but her project morphs into something more. Ultimately, as readers discover, the "note" in the last pages of the paperback version of *Just Kids* returns to voice—specifically the embodied voice shared by Robert and Patti, which can still contain, if not "awake," the dead.

Let us begin with the two-page epilogue, "A note to the reader," as a reflexive afterword to the story of *Just Kids*, describing how Smith's search for a voice to tell the story of Robert and Patti was a challenge in writing: "Our story was obliged to wait until I could find the right voice . . . . It is the one ['story'] he wished me to tell and I have kept my promise" (288)—that is, Smith insists that her tale is not a chronicle of events recounted by a monologic "I," but an evocation of the texture of two "kids'" time together that requires a different mode of telling. Although told by one author, the narrative strives for the shared voice that can capture their entry into New York City's artistic subculture at a transformative moment. Unlike the focus on the moment of loss in the "Foreword" of *Just Kids*, the "note" begins with the day, shortly before Mapplethorpe's death, when Robert and Patti have their final conversation. The passage, moving between their two voices in sentences without quotation marks, fuses indirect discourse with sentences of recollected dialogue, suggesting their emotional reciprocity. Its flow, without demarcation or quotation marks separating the speakers, creates a shared "third" voice. Robert begins, and the passage goes on: "Will you write our story? Do you want me to? You have to he said no one but you can write it. I will do it, I promised, though I knew it would be a vow difficult to keep" (287). Individualities merge in the back and forth of this interchange. In a few pages, their last conversation is presented as a dialogue unmarked by quotation marks, obfuscating who is speaking; rather, their words flow into one another's. The intersubjectivity created encapsulates Patti's sense that she and Robert became extensions of each other; he was "someone who had never been a stranger" (283).

Patti as narrator, then, continues their collaboration beyond Robert's death by finding "the right voice" in two senses: she crafts a narrative voice to convey the tenor of their early experiences together, but this voice also displays how their separate voices blended at times in the momentary mutuality of transpersonal union. Through that intersubjective voice, Smith situates the memoir as a place still to "hear" Robert's voice beyond the silence of the grave.

As the "note" goes on to explain, "the right voice" in *Just Kids* is akin to that in a fairy tale: "We were as Hansel and Gretel and we ventured out into the black forest of the world. There were temptations and witches and demons we never dreamed of and there was splendor we only partially imagined" (288). In Smith's allusion to the Grimm Brothers' tale, she references its "once upon a time" voice of enchantment and awakening, which the voice of *Just Kids* takes up, particularly in the memoir's first two chapters. There, the linked stories blend anecdotes of the "kids'" experiences of terror and privation with rushes of joy and wonder in narrating how Patti and Robert, as innocents abroad, found their way. Of course, the charms of this fairy tale are challenged by the complexities of adult "real life" when other voices—some darker, others occupied with the cultural moment—emerge in subsequent chapters of the memoir.

But Smith asserts in the "note" that their story belonged to both of them and extends throughout both their lives as a fundamentally relational tale: "Only Robert and I could tell it. Our story, as he called it. And, having gone, he left the task to me to tell it to you" (288). "The right voice," then, has to combine Patti's and Robert's voices, and situate them within the voice of Smith, the narrating "I." Ultimately, a transpersonal and intersubjective voice emerges, unique to relational life writing, shuttling between Patti and Robert, and speaking as "our story."

Autothanatography and the Memory Museum

With the publication of *Just Kids*, Patti Smith made a triumphant return to center stage in multiple media, as critics acclaimed her ability to create haunting and memorable voices. Its brilliant language, stylized reconstruction, and network of allusions that her "kid" self could not have mustered underscore her literary tour de force. Smith's exuberant narration of the New York scene, however, becomes pressured as the chronology of *Just Kids* moves beyond the late 1970s, when the threat of AIDS, which Mapplethorpe eventually contracted, began to shock and devastate the artistic world. That moment presents a narrative challenge to her personal aim to reassert her partnership with Mapplethorpe and enshrine their memories for a younger generation. The fifth, final chapter of *Just Kids* returns to the underlying elegiac tone of mourning announced in the retrospective bookend of the "Foreword," and in what readers of the paperback find in the concluding "note." With it returns the question of whether writing a memoir can offer consolation or satisfaction to the bereft partner who wants to "awake the dead." Formally, as the grieving voice of autothanatography reasserts the memorial project of *Just Kids*, Smith's act of "kicking in" the biographical wall that separates the dead from the living also returns.

The added epilogue in the paperback version of *Just Kids* provides an additional layer of reflection as a fragmentary archive of moments of Patti and Robert's young lives together. The archive includes Smith's melancholy "Memorial Song," written for the commemoration of Mapplethorpe's death; photographs and drawings of the young Robert and the young Patti (always separate); photographs of iconic details of 1970s New York (a Chelsea Hotel plaque, a Nathan's Hot Dogs sign); a memorial card for Mapplethorpe's death, with a self-portrait photograph; two letter fragments from Patti; a note about her recovery of his prized antique desk, an icon of his creative work and sensibility; and Smith's handwritten poem entitled "Just Kids." This coda of visual fragments, without comment by the narrating "I" except for the "desk" page, transports the narration to a zone of imagination, where words and images interact as a kind of "memory museum" for readers—a melancholic trace that brings the past into Smith's own—and our—present.

In this memory museum, images echo the resonant voices of the "kids" throughout the narrative, as if their past has come to life in a kind of synaesthetic, neo-Symbolist set of correspondences. Although Smith cannot literally awaken Robert, by juxtaposing his voice with the sequence of photographs, documents, and talismans from their young lives, she attempts to make these artifacts "speak" again. While, as a memoir, *Just Kids* inevitably attests to the impossibility of awakening the dead, its final pages gesture toward Smith's reanimating of Mapplethorpe's remembered voice and sensory presence through the conjunction of language and image.

We may, of course, ask in what sense this coda to Smith's project of "relating" moments and subjects can perform a counterfactual act to "awake the dead"? After all, Smith depends on "analog" technologies—writing and photography—at a time when the media of film and video can capture a subject in the act of speaking, and the digital technologies of social media now make the capture of others as voice-image simulacra an everyday experience. But using the materiality of the book to contain and project her subjective view of Mapplethorpe, photographically and verbally, as her "speaking" second self relies on illusion and the evocative power of narrative to "pierce" readers, in Barthes's sense of the photographic punctum. The final, near-wordless section of *Just Kids* "kicks in" a wall between representation and lived life by staging for readers an encounter with a gallery of images brought to life through the power of written voice. Its photographs of objects, conjoined to the verbal portraits of Mapplethorpe and Smith as kids, unroll their past again, embodied in photographed documents, as the trace of an unrecoverable past that gestures toward an inter-subjective self-in-relationship. Smith's attempt to defy temporal and material boundaries between the living and the dead by concluding with an evocation of Robert and their shared life becomes a poignant counterfactual insistence that, through the agency of memoir, "He is still alive" (277).

The Voice of Enchantment and the Artists' Story of Two "Kids"

In order to explore how the vocal effects of *Just Kids* as an "outlaw" form disman-tle the wall, or "rule," that normally separates *autos* from *bios* in life writing through a remarkable performance of voice,[17] I turn to the particular genres of life writing in which the story of *Just Kids* is composed. Smith's emphasis on find-ing "the right voice" to narrate the story of Patti and Robert's shared coming of age as a Hansel-and-Gretel pair of artists points up her use of the fairy tale's once-upon-a-time voice of innocence and wonder to present them as trailblazers in and emblems of a cultural moment. She adopts a particular kind of fairy tale—the romantic or visionary *Künstlerroman* of discovering one's inborn artistic vocation,[18] which was widely used by the German Romantics (Eichendorff, Novalis, the early Goethe); was riffed upon by a later generation of European Symbolists including Baudelaire, Huysmans, and Valéry; and was central to the voyages of Smith's hero, Rimbaud,[19] and, in different terms, to Blake's vision-ary poems.[20] In the first chapters of *Just Kids*, the narrating "I" adopts the per-spective of an experiencing child-I as she describes her own and Robert's origins and their voyage into the wider urban world of new-guard artists. Their rela-tionship is presented as a mystique of partnership and shared creative energy: "'Nobody sees as we do, Patti,' he said again….it was as if we were the only two people in the world" (104). Presented in juxtaposed sections, Robert's and Patti's experiences are paralleled as recognitions, even before the two met and began their life together.

The narrating "I" moving between Patti's and Robert's childhood stories of coming to artistic consciousness emphasizes that this is "our story," rather than just Patti's autobiography. Smith begins with her own childhood as the eldest sibling in a working-class post-World War II family, but she emphasizes moments of her awakening to "the radiance of the imagination" (4). The first memory presented is that of the three-year-old glimpsing a swan in flight while her mother teaches her the word "swan," linking the word to the image of pure, fluttering motion. Although the child is unaware (and the narrating "I" does not gloss this, but Smith surely knows), the swan is an iconic figure in Symbolist poetry, incarnating the word as image, from Mallarmé through Yeats, Valéry, and Rilke.

The stages of Patti's childhood are consistently presented as moments of awakening to the power of art: she leads her brother and sisters in fantasy games she invents; she discovers a larger, darker world after the shock of a childhood friend's illness and death; she is—at the time inexplicably—attracted to totemic objects, such as the skater pin that she, in an early transgressive moment, steals from the friend before she dies (8). These anecdotes condense events into what the narrator retrospectively interprets as signs of an artistic sensibility, marking her inborn vocation as an artist and rebellion against bourgeois life. What could have been told as the story of a bleak working-class childhood in Chicago and New Jersey is transformed by the adolescent's sense of election as she learns to "see" beyond the visible: "to be an artist was to see what others could not" (11). Smith frames her story as a tale she repeatedly recited to Robert when they first shared a Brooklyn apartment as lovers; his responses of "Patti, no" (9) at key moments of her transgressions are threaded through her telling, as if they together are recreating the story that readers encounter on the page.

Smith, however, must confront the challenge of managing this story of artistic development when life troubles threaten to take it in different directions: the birth of a child when she was 17 that she gave up for adoption, her factory job, and her years at a New Jersey college studying to become a teacher (17). But the narrator subordinates these events to the vow guiding her life that "I would be an artist" (18), which motivates her dropping out to move to New York in 1967. In her narrative, life events are aligned to those of Rimbaud, who "held the keys to a mystical language that I devoured even as I could not fully decipher it" (18).[21] As her literary mentor, Rimbaud influenced her to recast her perceptions of daily life as moments of illumination in all their sensuous particularity, like those of his poems, in order to escape mundane working-class life in pursuit of her vision (23).

At several points throughout the first chapter, Smith inserts the parallel story of Robert growing up in a middle-class Long Island family, where he was both a mischievous imp and a Catholic altar boy. The central truth of his childhood was also the discovery of his inborn vocation: "He was an artist and he knew it" (13). Mapplethorpe's recognition, induced by LSD, is also linked to vision, but a more rebellious one than Patti's: "He was an artist....He would no longer be a slave" (22). Similarly, the chapter juxtaposes photographs of the two as children (14—15) that show their parallel transformations from angelic "kids" into young hippies acting as artists of life, even before they found their art forms.

Thus, Smith's and Mapplethorpe's lives from 1967 to the early 1970s are presented as a shared artistic coming of age—a visionary process of discovering their commitment to art as a vocation. Totemic objects, another marker of the *Küstlerroman*'s visionary quest, symbolize and suture their bond. When Patti admires a violet Persian necklace in Brentano's, a Manhattan bookstore where she clerks, Robert eventually finds enough money to buy it for her (36, 51). The necklace intriguingly resembles the "blue flower" of German romanticism, a secret sign shared among the artistic elect, and becomes an icon of the symbolic "blue star" of mystical art that binds them.[22] Patti and Robert's days together are narrated as discoveries of their mutual dedication to the visionary in art and poetry—Blake's engravings, mandalas, the paintings of Dada and Surrealist artists. Invoking the language of chivalry, Patti casts her recognition of Robert as her second self and beloved: "I knew he was my knight" (42). Romantic tropes drawn from various periods and traditions thus provide an interpretive framework that overlays and recodes childhood experience.

While Patti, as a poet, vocalizes in lyrical form, Robert, as a visual artist, expresses his "energy" more in objects than dialogue, creating images that "infused objects, whether for art or life, with his creative impulse, his sacred sexual power." He exacts his transformative "genius" in acts that are simultaneously the creation and the recognition of "perfect object[s]" (136). Like artists and children, both impart a "magical life-breath" into the objects they engage: "The artist animates his work as the child his toys" (136). And, as in Baudelaire's "forest of symbols," the energy they evoke in each other during their early days together is "a sign that we were on the right path" to artistic fulfillment (137). In Smith's Romantic shaping of artists' lives, sharing their early days creates a transcendent bond based on their awakening and dedication to art: "Our work was our children," Patti assures Robert as he lies on his deathbed (274). Yet Robert's more sexualized and transgressive imagination will emerge as they gradually grow apart.

Importantly, the parallel lives narrated in the first chapters of *Just Kids* are fully relational, tracking similarities and differences in the backgrounds, physical identities, and visionary goals of Robert and Patti. They cannot be read as solely either autobiography or biography—Smith is among the few who achieve, in Eakin's phrase, "the autobiography of the other" (56). But the narrative of filiality linking the two young artists wandering "like Maeterlinck's children seeking the bluebird" in the depths of Lower Manhattan is challenged when their life choices—in artistic media, sexualities, and lovers—and ways of cultivating fame start to shift (*Just* 79). As Patti's and Robert's life trajectories increasingly diverge, the fairy-tale story of the mutual dedication of two "mirror selves," in Egan's term, committed to art is challenged. The story shifts to tracing their polar oppositions—across genders and sexualities, media and lifestyles—when the different possibilities opening for Robert and Patti created tensions. As their separate personal paths emerged, the narrating "I" tries to hold their divergent stories in relational equilibrium by a logic of similarity within difference.

By itself, however, Mapplethorpe's story could be told quite differently (and in most biographies has been): as a gay-male coming-out narrative, in which his sense of inborn homosexual identity and relentless push, in life and art, against taboos about sadomasochism form a transgressive frame for the tragic thanatography of AIDS-related death in the 1980s, when there was no effective treatment for its ravages. Another divergence—Robert's shift from their partnership to a focus on his career and opportunistic contacts with wealthy art patrons who supported his rise to fame (notably his life partner, Sam Wagstaff)—also threatens to unsettle the importance of what Smith makes central, and arguably redemptive: his partnership with Patti.

As a narrator trying to sustain her relational auto|biography, Smith adopts various strategies to forestall the collapse of their shared story into separate tales. Framing Robert's increasing attraction to a darker world of drugs, sexual aggression, and social ambition, she introduces a second explanatory "fairy tale"—the story of Faust's pact with the demonic Mephistopheles, which involved trading his soul for access to knowledge in all its sensuous forms and a refusal to ever stop exploring. The Faust myth, of course, offers no place for Patti: Gretchen drowned her infant and was arrested, Faust had multiple transient lovers, and he was "redeemed" at the end of Part Two when Mephistopheles lost the bet. (In fact, Smith conflates Faust and Mephistopheles as two sides of Robert.) Faustian or "Dionysian" in "embracing freedom and heightened experience" but also tireless in selling himself, Mapplethorpe rose to fame-as-notoriety in part for his sadomasochistic photographs (188).[23] As Mapplethorpe explores sexual shores wilder than any in *Faust* and Patti watches him "come into his own" amid a moneyed class of art patrons, their friends and social circles increasingly diverge (150). Finally, she emphasizes her separation from Mapplethorpe's artistic focus on "hardcore" images that "produce visuals of self-inflicted pain" (236). Summing up the split in their artistic paths, she observes, "I left Mephistopheles… saying, 'I choose Earth'" (256).

Yet Smith, the present-time narrator, also reiterates her insistence that "[n]either would leave the other….My picture of him remained intact. He was the artist of my life" (157). She tries to hold their differences together as a dynamic of mutuality and recognition that fueled the best moments of "our work, our collaboration for as long as I live" (287), a magic mirror of relationship as symmetry—resemblance within difference within resemblance. And she presents their parallels as able to contain oppositions because each was shaped by the other: "We came to accept our dual natures. We both contained opposing principles, light and dark" (9). However dissimilar their lifestyles, art forms, and career trajectories, in Smith's narration they remain linked as mirror selves.

"Light Writing" and the Photographic Story

Incorporating multiple differences as part of the relational structure of Robert's and Patti's lives, Smith tracks how their embodiments fractured cultural norms of masculine and feminine, even as their various "looks" sutured their bond as hippie artists. While a discussion of the photographs (30 in the hardcover edition, 40 in the paperback) is not my main focus, I see them as comprising another kind of relationality—that of word to image. More than a paratext, the "light writing," in Timothy Dow Adams' lovely term, of photographed faces, artifacts, and documents textures the memoir's voice as its visual equivalent.[24]

Some photographs of the time show Patti and Robert as strikingly similar to each other in body and affect, though their gendered appearances vary with the image. *West 23ʳᵈ St. Fire Escape* depicts them as frail yet tough, with Smith's leaning body and averted eyes suggesting "feminine" dependency on Mapplethorpe's confident "masculine" embrace of her (201). Other photographs, by contrast, exhibit their undermining of gendered difference as new-guard artists of the early 1970s, enacting what Judith Butler terms gender performativity—impersonation improvising on and intervening in an arbitrary binary system of sexual difference. In photographs, Robert and Patti often appear as equals in "cool"— for example, in the cover image of the original hardback, where they are dressed as young hippies in bell-bottoms at Coney Island, or in the close-up of them kissing in a photo booth, both in men's hats, which is the back-cover image of the paperback. Elsewhere, in the photograph of the couple on the cover of the paperback edition, their affects are contrasted: Robert's eyes are closed in apparent bliss, while the ever-reflective Patti gazes seriously at the camera, eyes open in scrutiny.

Mapplethorpe, in particular, sought to undermine stereotypes of masculinity and femininity, butch and femme, in his photographic work as well as his physical identity. He not only enacted, but embodied gender drag as his identities shifted: growing up as a Catholic-school altar boy (15); in New York first as a "shepherd" in apocalyptic hippie garb, a sheepskin vest over his bare chest adorned with multiple necklaces; and after deciding, "I'm tired of looking like a shepherd boy" and shifting to a "city" look (138–39), coming out as a sadomasochistic gay man, and consciously mimicking the dress of sailors and leather boys (202, 236). Smith's narration of their transgressive gendered affect, however, frames it as simultaneously youthful experimentation in search of identity and an avant-garde aesthetic incorporated in their performance of artistry. As fairy-tale characters, they slip in and out of costumes that only gradually come to have more enduring implications for the identities they eventually inhabit.

It is true that, in *Just Kids*, women writers' and rock artists' work and voices appear with less frequency than men's, which to some suggests Smith's masculinist dominance.[25] But, as Shank has convincingly argued, "Smith was able to command a position in the field of rock that had long been denied to women singers and musicians" as a "female machisma" with "a kind of tomboy appropriation of masculine values and subject positions" that she could assert was "beyond gender," even as she operated within its contradictions (167). This complex interplay of gendered positions and their undermining, which both Mapplethorpe and Smith powerfully worked, is perhaps most visible in the range of photographs in *Just Kids*, which are striking for both the vulnerability of the "kids" and the challenging of bourgeois convention that they suggest. In photographs, then, "the right voice" is captured as a mode of "speaking back" to heteronormative values through relational portraits that reference both a bohemian artistic tradition and an emerging postmodern photographic style.

Performing Autoethnography

The memorial framing of the fairy-tale voice, in which *Just Kids's* narrative begins, shifts as Patti and Robert move to Manhattan, where they encounter a world of bohemian artists, writers, and musicians, who contribute to shaping their protean selves. From chapter three on, Smith narrates more often in the voice of an autoethnographer,[26] serving as an insider-outsider observer, a historian of a moment who is on, but not fully of, the scene, chronicling memorable artists and places in rich sensory detail. After Robert and Patti arrive, in every sense, at the Chelsea Hotel, their parallel stories begin to diverge,[27] as they encounter famous, up-and-coming, and would-be artists and intellectuals. Smith's narration incorporates the dialogism of the jarring voices that texture the urban scene. *Just Kids*, as a mosaic of a cultural moment, depicts multitudinous urban sounds and sights, and moves through iconic places—Brooklyn's then-gritty Clinton Hill, the Chelsea Hotel in its heyday of musicians and poets, Manhattan galleries mounting new work, coffee houses and clubs such as Max's Kansas City and CBGB, and the seedy pleasures of Coney Island. At their best, Smith's word portraits of rock and visual artists, like Mapplethorpe's photographs, anecdotally catch "the magic" of a moment as a Rimbaudean illumination. An ethnographer of a "moveable feast" à la Hemingway's memoir of expatriate Paris,[28] Smith chronicles meetings with artists swirling around Lower Manhattan, from the 1967 "Summer of Love" up to the outbreak of HIV at the end of the 1970s, filtering out the national scene—there are no allusions to Watergate or Nixon's China visit. Rather, New York's fabulous characters are evoked in a collage of vocal scraps that reference the revolutionary energy of rock 'n' roll fueled by sex, drugs, and a hunger for the edge and the new. Typically, Smith shapes these vignettes, saying, for example, in a pithy epigram characteristic of the participant-observer, about Beat poet Gregory Corso that he "could enter a room and commit instant mayhem, but he was easy to forgive because he had the equal potential to commit great beauty" (137).

This autoethnographic voice encompasses many of the artists and writers, living and dead, whom Smith, a tireless autodidact, read voraciously. She disarmingly narrates encounters with writers including Allen Ginsberg, who, she claims, on meeting her in a lunch automat, thought she was a boy and made a pass at her. And her crush on the extraordinary William Burroughs, her "guardian angel," is endearingly ironic.[29] In this visionary company, Bob Dylan is an intriguing figure, claimed as an exemplar for her music and, perhaps, her memoir. He is "the one I had modeled myself after" in his vocal style of prophetic song, although he remained inscrutable, even to Patti (248).

Although Patti's flirtation with patrons and "stars" was more tentative than Robert's, in New York she occasionally found alternate others for her experimental young self. Notably, playwright Sam Shepard, whom she initially knew as Slim Shadow, the drummer for The Holy Modal Rounders, briefly became her partner in writing and life, and *Cowboy Mouth*, the play they cowrote, memorably captured her in-your-face style.[30] But Shepard is not foregrounded as an alternate relational self; the underlying memorial dedication of the memoir to Mapplethorpe is unswerving.

Celebrity Memoir as a Narrative for "the People"

As *Just Kids* moves into the mid 1970s, when Smith and Mapplethorpe became famous, it strives to resist the pull of what celebrity memoir is generally considered to be: a chronicle of the sensational highlights of a star's public life for inquiring readers seeking vicarious pleasures in personal dirty laundry.[31] While celebrity memoirs are typically collaborations "as told to" a ghostwriter, who is at best recognized on the copyright page but has suppressed her or his separate voice in crafting the star's, Smith's narration problematizes the celebrity memoir as a form in ways that point up the difference of her personal voice and dedication to lyrical writing. Her narrative is written solo, although designed collaboratively, as the coherence and authority of her voice indicate.[32] Admittedly, Smith's claim to tell a relational story, including Patti's and Robert's distinct voices and creating their "third" shared, intersubjective voice, confronts some biographical problems that threaten its underlying melancholic purpose. The narrator must negotiate how to incorporate an other who has been dead for nearly two decades without having the autothanatography of grief overwhelm it or make it a "just personal" act of mourning. Crucially, Smith must also counter readers' suspicion that Patti's account of her life with Robert is an act of ventriloquism after the fact of his death. In the spaces the narrative clears for the voice and the difference of Robert, Smith's memorial project is in tension with its public chronicle as an autoethnography. Her relational strategy, shuttling between the two "kids'" stories as a dual portrait, contrasts Patti's embrace of her artistic vocation with the unrelenting pursuit of fame that drove the equally artistic Robert,[33] while emphasizing their differing versions of celebrity.

This is, then, a bifurcated story of celebrity, although the narrating "I" has a retrospective assurance about her accomplishments that Patti, the narrated "I" who dropped out of the scene, lacked. As Marjorie Garber trenchantly observed, "in accepting the National Book Award, Smith's memories were of a teenage girl who longed to be a writer… [but] her tears were the tears of a star" (1084). The sense of autocreation and generative energy that Smith portrays Patti and Robert as sparking in each other in *Just Kids* unquestionably produced creative innovations beyond the ephemera of the Warhol Factory stars with whom they at times hobnobbed, but it also generated a memoir superior to the kiss-and-tell jottings of, say, Viva of the Warhol Factory in *Superstar*.[34] Despite its portrayal of Robert's determined quest for fame and notoriety, *Just Kids*, unlike such "star" memoirs, demystifies stardom as one-tenth genius but nine-tenths sweat equity, luck, connections, and staying power. Indeed, *Just Kids* might be thought of as an anti-celebrity memoir in counteracting the usual vanity of the form. It implicitly cautions aspiring artists on what is required psychically, emotionally, and materially to realize an inborn vocation through apprenticeships to masters and mentors. Its stories combine practical advice with a manifesto's urgency about how young people must starve and suffer in pursuit of an artistic dream, rather than just become pop stars who recycle consumer culture. Its voice at some moments becomes politically edgy, if gently didactic, in emphasizing the dedication to craft and schooling in the visionary traditions required to become revolutionary anarchists and priests of the imagination.[35]

The public voices of *Just Kids*, then, work to reactivate the avant-garde energy of rock music and performance by recounting for the younger generations of her audience the legacy of art as both aesthetic and political action, even as the memoir's last third subordinates Smith's personal project of remembering Mapplethorpe to its focus on aesthetic and political tales of artists.[36] When Smith appeared on the popular fake-news television show *The Colbert Report*, she summed up *Just Kids's* depiction of the Lower Manhattan scene at the turn of the 1970s, saying, "When I was writing [the book], it was like writing a movie for the people." This is yet another way of "kicking in" the rules of writing memoir, imagining it as a site where diverse audiences can immerse themselves in an earlier era. Voices and images become coterminous as aspects of "the right voice," ways of evoking the past as present, almost to "awake the dead"—as we discover in its last chapter, added "note," and photograph gallery. There, the recursiveness of an autobiographical story that ends in the "memory museum" of lived experiences from which it originated and which now resonates for readers achieves the resonance of truly relational storytelling.

Conclusion

Just Kids's narrative voice works, above all, as a kind of enchantment conveyed in the seeming modesty of the narrative's project of intimate remembrance. As the narrating "I"'s sense of wonder about how the cool Lower Manhattan scene opened up for a poor girl from New Jersey and an altar boy from Long Island, its engaging voice repeatedly moves between *autos* and *bios* to tell its story as a partnership with two subjects. In the polyphonic performance of *Just Kids*, we observe the play of personal voice within, and against, the narrative genres of the *Künstlerroman*, autoethnography, and autothanatography as aspects of celebrity memoir. And we observe the interplay of voices across *autos* and *bios*: the memoirist's reflective voice; the narrated "I"'s recounting of its story in a child's "and—then" sequence of events from an experiential past; the dialogues of the two "kid" protagonists, Patti and Robert; and the emerging intersubjective voice of their collaboration that seeks to evoke a counterfactual "presence" of Mapplethorpe two decades after his death. In its focus on the intersection of voice, visual artifacts, and genres, *Just Kids* offers a model for how we, as life-narrative theorists, might also "kick in" the walls or boundaries that have separated auto- and biographical forms to rethink the presentation of subjectivity beyond an individual consciousness in contemporary memoir.

The Ohio State University

Acknowledgments

This essay was first presented as a paper at the 2012 International Auto|Biography Association conference in Canberra, Australia, where I had a long and illuminating conversation with a young woman scholar about Patti Smith's music and the differences of, and interplay of voices in, Smith's written work. Charron Andrews provided helpful information for websites with photographs of Patti Smith. Comments on various versions of the essay by Linda Haverty Rugg, Craig Howes, Julie Rak, Jim Phelan, Christian Moser, Norma Coates, David Shumway, Barry Shank, Danielle Marx-Scouras, Bella Brodzki, Ricia A. Chansky, and, as ever, Sidonie Smith, were also helpful. Any errors of fact or judgment are my own.

Disclosure Statement

No potential conflict of interest was reported by the author.

Notes

1. For a discussion of the concept of relationality and theorists who have employed it productively, see Smith and Watson (esp. 215—18). While Eakin has helpfully defined it as "the other's story" (56), the concept is often loosely applied to all life narratives that engage the stories of others. But as Eakin, Miller, and Smith and I have all observed, very few autobiographical texts do *not* involve the lives of others. A new German study by Anne Rüggemeier, *Die relationale Autobiographie*, proposes to study relationality as a new genre in English narrative.

2. In 2012, the Detroit Institute of Arts hosted an exhibition of her Polaroid photographs entitled "Patti Smith: Camera Solo," which later moved to the Wadsworth Atheneum.

3. On Arista Records, recorded at Electric Lady Studios (which Jimi Hendrix established and where he recorded) in New York City.

4. While Smith refers in *Just Kids* to dressing in her favorite striped sailor's shirt and long gray raincoat as a kind of flâneur of ambivalent sexuality, both the narrative and the photographs show that Smith also attired herself in a favorite black-velvet dress with a lace collar, a "feminine" costume. But she told an interviewer from *Mademoiselle* magazine that "You can't worry about gender when you're doing Art on its Highest Level," and she had to learn how to dress like a woman (Shank 167).

5. As her appointment as a commander of the Ordre des Arts et des Lettres in France in 2006 signals.

6. It was the apparatus used to shoot the Polaroid photographs exhibited at the Detroit Institute of Arts.

7. Smith is also an astute literary critic. See her insightful review of Haruki Murakami's 2014 novel, *Colorless Tsukuru Tazaki and His Years of Pilgrimage* ("Deep Chords").

8. Dillingham suggests that *Just Kids* may soon be a motion picture with script and production by Smith, but, as of this writing (2015), it is not on the horizon. And a follow-up volume to *Just Kids*, tentatively titled *F Train*, may appear in fall 2015.

9. Sidonie Smith and I have argued that "voice" should be considered as simultaneously inflected speech, a set of templates for telling, and an effect to which readers respond. For a longer discussion of voice, see Smith and Watson (esp. 79–85, 250–51). Narrative theorist James Phelan helpfully defines voice as "a metaphor in which writing gets treated as speech," and argues that readers experience words on a page as "a learnable kind of synesthesia: as we see words on a page we can hear sounds" (138)—that is, two senses converge as we convert what we read into the "sounds" of a text to evoke the rhythms and tone of a speaking person. (Intriguingly, this notion of synesthesia recalls the French Symbolists' use of the trope to image the confusion of the senses in states of artistic exaltation that poetry can conjure.) In writing, various narrated and narrating "I"s join to form what Bakhtin termed the "double-voiced discourse" of narration, communicating to readers a sense of the narrating "I"'s subjectivity and ethical values—what might be called the texture of an experiential history (Phelan 139). Narrators may present a range of conflicting inner voices linked to the genres they take up, and the voices of others may be incorporated not only as external dialogue, but in free indirect discourse, across distances of time, shifting belief, and emotions. Voice

in writing, then, rather than being a monologic performance, is a hetero-glossic mix of multiple utterances, both internal and external.

10. It was written in memory of Maria Schneider of *Last Tango in Paris* fame.

11. She makes this comment in her film *Dream of Life*.

12. The pagination in hardback and paperback editions is identical, except for the nine additional paged pages and eighteen unpaged pages, a total of twelve added photographs, for 42 in the paperback, 30 in the hardback, and the different front and back covers.

13. I have given each chapter a number rather than repeating their titles: "Monday's Children" is chapter one; "Just Kids" is chapter two: "Hotel Chelsea" is chapter three; "Separate Ways Together" is chapter four; and "Holding Hands with God" is chapter five. The "Foreword" and the con-cluding "A note to the reader" are identified by name.

14. *Just Kids's* copyright page and "Photographs and Illustrations" page credit Mary Austin Speaker with the editorial design (of both the hardback and paperback editions).

15. I will refer to the memoir's protagonists by their first names and to the flesh-and-blood artists by their last or full names.

16. See Miller's observation in "Representing Others" that "every autobiogra-phy, we might say, is also an autothanatography," because each writer confronts the inescapability of death (12). Egan, in *Mirror Talk*, explores the centrality of autothanatography because its "focus on illness, pain, and imminent death [is] crucial to the processes of that life" (224). This topic is explored in more detail in Smith and Watson (138–41).

17. See Kaplan's discussion of "outlaw genres" as hybridized forms that flaunt the implicit rules of genre.

18. The *Künstlerroman* is understood as the narrative of "the figure of the artist as social outsider, who struggled with conflicts between the internal crea-tive impulse and the external constraints of bourgeois social reality" (Martin 61). It has been revived by both Patti Smith and Keith Richards, in *Life*, as Leigh Gilmore notes. In Romantic literature, it was considered an exclusively "masculine" genre, but feminist critics have pointed out that its features merge with the "feminine" genre of the sentimental or the domestic novel (Martin 63). Smith situates herself predominantly within the masculine tradition.

19. Smith's lifelong dedication to French Symbolist poet Arthur Rimbaud is discussed in *Woolgathering* ("To the Reader" n. pag.) and chronicled in the journey to his grave that she details in *Just Kids*.

20. Smith entitled her 2005 poetry collection *Auguries of Innocence*. She also compiled and introduced an edition of Blake's poetry, including Blake's 132-line "Auguries" poem, for Vintage.

21. Famously, Rimbaud fractured the "I" into fragments of subjective perception ("*je est un autre*")—a quite different trajectory of self-presentation than Smith takes.

22. The *blaue Blume* or glowing "blue flower" of German romanticism features centrally in Joseph Freiherr von Eichendorff's important and charming *From the Life of a Good-for-Nothing* (*Aus dem Leben eines Taugenichts*) and in Novalis's essays. The leitmotif continued to signal artistic vocation throughout the German nineteenth century. It recurs as a trope for the mystical quest in Leni Riefenstahl's silent film *The Blue Light* (*Das blaue Licht*, 1932), where the Fascist overtones it has acquired become evident.

23. Notably, in the censoring and closing of "The Perfect Moment" exhibit at the Corcoran Museum in Washington, which reinforced Mapplethorpe's notoriety.

24. See Adams' discussion of photography as "light writing" (1—21, 232—42).

25. See Coates' argument about the difficulty that women rock singers had both in being recognized as independent performers, rather than the girlfriends of male performers, and in telling their stories of trying to become visible within the evolving masculine narrative of rock performance.

26. For a discussion theorizing the terms and narrator position in autoethnography, see my essay "Strategic Autoethnography."

27. Quinby's essay, "The Subject of Memoirs," remains definitive on the distinction between the diaristic and inner-directed genre of memoir and the socially oriented practice of writing memoirs, a kind of precursor to autoethnograpy (see esp. 297—99). Smith could be said to combine both forms.

28. Posthumously published in 1964.

29. In *Dream of Life*, when she admits to Burroughs her long-term crush on him as her "guardian angel," he replies wryly, "Patti, I'm a homosexual."

30. Smith performed in *Cowboy Mouth* only once, in 1971, thinly disguised as Cavale, one of the two protagonists in the brilliant, edgy, obscenity-filled play, with Sam Shepard playing "Slim." Smith insists that the "cowboy mouth" was Shepard, not she, as is commonly assumed (*Just* 171, 185—86).

31. Rak observes that, in the US, "celebrity" as "the liberal democratic ideal of sharing one's life in the public sphere" is "the condition for public identity of any kind" but also, inescapably, an act by which public figures turn their lives into commodities (208). She also argues for rehabilitating a negative view of celebrity memoir as cheap thrills by including famous artists, politicians, and thinkers in the category. Readers engage with

their stories—and Smith's, in my view—for instruction as well as pleasure in their nonfictional character.

32. She has not, however, included the diaries from which particulars of *Just Kids* are drawn; they would give it a different, documentary kind of authority.

33. While Smith seemed not to cultivate fame as assiduously, the back cover of the initial hardback edition is a copy of a note that young Patti writes to Robert on their first "anniversary," signed with a blue star: "We'll have a real home soon one way or another and it's then that we'll be famous—with or without the shit of the world."

34. Mick Jagger voiced a dissenting view, seeing Smith as a musical poseur (McNeil).

35. For example, she recalls how at the Fillmore East in 1970 she saw Crosby, Stills, Nash, and Young, who as a group did not impress her; but she praised Young for his song "Ohio," which "seemed to crystallize the role of the artist as a responsible commentator" (*Just* 157).

36. See Paytress on Smith's belief in the redemptive and "revolutionary power of rock'n'roll" (37).

Works Cited

Adams, Timothy Dow. *Light Writing and Life Writing*. Chapel Hill: U of North Carolina P, 1999. Print.

Berger, Kevin. "When Patti Smith and Robert Mapplethorpe Were 'Just Kids.'" *Los Angeles Times*. 17 Jan. 2010. Web. 15 June 2012.

Coates, Norma. "Whose Tears Go By? Marianne Faithfull at the Dawn and Twilight of Rock Culture." *She's So Fine: Reflections on Whiteness, Femininity, Adolescence and Class in 1960s Music*. Ed. Laurie Stras. Farnham: Ashgate, 2010. 183−202. Print.

Dillingham, Maud. "Patti Smith: *Just Kids* Autobiography to Be a Major Motion Picture." *Christian Science Monitor*. Christian Science Monitor, 24 Aug. 2011. Web. 13 Nov. 2014.

Dream of Life. Dir. Steven Sebring. Perf. Patti Smith. Celluloid Dreams, 2008. Film.

Eakin, Paul John. *How Our Lives Become Stories: Making Selves*. Ithaca: Cornell UP, 1999. Print.

Egan, Susanna. *Mirror Talk: Genres of Crisis in Contemporary Autobiography*. Chapel Hill: U of North Carolina P, 1999. Print.

Garber, Marjorie. "Dig It: Looking for Fame in All the Wrong Places." *PMLA* 126.4 (2011): 1076−85. Print.

Gilmore, Leigh. "*Just Kids*, and *Life* (review)." *Fourth Genre* 13.2 (2011): 123−26. Print.

Kaplan, Caren. "Resisting Autobiography: Outlaw Genres and Transnational Feminist Subjects." *De/Colonizing the Subject: The Politics of Gender in Women's Autobiography*. Ed. Sidonie Smith and Julia Watson. Minneapolis: U of Minnesota P, 1992. 115—38. Print.

Martin, Judith E. "The Nineteenth-Century German *Künstler(in)roman*: Transforming Gender and Genre." *New Comparison* 33.4 (2002): 61—71. Print.

McNeil, Legs. "Getting Stoned with Patti Smith." *Vice.com*. Vice, 10 July 2014. Web. 17 Nov. 2014.

Miller, Nancy K. "Representing Others: Gender and the Subjects of Autobiography." *differences* 6.1 (1994): 1—27. Print.

"Patti Smith." *The Colbert Report*. Comedy Central. 23 Dec. 2010. Television.

Paytress, Mark. *Patti Smith's "Horses" and the Remaking of Rock 'n' Roll*. London: Piatkus, 2006. Print.

Phelan, James. "Voice, or Authors, Narrators, and Audiences." *Teaching Narrative Theory*. Ed. David Herman, Brian McHale, and Phelan. New York: MLA, 2010. 137—50. Print.

Quinby, Lee. "The Subject of Memoirs: *The Woman Warrior*'s Technology of Ideographic Selfhood." *De/Colonizing the Subject: The Politics of Gender in Women's Autobiography*. Ed. Sidonie Smith and Julia Watson. Minneapolis: U of Minnesota P, 1992. 297—320. Print.

Rak, Julie. *Boom! Manufacturing Memoir for the Popular Market*. Waterloo, ON: Wilfred Laurier UP, 2013. Print.

Rüggemeier, Anne. *Die relationale Autobiographie: ein Beitrag zur Theorie, Poetik und Gattungsgeschichte eines neuen Genres in der englischsprachigen Erzählliteratur*. Trier: Wissenschaftlicher Verlag Trier, 2014. Print.

Shank, Barry. *The Political Force of Musical Beauty*. Durham: Duke UP, 2014. Print.

Smith, Patti. "Deep Chords." Rev. of *Colorless Tsukuru Tazaki and His Years of Pilgrimage*, by Haruki Murakami. *New York Times Sunday Book Review* 10 Aug. 2014: 1, 16. Print.

—. *Just Kids*. New York: Ecco, 2010. Print.

—. *Just Kids*. Paperback. New York: Ecco, 2010. Print.

—. *Woolgathering*. 1992. New York: New Directions, 2011. Print.

Smith, Sidonie, and Julia Watson. *Reading Autobiography: A Guide for Interpreting Life Narratives*. 2nd ed. Minneapolis: U of Minnesota P, 2010. Print.

Viva [Janet Susan Mary Hoffmann]. *Superstar*. New York: Putnam, 1970. Print.

Watson, Julia. "Strategic Autoethnography and American Ethnicity Debates: The Metrics of Authenticity in *When I Was Puerto Rican*." *Women's Life Writing and Diaspora*. Spec. issue of *Life Writing* 10.2 (2013): 129—50. Print.

Public Memory and Public Mourning in Contemporary Colombia

Memoria pública y luto público en la Colombia contemporánea

By Gabriel Jaime Murillo Arango

Translated by Karla Marie Rodríguez Acosta and Carlos Agudelo Castro

Colombia today has advanced in setting experience narratives as a resource in the pedagogical practices, cultural agenda, mass media and political action. Beyond classrooms, these narratives include short stories from victims and victimizers of internal war, historical memoirs, artworks, movies, soap operas and testimonial narrative. Rather than simple historical randomization, these phenomena project the dignity and greatness of "small lives" above powerful metanarratives within the current cultural transmission crises. This paper reveals the existing asymmetrical relationship between the social practice of historical memory, as reflected on the "places of memory," artworks, cinema, testimonial narrative, and the political as well as judicial practice of memory, as manifested in struggles for both dignity and restitution of rights, lands, and property to victims. However, the pedagogical practice of historical memory remains as an unachieved goal in Colombia.

La Colombia de hoy ha avanzado en utilizar las narrativas de experiencia como recurso en las prácticas pedagógicas, la agenda cultural, la comunicación en masa y en la acción política. Más allá de los salones de clase, estas narrativas incluyen cuentos cortos de las víctimas y victimarios de las guerras internas, memoirs históricos, trabajos de arte, películas, novelas y testimonios narrativos. En lugar de ser una simple aleatorización histórica, estos fenómenos proyectan la dignidad y la grandeza de las "pequeñas vidas" sobre las metanarrativas poderosas dentro de las crisis de transmisión cultural actuales. Este trabajo revela la relación asimétrica existente entre la práctica social de la memoria histórica, la cual se encuentra reflejada en los "lugares de memoria", trabajos de arte, cine, testimonios narrativos y la política, así como la práctica judicial de memoria manifestada en las luchas por la dignidad y la restitución de derechos, tierras y propiedades para las víctimas. Sin embargo, la práctica pedagógica de la memoria histórica permanece una meta inalcanzable en Colombia.

Today, educators in Colombia have advanced by using narratives as a resource in pedagogical practices, the mass media, and political action. These narratives include fictional texts, visual narratives, and testimonies. Importantly, these phenomena project the dignity and greatness of small lives above powerful metanarratives within the current cultural-transmission crises. This essay explores the existing asymmetrical relationships between the social practices of historical memory, as reflected in places of memory, including artwork and testimonial narratives, and the judicial practice of memory, as manifested in struggles for both dignity and the restitution of rights, lands, and property to victims. However, the pedagogical practice of historical memory remains an unachieved goal in Colombia.

For over fifty years, Colombia has experienced eruptions of violence that have turned it into a country of unrest, uncertainty, and precarious democracy. Among them, the confrontations between the Fuerzas Armadas Revolucionarias de Colombia (Colombian Revolutionary Armed Forces)—which is considered to be one of the oldest guerrilla groups in the world—and the Ejército de Liberación Nacional (National Liberation Army) stand out the most. The state is currently trying to achieve a peace treaty with these entities that will lead to the end of armed struggle and the transformation of the social and political order. In the early years of the twenty-first century, the government, with the conspicuous sponsorship of drug cartels and the hidden support of the powerful political elites of the region, partially demobilized the paramilitary forces, which had controversial effects. These same paramilitary forces obliterated both small and medium-sized properties that had belonged to campesinos According to the authors of *Justica y Paz ¿Verdad Judicial o Verdad Histórica?*. Significantly, this dispossession led to the expansion of large illegal estates located in the countryside, as well as the forceful displacement of five million poor to the big cities.

The intricate peace process led to the adoption of a normative framework responding to the principles of truth, justice, and symbolic atonement. These are the principles that condense the philosophy of transitional justice expressed in the Law of Justice and Peace, or Law 975 of 2005. According to the authors, this law can be seen as a "pedagogical, political, and historiographical" pledge (Orozco et al. 19), in which the normative framework attempts to articulate the meaning as characterized by Pierre Nora. This law is enacted through a judicial institution embodying a civic tradition that resists authoritarian attempts at control, such as replacing the law with an ephemeral loyalty to a caudillo and appeals to the force of law.

Since then, other proposals have emerged with the intent of adopting a strategy to pay respect to the historical bereavement of the tragedy of war. Under Law 1448—also known as the Victims' Land Restitution Law—9 April 2012 was declared a national day of remembrance and solidarity for the victims. The promulgation of this law combines the remembrance of the victims of the previous period known as "La Violencia" (always written with a capital "V")—which began following the assassination of the liberal populist leader Jorge Eliécer Gaitán on 9 April 1948—with the victims of today. The day of remembrance is designed to facilitate public engagement in the cultural work of building a historical memory. In turn, the event calls for developing ways of social resistance and generational change, because it is directed specifically at the youth, who have largely grown up giving its strength to traditional bipartisanship in the middle of diverse conflicts. All hope of ending the interminable war has been placed in this cultural pledge, along with other political rituals and discourses.

Nevertheless, the legislators committed to the duty of historical memory have not appropriately used the space of the classroom to discuss violence; on the contrary, this topic has been consistently omitted or absent in history, ethics, or civics courses in the official curriculum. Therefore, successive generations of Colombians, who have frequently engaged with news about terrorist bombings, waves of poor campesinos displaced to the cities, and kidnappings, have not been adequately educated in the exercise of historical memory—that is, schools and other public institutions have not considered how to cope with the collective grief of the people in any meaningful way.

The importance of the issue reveals a disagreement and an inconsistency between the social practice of historical memory—reflected in the proliferation of narratives in art and film, and in personal testimonies—and the legal and political practice—expressed most recently in the arduous efforts by the judicial establishment for the restitution of victims' dignity, civil rights, and assets. However, despite the aforementioned achievements, the pedagogical practice of historical memory still remains a largely untapped resource. To this day, intimate or domestic memory fragments, rituals of homage, well-timed collective actions, and memorials all contribute to the historical accumulation of the social practice of memory and remembering. Consequently, these actions have started a social movement that, in the name of the victims of war, challenges the state's power to exclude, uproot, and exempt victimizers from the consequences of their actions. The movement's force has been felt in recent normative processes by the state, which has gradually yielded before both national and international pressure.

For the past decade, the intimate details of the war against a civil, unarmed population have been unveiled, thanks to the countless testimonies of those accused before tribunals, as well as the identification of partnerships between criminal paramilitary gangs and thousands of state officials at all levels. These findings would not have been possible if judicial investigators had not been determined to bring the executioners to justice and establish the truth concerning their actions. Yet, at the same time, the ambiguity that surrounds the work of the Congress has also been scrutinized. This Congress, which is the premier legislative body of the nation, has had close to one hundred of its members criminally convicted in the so-called "parapolitical trials." At one time, it was estimated that 35% of the Congress had been co-opted by paramilitary forces. Importantly, this Congress is the same legislative body that enacted the Law of

Victims, among others—a fact that signals the contradictions underlying the often complicated role that the juridical-political has played (and continues to play) in the production of historical memory.

Regardless of the hazards and tensions that accompany this process, nothing has prevented the notable achievements and academic research of the former Group of Historical Memory, which is now legitimized, from an institutional standpoint, as an organization called the Centro Nacional de Memoria Histórica. The Group of Historical Memory was established in 2006 at the request of the Constitutional Court, as an autonomous academic commission dedicated to the search for truth, with the important goal of restoring the dignity and rights of the victims of violence. In 2012, this mandate turned into the Centro Nacional de Memoria Histórica. Since its foundation, it has been under the direction of historian Gonzalo Sánchez, Professor Emeritus of the Universidad Nacional de Colombia, who started the Commission of Studies on Violence during the 1980s, which was also colloquially referred to as La Comisión de Violentólogos (The Commission of Violentologists). The organization's task was to record a narrative capable of recognizing the inseparable relationship that exists between memory and democracy. This relationship is, in itself, a form of justice, and it implies standing up to silence and oblivion. The linkage is a means to realize that a past of violence transcends the space of an individual life history—hence the need to configure a public space that can, and must, carry meaning in the rituals of social acknowledgement, in the judicial processes, and in the corresponding reparations.

The methodology used with the victims in the memory workshops conducted by the Centro Nacional de Memoria Histórica involves various techniques drawn from the field of the social sciences: oral histories, written and visual narrative registries, timelines, and visual biographies. Women, in particular, participate in quilting (patchwork) as a form of storytelling, with visual metaphors to represent collective memory and the "knitting" of solidarity. Another visual project—body maps—creates a graphic representation of bodies, registering marks and footprints of the experience of suffering and violence, as well as resistance and pleasure. In-depth interviews are an effective instrument for the public reconstruction of individual memories pertaining to witnessing, victims, and victimizers. Many cases pertaining to life stories start by restoring the name of a person who was thrown into a common grave as an "NN" ("No Name"); this process begins with interviews with surviving witnesses and the collection of materials such as pictures, personal documents, and mementos. The workshops involving the collective recovery of memory seek to integrate self-report with group therapy through the shared creation of narratives about traumatic episodes. This aspect initiates a learning process based on listening to memories of the past through the exchange of experiences, reflections, and expectations for the future. In short, the workshops are based on a pedagogy of memory—one that is capable of surpassing the devices of mistrust (Sáenz 19), which have historically impeded the process of constructing civility after war.

Stories of Mourning

Understanding the political function of historical narrative means understanding that there are also multiple narratives of war. Until now, the state's version, the testimonies of victims, the media's narratives, and academic articles have been prioritized, while the narratives of the rest of the people have been lost; they do not make up part of the nation's narrative history. However, as long as the narrative impulse is present, there exists the possibility of being and of having an identity, in accordance with the theoretical affirmation that we are the stories we tell about ourselves, as well as the stories that are told about us. The role of historical narrative in this political scenario, then, takes the form of a medium that is used to construct coexistence and achieve national peace. This has resulted in the creation of a collaborative narrative project directed toward "finding ways, tactics, and strategies to say, to resist, and to tell that which people cannot, or do not want to, tell" (Franco, Nieto, and Rincón 7).

The production, compilation, and circulation of the stories that surfaced from the most diverse social strata, levels of education, and regions in the country draws both a testimonial geography and a sociology of narrative. With their voices and their ways of threading memories, they contribute to the defeat of the official history, prevent cultural amnesia, and result in the disclosure of a different Colombia. As a consequence, this type of narrative marks an epistemological turn as soon as a new subject appears and produces, from the beginning, a type of situated recognition outside of academia. It is also located outside the official discourse, traversing various stages: narrating, listening, transcribing, narrating once more, and assembling the text in order to understand the reason for being and the state of the relationships of power mediated by language and the daily life of common folk living in the middle of a war. The relationship woven between the oral narrator, the transcriber, and the assembler of the texts creates a field of mediation that opens a core space characterized by the type of writing that aspires to reappropriate a common history. The hybrid character of testimonial writing transgresses traditional literary categories and imposes new conditions of reception and circulation. It starts by highlighting first-person subjects who, with time, will build an identity to find the right means of expression as they narrate their lived experiences. The situation of understanding shared experiences through the narrating of these experiences, however, is not in vain, though it is hard to cross the barriers between narration as a literary object and the setting of a collective catharsis or a type of psychological therapy. Clearly, the testimonial genre becomes part of a linguistic game that reveals an evolution of the bonds established between language, social position, and power. As Marie Estripeaut-Bourjac states,

> These stories, the ones that belong in the category of testimonials, and generally all writing that pretends to "make another person talk," implies

diverse de facto strategies for transcribing the presence of two social languages within a single text. In turn, techniques of awareness are used in the
relationship between the transcriber, or mediator, and the witness in order
to go from one language to the next, and power relationships are established
this way. Testimonial writing is a melting pot of linguistic syncretism, and
each narrative submits a state of negotiation between a balance that is both
unstable and precarious. (174)

The Enlightened Eye

In Colombian visual art, the representation of violence cannot necessarily be
explained by the influx of a new artistic vanguard; instead, it coincides with the
emergence of modern art in Colombia. Certainly, since the time of Alejandro
Obregón, Luis Caballero, Fernando Botero, and Débora Arango through to the
young artists of today, representations of the body and its relationship to acts of
violence have continued to appear on canvas and in sculptures, murals, and
installations, regardless of whether this art appears on the streets, in galleries or
in museums. On the contemporary scene, we typically cite three visual artists
who explore, in their works, the fragile balance between beauty and horror,
reflecting the immediate history of the country: Doris Salcedo, Oscar Muñoz,
and Juan Manuel Echavarría. They oscillate between the contained expression of
a feeling, the open and public manifestation of muteness and screams, and attention to aesthetic detail and the ironic gesture. This art is commonly based upon the
techniques of field research, specifically interviewing witnesses, gathering information, and transmitting the voices of the victims. Furthermore, the art typically
includes reappearing iconic figures or the multiplication of incendiary objects,
recycled materials or reiterated tones and hues, echoing the sardonic words credited to Beatriz González: "Colombians like repetition" (García-Moreno).

In collaboration with Doris Salcedo, González has intervened in the public
space with *Auras Anónimas*, an installation of some nine thousand graves, featuring eight different designs, in the columbarium of Bogotá's Central Cemetery.
To the viewer, the black silhouettes in this piece look as if they are fading and
turning gray until they encounter a line that explodes and then disappears. The
artist explains how, unlike in the nineteenth century when humans carried
the deceased on their backs through the very difficult Colombian mountain, in
the twentieth and twenty-first centuries the dead would be transported wrapped
in plastic, fabric, and hammocks. In *Auras Anónimas*, as in González's public art,
the idea of repeating the iconic figures stresses the necessary condition of a
memory that prevents the testimony of witnesses from fading like silhouettes.

Similarly, approximately one hundred and twenty units, each consisting of
two redwood tables, one atop the other, sandwiching a thick layer of earth and
organic materials, comprise Salcedo's installation piece *Plegaria Muda*. This

Figure 1. Doris Salcedo, *Plegaria Muda* 2008–2010. Wood, mineral compound, metal and grass. 166 units as installed. CAM, Funacao Calouste Gulbenkian, Lisbon, November 12, 2011–January 22, 2012. Photo by Patrizia Tocci.

dynamic allows the grass to grow from the soil and through the wood into an irrepressible testimony of life surrounded by a sepulchral silence (see figure 1). The coffins in this piece represent the absence of grief rituals for the *falsos positivos* or "false positives"—the thousands of youngsters who disappeared at the hands of Colombia's armed forces as they fell prey to the game of ransom paid to soldiers and officers for each presumed guerrilla fighter killed in combat.

Unlike some of Salcedo's preceding works, however, viewers do not find visible objects, dresses, furniture, or other signs of personal items belonging to individuals who have become victims; in this case, viewers are able to see only the dispossession that points toward the radical limit imposed by death. In the catalog from the exhibition at the Universidad Nacional Autónoma de México, the artist marks the tone of the tragedy:

> I consider Colombia to be the country of dead unburied, of the common pit, of the anonymous dead....Each piece, despite being unmarked, can be found sealed and with an individual character that indicates the mourning that took place.... I believe that the repetition also focuses on the traumatic character of those deaths considered irrelevant by the majority of the population. By individualizing the traumatic experience through repetition, I hope that this work can one day evoke and restitute each and every one of

those deaths in their true dimensions, allowing [their] re-entry to the human sphere....Despite it all, I hope life prevails through difficult conditions... As it happens in *Plegaria Muda*. (Salcedo, *Catálogo* 23)

The critical conception of memory, as well as the function of art as witness, is condensed in the notion of deliberate forgetfulness. Salcedo states that Colombia "needs a strange mix of memory and oblivion, by which I mean memory that [can] be mediated, that can evolve, that is capable of establishing distance, and not getting locked in to a vicious circle of useless vengeance" (Salcedo, "Interview"). The forgetful memory articulates that art gives the spectator access to a lasting experience in the midst of the chaos, as he or she faces the silent intelligence of the aesthetics: "I am a witness. I must stay in order to testify. Otherwise, what is my reason for being?" (Salcedo, "Interview").

Oscar Muñoz continually experiments with the most unpredictable materials to document the processes of disappearance and reappearance of images. His work *Las Cortinas de Baño* (*The Bathroom Curtains*, figure 2), which intended to represent the normal postures of a bather's body as it is blurred by the vapor of

Figure 2. Las Cortinas de Baño *by Oscar Muñoz (1992). Acrylic on plastic. Reprinted with permission of the artist.*

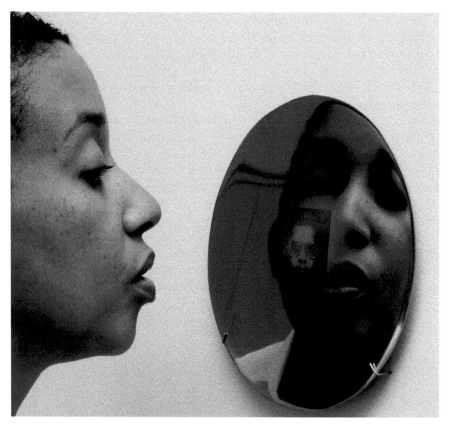

Figure 3. Aliento *by Oscar Muñoz (1996—2002). Installation of mirrors, altered photographs, and human breath. Reprinted with permission of the artist.*

a shower, initiated his attempts at working with materials such as water, carbon powder, and human breath. One of these pieces, for instance, unveils the millions of people who were displaced from the country to the cities, the missing people, the NNs, the prisoners, and the floating bodies in the rivers. In another work, *Aliento* (figure 3), he mounted half a dozen stainless-steel circular mirrors onto a wall in order to produce an effect: the spectator's own image fades the moment he or she breathes on the surface of a mirror, but this act also triggers the sudden appearance of pictures of unnamed missing people that were published in newspapers. Therefore, as spectators, we discover the image of someone else who no longer exists, the reality of a ghost of someone who has vanished (Jiménez).

Like Muñoz, Erika Diettes experiments with the medium of her craft, as seen in *Río Abajo (Down the River)*, which displays pieces and objects belonging to the disappeared as they float in transparent waters and inspire ideas relating to the purity and fragility of life. She explains, "After I took the first images, I felt the need to ensure the transparency of the project. As I began to find the elements, I understood that I was photographing a ghost. I concluded that the images had to be printed in glass. They also had to be monumental, big and loud; they had to generate an impact, which is what I felt when I felt their history. However, I also wanted the pictures to have a sense of fragility and ephemerality" (qtd. in Gualteros and Simbaqueba 128).

The moment he turned fifty, another significant Colombian artist, Juan Manuel Echavarría, experienced a radical rupture in his artistic trajectory: he wished to pursue the exploration of violence through metaphors and the creation of photographs or videos that would capture the horror behind what appeared to be beautiful. In recent years, he has directed artistic workshops for victims and victimizers of the war in Colombia, which has resulted in the exhibition "La Guerra Que No Hemos Visto" ("The War We Have Not Seen"). The paintings in this exhibition expose the naturalization of violence, which has become more lethal with greater anonymity. The tombstones that individuals adorn and worship in the cemeteries of Puerto Berrío, a town on the shores of the Magdalena River, appear anonymous and nameless as well. Echavarría, in the artistic work *Réquiem NN*, explores these sites of collective prayer and even extends a cover of eternal protection over the corpses pulled from the waters of the river. Furthermore, Echavarría's *Corte de Florero* (*Flower Cut Vase*) ironically displays skeletal remains that are arranged to mimic the beautiful drawings of the Botanical Expedition's floral collection.

Echavarría's *The "O"* features a series of photographs of demolished school buildings that the jungle has swallowed up in some twenty hamlets, most of them in Montes de María, a group of small mountains located in the north of the country that was isolated by the war throughout the last two decades (see Figure 4). This particular series consists of the repeated image of a dilapidated board behind a cracked wall, through which the feral vegetation of the tropics seeps. For this reason, the artist assigns similar names to the photographs: *Silence...*, *With Tree*, *With Light*, and *Withered....* The emptiness of the classrooms is a testimony to an absence that makes visible the advances of terror, as expressed in the series *Escuela Nueva*. This series puts together notebooks illustrated by children about the moment of an assault by a nameless armed group—notebooks that are randomly collected by the artist like the remains from a shipwreck.

The Duel of Memories

It is not surprising that the vicissitudes of war in Colombia, as in any other past or present war, also shows a transfer of mourning from the battlefield to the field of speech and memories. The control of memory is not an exclusive feature of the totalitarian regimes of the twentieth century; in truth, it is always seen as a trophy, coveted by antagonistic forces. In this game, it holds up to the most horrific methods: the disappearance of tracks, converting corpses to powder in cremation ovens, the burning of files, intimidation and prohibition to receive and transmit information, and the use of euphemisms, systematic lying, concealment, and propaganda through the mass media (Todorov 140–42). The pedagogical work of memory is not so much the essence or the substance of being identical, but the inquiry about the circumstances or contingencies; it is not so much an identity as the identification process, or how we have become to be who we are and how we can live.

Assuming that the deep wounds which mark warring nations are measured by the collapse of the host structures, reconstruction work is colossal and extends through several generations. In the words of Lluís Duch, "Socialization, identification, [and] symbolic anticipation [can] only go on to become something really important in the fabric of human existence by means of the host structures, which are those relational elements in and from the present [that] allow a creative link with the past in order to imagine and shape the future" (27). The pedagogical work of narrated memory, then, is conceived as an action—one capable of raising the imagination and, at the same time, ready to transmit what has been said as a common heritage, as well as what still remains to be said, which is the promise held by every birth (Arendt 185).

Facing the threat of *la peste del olvido* ("the stink of oblivion") in Macondo, artists highlight the value of hosting a welcoming recognition of the Other in its irreducible Otherness. This concept is part of a "welcome ethics" that functions as a kind of courteous and hospitable invitation to the newcomer, as if to say, "this is our world" (Bárcena and Mélich 87). This welcome provides for the possibility of socialization and the construction of the reality of each subject. Because of these issues, the individuals identify with a continuous process of building meaningful relationships in the world—ones that welcome and integrate them into the flow of a particular cultural tradition, which also makes it possible to acquire a personal identity. They also provide the necessary elements for the rich display of the symbolic power of the human being, figuratively and literately placed in a present, from which to recall the past and anticipate the future. In short, the structures of these works of art unleash the power to recall the process of the *empalabramiento* of reality, which has, as a consequence, the "coming into existence" of subjects. This hosting can and should be realized in educational spaces that are designed as safe spaces in which students are allowed to try without being ridiculed, to make mistakes, and to begin again without their mistakes being held against them. Therefore, the educator has two essential responsibilities: to build safe spaces for learning and to stimulate the senses in order to make available for learners the energy to mobilize them toward knowledge. Thus, the two origins of the word "education" are combined: *educare* ("to nurture") and *educere* ("to lead," "direct toward," "involve," and "elevate").

Figure 4. *Silencio con mapas politicos Juan Manuel Echavarría* (2014). C-print mounted on dibond. Reprinted with permission of the artist.

The immense power of narrative in education lies in its ability to promote the cognitive and moral development of individuals through the process of decentering—that is, opening oneself to an other. The act of telling our own lives to others, as well as hearing their stories, ultimately brings about a process of transformation in oneself that affects how an individual understands the world and his or her life. In this sense, being yourself is being a bit of others: I am an other. We are not so absolutely transparent as to feel alienated to the experience of relating to others. In the words of Juan Gabriel Vásquez in *El ruido de las cosas al caer* (*The Sound of Things As They Fall*), "Experience, that thing that we call experience, is not the inventory of our pains, but the learned sympathy toward others' pain" (85).

Universidad de Antioquia

Works Cited

Arendt, Hannah. *Between Past and Present*. New York: Penguin, 1993. Print.

Bárcena, Fernando, and Joan-Carles Mélich. *La educación como acontecimiento ético: Natalidad, narración y hospitalidad*. Barcelona: Paidós, 2000. Print.

Duch, Lluís. *La educación y la crisis de la modernidad*. Barcelona: Paidós, 1997. Print.

Estripeaut-Bourjac, Marie. "[Pensar las historias] La urgencia del relato, hoy, en Colombia." Franco, Nieto, and Rincón 171—80. Print.

Franco, Natalia, Patricia Nieto, and Omar Rincón, eds. *Tácticas y estrategias para contar (Historias de la gente sobre conflicto y reconciliación en Colombia)*. Bogotá: Centro de Competencia en Comunicación para América Latina and Friedrich Ebert Stiftung, 2010. Print.

García-Moreno, Diego. *¿Por qué llora si ya reí?* Bogotá: Producciones La Maraca, 2010. Film.

Gualteros, Vladimir Olaya, and Mariana Iasnaia Simbaqueba. "Estetización de la memoria: Formación y espacio de lo político." *Revista Colombiana de Educación* 62 (2012): 117—38. Print

Jiménez, Carlos. "Los pliegues del instante." *Lápiz* 128|129 (1997): 20—27. Print.

Nora, Pierre. "Between Memory and History: Les Lieux de Mémoire." *Representations* 26 (1989): 7—24. Print.

Orozco Abad, Iván, María Victoria Uribe, Gina Cabarcas, and Luis Carlos Sánchez Díaz. *Justicia y paz: Verdad judicial o verdad histórica?* Bogotá: Taurus|Semana, 2012. Print.

Sáenz, Javier. *Desconfianza, civilidad y estética: Las prácticas formativas estatales por fuera de la escuela en Bogotá, 1994—2003*. Bogotá: Instituto para la Investigación Educativa y el Desarrollo Pedagógico, Universidad Nacional de Colombia, Facultad de Ciencias Humanas, 2007. Print.

Salcedo, Doris. *Catálogo Museo Universitario de Arte Contemporáneo (MUAC)*. México, D.F.: Universidad Nacional Autónoma de México, 2011.

—. "Interview by Marguerite Feitlowitz." *Marguerite Feitlowitz*. n.d. Web. 29 Jan. 2015.

Todorov, Tzvetan. *Memoria del mal y tentación del bien: Indagación sobre el Siglo XX*. Barcelona: Península, 2002. Print.

Vásquez, Juan Gabriel. *El ruido de las cosas al caer*. Barcelona: Anagrama, 2011. Print.

(Auto)Biography in Pre-Service Teacher Training: Rural Education in Bahia, Brazil

(Auto)Biografía en el entrenamiento de maestros pre-servicios: Educación rural en Bahía, Brasil

By Elizeu Clementino de Souza

Translated by Lorena Paccini Lustosa

This essay explores the potential that narrative inquiry holds for pre-service teacher training as both a methodological resource for pedagogical researchers and as a self-reflexive practice for teachers. Focusing on an interdisciplinary, international, collaborative research project conducted in the rural school district of Bahia, Brazil, this paper establishes the need for and benefits of an inclusion of (auto) biographical texts and acts in the pedagogical formation of instructors teaching in understaffed, multi-grade elementary schools.

Este ensayo explora el potencial que la interrogación narrativa sostiene para el entrenamiento de maestros en pre-servicio tanto para un recurso metodológico para investigadores de pedagogía como para una práctica de auto-reflexión para maestros. Con un enfoque hacia un proyecto interdisciplinario, internacional y colaborativo conducido en los distritos de escuelas rurales en Bahía, Brasil, este ensayo establece la necesidad de beneficios que emergen por la inclusión de textos (auto)biográficos y actos de formación pedagógica de instructores enseñando en escuelas elementales de multi-nivel que están faltas de personal.

In the last decade, a significant body of scholarship has been produced in Brazil on the role of (auto)biographies in pedagogy and teacher training. Discussions of (auto)biographical research emerging from the Brazilian educational field have focused, quite specifically, on studies that take into account the methodologies of pre-service or junior teacher training with continuing emphasis on aspects related to professionalism on the job, integration of new teachers into schools and communities, and furthering the professional development of teachers of different grade levels and diverse knowledge areas. It is important to note that many of these studies have been developed within regional, national, and international research networks, a practice somewhat common in the field of biographical research, thereby allowing scholars to form partnerships and cooperation between research groups. This collaborative approach to studying (auto)biography and pedagogy has afforded Brazilian researchers, through the implementation of different methodologies emerging from international and interdisciplinary research norms, the opportunity to develop four axes of (auto) biographical research and key courses of action and investigation, as discussed in this essay.

The first axis of (auto)biographical research focuses on the act of narration as an anthropological and humanistic phenomenon that different semiotic systems perform, most notably oral and written language. The second axis considers the creation and analysis of (auto)biographical sources to investigate the historical, social, multicultural, and institutional formation and professional development of teachers. The third takes (auto)narratives as a practice of (auto) formation, seeking to investigate self-reflective activities and their impact on the formation of and integration into the professional life of a teacher. Because training practices involve trainees and trainers, the fourth axis investigates the use of (auto)biographical narratives as educational intervention procedures, focusing on teacher formation through the monitoring of (auto)writings.

With these initial points in mind, I here review, in an abbreviated form, my reflections on the configuration of the (auto)biographical movement in Brazil as it relates to pedagogical practices. I will further share some of my experiences of participating in a collaborative research project to study rural education in Bahia, Brazil. These musings are intended to highlight the ways in which we have applied theoretical and methodological principles of (auto)biographical research in rural areas of Brazil to the benefit of teacher education and student learning.

Work on the construction, collection, and analysis of life narratives in pedagogical research and teacher formation—what may be called (auto)biographical methodologies—responds to the demands present in the educational field. Let us begin by considering that the forms of conducting research, choice of procedures, and arguments used to justify and substantiate scholarship are extremely varied and, in order to understand the decisions that a researcher makes, the academic space in which such works emerge must be understood. Studies in the field of pre-service teacher training that incorporate (auto)biographical narratives as a means of cultivating more meaningful teacher development tend to favor the model of extending the curriculum to include the reading of published texts and asking students to consider how they might appropriate or adapt relevant ideas to their own teaching. This appears to be an especially popular instructional model in Europe and North America.

Similarly, in viewing life histories as a resource for the development of socio-historical studies of educational processes, it may be understood that these narratives are potent sources in thinking about the progression of meaning-making from what the subject experiences and subsequently records. Life histories are currently used in different areas of the humanities and "formation sciences," through the adaptation of their epistemological and methodological principles to other aspects of adult education, from tacit knowledge or experiential learning, and from the learning built throughout a lifetime as a metacognition or meta-reflection of self-knowledge. In Brazil, however, the routine, self-reflexive act of creating life narratives is also being explored as an important aspect of pre-service teacher training. The history of education, pre-service teacher training, and teaching itself have been, in the Brazilian context, important aspects of identity formation that are routinely present in the life histories, oral histories, and narratives of pre-service and active teachers.

The use of life narratives in Brazil stems from the influence and tradition of oral history. Oral history was popularized in Brazil as a means of testimony and public record in the 1960s through the oral-history program of the Center for Research and Documentation of Contemporary History of Brazil at the Fundação Getúlio Vargas. This project was developed in order to gather testimonies from the national political elite and was so successful that, in 1994, the Brazilian Oral History Association was founded to hold seminars and disseminate research. This mode of research has become so ingrained in Brazilian culture that bodies such as the Center for Urban and Rural Studies rely heavily on oral-history methodologies to conduct their research.

While certainly influenced by oral-history methodologies, the (auto)biographical research conducted within the parameters of education and teacher training in Brazil has, out of necessity, developed its own unique research framework. According to Elizeu Clementino de Souza et al., the contemporary biographical movement in Brazil is rooted in its connection to research in the field of education—including pedagogy, pre-service teacher training, and the history of education—and branches out into other areas that use narrative inquiry as a research perspective of (self-)formation. The diversification of the thematic and methodological approaches used in such biographical research resulted from the accumulated body of analysis in projects concerning the initial and continued identity formation or life narratives of educators. These include the experiences of educational innovators who sought to make visible the socio-historical dimensions of a teaching career, professional identity, school organization, and the daily life of a school.

The creation and work of the first phase of the Teaching Study Group: Memory and Gender marks the initial experience with (auto)biographical research and the practices of teacher training in Brazil, accessed through gender studies and following the criss-crossing paths and memories of teachers on their courses and teacher-training programs. The work of Belmira Oliveira Bueno et al. constitutes the first assessment of the methodology used in research on life histories and (auto)biographies as materials for investigation in Brazil from 1985 to 2003. Their analysis provides an overview of national scholarly production, including abstracts, dissertations and theses, books, and peer-reviewed scholarly essays, with an emphasis on pre-service teacher training and pedagogy. Bueno et al. highlight the emergence of and interest in new themes of study in both the profession and identity development, and they emphasize the need for further discussion about cultural appropriations, definitions, methodological research perspectives, and training practices in (auto)biographical research and narrated lives. In the Brazilian context, the research developed in the fields of education and, more specifically, teacher-training practices has shown different ways of working with memories, life histories, and (auto)writings, which have greater implications within the process of teacher training and the larger scope of the initial and continued formation of identities.

Since the late 1970s, biographical methods have been prominently used in Brazilian approaches to teacher education, including the writing of diaries and other forms of (auto)writings as a formative practice. This curricular development also includes the incorporation of published (auto)biographical narratives, particularly educational (auto)biographies that demarcate perceptions related to the path of teacher formation, as well as those that confront dominant methods in the field of educational research. The practices of educational research and teacher training, interwoven with life histories, embrace a variety of sources and collection procedures, which may be grouped in two general sets: various personal documents (memoirs, diaries, letters, photographs, and other personal items) and biographical interviews, which may be oral or written. Because published (auto)biographies are widely used as historical sources in research in educational fields, each text created in teacher-training programs ought also to be used as an object of analysis, considering, above all, the context of its production, its textual form, and its content in relation to the research or training project to which it is linked.

Maria da Conceição Passeggi signaled these developments when she argued—in regard to francophone narratives—that educators' life histories emerge within the context of lifelong identity formation, which is strongly influenced by the global impact on work structures. Contemporary research on and practices of teacher training are, therefore, constructed to make life histories visible during teacher training—a movement that has put the adult at the center of the process in an attempt to value the experiences recorded in (auto)biographical projects as essential to professional orientation and development.

Within the paradigm of singular|plural, as Marie-Christine Josso tells us, lie potent reasons for the choice of the biographical approach—with its emphasis on life histories and on using oral or written reports—as an investigation and training practice for teachers. A diverse biographical-narrative approach allows us to understand the uniqueness and universality of (auto)biographical narratives and the formation of memories, which reveal individual and collective approaches in subjects who both learn and teach. This revaluation of life stories lies at the turn in hermeneutics that understands social phenomena as texts and interpretation as assigning meanings to individual and collective experiences.

In light of the work done as part of my project "Rural Diversities, Diverse Ruralities: Individuals, Institutions, and Pedagogical Practices in Rural Schools in Bahia, Brazil," I will refer to the research and training experiences in the field of experiential pedagogy and the construction, collection, and analysis of the life narratives that were collectively studied by the Research Group on (Auto)Biography, Formation, and Oral History, which is also linked to Research Line II: Education, Pedagogical Praxis, and Teacher Formation. The projects and activities of this group derive from interdisciplinary and international perspectives in the fields of life history and (auto)biographical research, since it is productive to gain knowledge from multiple perspectives and places about the everydayness of schools and the questions that arise regarding teaching and teacher training. Our inquiry was specifically focused on the shape of multigrade elementary schools, with emphasis on studies of individuals, institutions, and the pedagogical practices that are implemented in rural schools in Bahia.

This research analyzes problems in rural education, with an emphasis on the pedagogical practices of teachers in multigrade classes. The research questions have been developed by the Research Group on (Auto)Biography, Formation, and Oral History, and the project has been strengthened through a collaborative research network developed between the Universidade Federal da Bahia and the Universidade Federal do Recôncavo da Bahia in Brazil, and the Université Paris 13 in France. This work is also supported through a partnership between several Brazilian research groups—the Research Group on (Auto)Biography, Formation, and Oral History; Curriculum, Assessment, and Formation; and the Center for Teacher Formation, Campus Amargosa—and the Centre de Recherche Interuniversitaire Expérience Ressources Culturelles Éducation, which is co-sponsored by the Université Paris 13 and the Université Paris 8. These groups have been developing a network of research on educational procedures and activities in different rural areas in the state of Bahia, Brazil, and in France, with an emphasis on (auto)biographical research and elevating studies on rural education. The specific thrust of the study has been on multigrade classes, pedagogical practices, and the state of rural education over the past decade in both the Brazilian and French educational systems.

The decision to carry out the study in rural areas of Bahia was made in large part due to the concentration in these areas of the lowest educational-performance indicators in Brazil and the state of Bahia. It is important to note, however, that the rural areas of Brazil, under the complex processes of urbanization, were historically omitted from government agendas and schedules for discussion. This mandate overlooked the specific characteristics inherent to the population in these areas and simply transplanted urban educational policies into the rural context. The lack of educational policies that met the specific needs of rural Brazilians meant that rural schools merely imitated urban schools (Leite). The academic calendar, system of organizing classes, teaching, and grading, discipline, subject content, and methods and teaching that inform the national style are inspired by the urban-school model, and teachers in rural areas struggle to apply it efficiently—hence the frustration when students drop out of school at harvest time or do not turn up on Fridays, as they are traveling to Saturday fairs in the cities in order to sell their goods. This distresses teachers, especially those in multigrade classes, by creating the expectation of a heterogeneous class. The illogicality of simply transferring the urban-school model to rural areas has already been demonstrated, making necessary the development of innovative pedagogical approaches that answer the specific needs of rural territories in a concrete way by allowing all subjects—even rural subjects—to recognize themselves in educational practices.

We understand rural as a category that emerges from entwined socio-historical, geographical, and cultural elements. It is fruitful to move beyond the concept of a rural space as one that is eminently agrarian, developmentally delayed, and inferior to the urban, and to turn instead toward contemporary rural spaces as those associated with nature and its productive processes. This idea of the rural is presented in the *Operational Guidelines for Basic Education in Rural Schools* (Brasil, *Resolução*), which understands the rural space as a space of forestry, farming, mining, and agriculture, but goes beyond this when it also accommodates fishing space, riverine space, and *caiçaras*. The rural, in this sense, is "more than a non-urban perimeter... [but] a field of possibilities that streamline the connection of human beings with their own production of the conditions of social existence and achievements of human society" (Brasil, *Resolução* 1). One might, according to these *Guidelines*, consider present-day rural space as a "living place, where people can live, work, study with the dignity of those who have their place, their cultural identity" (Fernandes 137). In this sense, it appears as a space of social relations, a "singular space and collective actor" (Wanderley 92). Thus, in the *Guidelines* there are two important foundations for rural education: overcoming the dichotomy between the rural and the urban, and becoming open to the world.

From this legal basis, a rural public-education system needs to be developed that enhances the identity and culture of the peoples inhabiting these localities. Any such system should support human development and sustainable local development, including an operationalized education outside of urban spaces. This attention is relevant and this discussion is necessary, especially since Brazil is characterized by a large number of municipalities in which social and economic values, lifestyles, and cultures derive from rural practices and values. In this context, it is fitting to discuss the education, schools, and teaching produced in these social spaces, and the educational innovations that emerge. Even though problems in education are present outside rural areas, education is complicated in Brazil because rural populations face distinct prejudices. Inhabitants of rural areas must live with the popular belief that their homes are devoid of elaborate economic arrangements and limited by their own way of life in relation to those of urbanized areas.

While analyzing rural education in Bahia, the aforementioned research team identified three interesting educational situations. The situation most salient to this project is present in "official" schools linked to the Municipal Education Department, where most schools strictly adhere to curricula from mass-marketed textbooks. Thus, the curriculum seems strange and even contrary to the local reality, inhibiting local dynamism and sustainable development. The practices of the "official" schools are a result of the policies adopted by the Brazilian government throughout the twentieth century—developed because of the absence of public policies to serve the interests of the rural populations. This resulted in an attempt to make education policies in rural areas imitate those in urban areas.

In the rural schools of the different territories studied in this research project, the classes take place in a single classroom combining students of various grades, ranging from kindergarten to fifth grade. In the milieu of rural education, those schools with multigrade classes are characterized by the simultaneous offering of various "series" of the same class, conducted by a single teacher, and are also called *unidocentes* or "one-instructor" schools. However, despite great concerns over this teaching format, this issue has been muted by public policies and also by universities, which have conducted notably sparse research on the issue and underplay concerns related to *unidocente* classes in training courses for teachers, especially courses pertaining to elementary education.

All this is despite Brazilian Law 9.394|96, which establishes the guidelines and bases of national education; proposes measures to adapt school curricula and policies to life in rural areas; offers operational guidelines that acknowledge alterity and confer respect for rural populations' unique needs; calls for building a school system that is designed specifically for rural people; and regulates specific strategies for rural-school assistance. This same law also makes clear that the professional training of teachers occurs at the start of their careers and continues throughout their tenure, emphasizing that the quality of teaching in Brazil can be improved and guaranteed only with financial and political investments contextualized in rural areas. Recent changes in public policy have encouraged the process of scholar centralization and the reduction of multigrade schools, but there are still approximately 93,623 classrooms in elementary education in Brazil that follow this model, according to the 2010 School Census (INEP). The state of Bahia has the largest number of such classes in the nation at 16,985, accounting for 18.14% of this standard of education in Brazil (INEP).

We therefore believe it to be necessary for teachers who are active in this type of classroom to have a well-defined background so that they may work successfully with the diverse student body presented to them. In this regard, rural education, at the core of its delayed and uneven implementation, still carries the marks of its precarious creation, but with some progress. At present, the successes and failures of rural schools are not fully known, nor is the relationship to their causes fully understood. We understand, then, that many things must change in rural education and, among them, the most urgent and analyzable is the development of teachers. Thus, we believe that the relation between teachers' knowledge, pedagogical practices, and the (re)construction of identities is a guiding principle of training and teaching.

The work of rural teachers is based on the assumption that culture and diversity are parts of everyday life, especially in consideration of the reality of multigrade classes and the demands placed on the teacher, as elements that affect the processes of teachers' development, educational practice, and students' development and learning. In order to study these "diverse ruralities," we have relied on (auto)biographical narratives as a methodological approach that adopts (auto)writing to gather information from pre-service and junior teachers. Because these narratives are marked as formative works through collective reflections of teaching experiences, they are undertaken as devices of investigation, formation, and action.

The dual function that characterizes narrative research, as both a source for examination and a self-reflexive practice of development, sets up, according to Nóvoa, both a means of investigation for the educational researcher and a pedagogical tool for the teacher. This dual purpose more than justifies the increasing expansion and implementation of narrative research in education and, more specifically, in contexts of development and teacher training. This research with (auto)biographical narratives involves making the life narrated the core of investigation, formation, and action projects, and requires that participants engage with some of the different memories, narratives, and subjectivities that the identity process holds, as well as recording some of the complexities that daily work in teaching requires.

This research on subject biographization, by adopting (auto)biographical theoretical and methodological principles in investigating narrative experiences, starts from everyday life in rural areas, including the awareness of institutional memory and pedagogical work in multigrade classes, the process of shifting from the countryside to the city in search of school identity, and the implications of the subject and the territory (Delory-Momberger). The problematic daily life of schools and the schools' failure to serve students in rural areas mark other analyses of evaluation policies and statistical data, as well as the narratives of different subjects in their interfaces with everyday living. We can see that various institutional silences, curricular and procedural gaps, and possible new horizons can be considered when using a biographical approach to historical issues related to multigrade classes in the national and international context.

Multigrade schools assume social and political relevance in the rural communities where they are located, especially because they ensure access to education for large numbers of Brazilians who would not otherwise be educated. Despite their importance, evidenced in the numbers presented earlier and their social importance to subjects in the countryside, issues with such schools have been invisible to public policy. This invisibility can be seen in the lack of policies for the construction of school facilities, teacher training, and the development of instructional materials that meet the needs of schools with multigrade classes. The only existing program in the country for multigrade classes is the Active School Program, which was established in 1997 and has not withstood the many criticisms that have been leveled at it, even after reforms (Xavier Neto; Gonçalves; FONEC).

These concerns have also been muted in the universities. As previously mentioned, research on the subject has been scarce, and disproportionate to the size of the affected population and social importance of their education on the national stage. A survey conducted using the Bank of Abstracts of Theses and Dissertations, housed at the Coordenação de Aperfeicoamento de Pessoal de Nível Superior, revealed that only forty-seven papers dedicated to the study of multigrade courses were defended in Brazil between 1987 and 2010. In this survey, we identified two studies in the 1980s, six in the 1990s, and thirty-nine in the 2000s. During the past decade, twenty-eight studies were defended between 2006 and 2010, which shows significant growth in recent years. Most of these projects were completed in the field of education, but it should also be noted that multigrade courses were discussed in several other fields, such as educational psychology and general psychology. Certainly, the low national production of scholarship at the graduate level on multigrade classes, as shown above, has contributed to training courses for pre-service teachers that disregard the difficulties of the multigrade classroom, even those courses that are located in the interior regions of the country. This practice obviously generates difficulties for teachers who teach in multigrade classrooms, as such discussions are markedly absent in typical Brazilian undergraduate courses in pedagogy.

In 2005, however, the Universidade do Estado da Bahia undertook some initiatives in courses for pre-service teacher training, in direct consideration of the provisions set forth in the *Operational Guidelines for Basic Education in Rural Schools* (Brasil, *Resolução*). This program has introduced the discipline of rural education, typically with a workload of approximately sixty credit hours. Of paramount importance to this pilot program is the production of self-reflexive (auto)biographical texts by the enrolled pre-service teachers, as both a means of preparing teachers to work in multigrade classes and a biographical methodology for researchers to study the preparation of these teachers.

It is understandable that students enrolled in schools with multigrade classes have great difficulty in learning and poor academic performance, contributing to the persistence of low educational outcomes in these schools. Given the scarcity of studies on these schools (with the notable exception of Bof), it is not surprising that indicators show these schools' performance to be very inefficient, with students lacking scientific literacy and having difficulties across the spectrum— in mathematical and logical reasoning, as well as reading and writing. Therefore, we emphasize the need for policies on teacher training and for institutions that train teachers to discuss, as part of the curriculum, the dynamics and singularities of multigrade classes. Thus, trainee teachers can recognize and analyze the cognitive distortions, negative representations, and prejudices around rural education, and understand that the derogatory discourse was historically constituted and why there is an absence of public policies specifically for multigrade classes. We argue that the incorporation of (auto)biographical textual production into the curricula of pre-service teacher training, pedagogy, and elementary education programs is an effective means of accomplishing this objective.

The biographical approach is considered to be both a means of investigation and a teaching tool, and it is precisely this dual function that justifies the use of the method in the educational sciences. This approach contributes to the understanding of daily school routines and issues related to the profession, in addition to being a fertile ground to develop and enable learning, knowledge, and growth through the experiences and ways of narrating our individual and collective histories. The key question, then, is what knowledge can be generated from (auto) biographical narratives, and what is the relevance of this knowledge to training professional teachers? The answer to this question is linked to the experiential learning forged in professional teaching practice and the assessment of its capability to fuel pedagogical theories. These ontological knowledges, elaborated and implicated with life experiences, are the basis from which the narratives of schooling trajectories and development are based.

Debates about the biographical method and life histories encourage us to observe and understand the importance of this method not only as a research tool, but also as a tool that helps pre-service teachers better understand their relationship to their educational training, allowing them to identify what was actually formative in their own life histories. This use of life narratives has triggered important theoretical debates in the course of its evolution, as it fights for recognition of its scientific value as a method of self-investigation. As a mediation between individual, social, personal, and professional histories, interest in the use of such a method has increased in past decades in different areas of knowledge. Research with life histories in Brazil has informed a variety of studies on the biographical approach and the lives of educators and their training paths, revealing their significant value and influencing educational research on personal dimensions in the process of formation.

Universidade do Estado da Bahia

Acknowledgments

"Rural Diversities, Diverse Ruralities: Individuals, Institutions, and Pedagogical Practices in Rural Schools in Bahia, Brazil" has received funding from the Research Foundation of the state of Bahia (2004-2007 Thematic Education Edict) and from Edictal of Humanities, Social Sciences, and Social Applied Sciences (2008—10, CNPq). It currently has funding from the Universal Edictal CNPq (2010).

Disclosure Statement

No potential conflict of interest was reported by the author.

Works Cited

Bof, Alvana Maria, ed. *A educação no Brasil rural*. Brasília: MEC|INEP, 2006. Print.

Brasil. Lei de diretrizes e bases da educação nacional—Lei 9.394|96 estabelece as diretrizes e bases da educação nacional. *Diário Oficial da União* 20 Dec. 1996. Print.

—. *Resolução CNE|CEB 01|2002, de 03 de abril de 2002, institui as diretrizes pperacionais para a educação básica nas escolas do campo*. Brasília: MEC|CNE|CEB, 2002. Print.

Bueno, Belmira Oliveira, et al. "Histórias de vida e autobiografias na formação de professores y profissão docente (Brasil, 1985—2003)." *Educação e Pesquisa* 32.2 (2006): 385—410. Print.

Delory-Momberger, Christine. *Biografia e educação: Figuras de l'indivíduo-projeto*. Trans. Maria da Conceição Passeggi, et al. São Paulo: Paulus; Natal, Rn: Edufrn, 2008. Print.

Fernandes, Bernardo Mançano. "Diretrizes de uma caminhada." *Por uma educação do campo*. Ed. Miguel Gonzalez Arroyo, et al. Petrópolis: Vozes, 2004. 133—45. Print.

Fórum Nacional de Educação do Campo (FONEC). *Nota técnica sobre o programa escola ativa: Uma análise crítica*. Brasília: FONEC, 2001. Print.

Gonçalves, G. B. B. "O programa escola ativa: Uma pedagogia em movimento para as classes multisseriadas rurais?" *III encontro nacional de pesqusia em educação do campo, 2010.* Mônica Castagna Molina, ed. Brasília: Observatório de Educação do Campo, 2010. Print.

Instituto Nacional de Estudos e Pesquisas Educacionais Anísio Teixeira (INEP). *Censo escolar 2010: Sinopse estatística da educação básica—ano 2010.* Brasília: MEC| INEP, 2010. Web. 29 Oct. 2011.

Josso, Marie-Christine. "Os relatos de histórias de vida como desvelamento dos desafios existenciais da formação e do conhecimento: Destinos sócio-culturais e projetos de vida programados na invenção de si." Souza, Elizeu Clementino de and ABRAHÃO, Maria Helena Menna Barreto (Orgs.). Tempos, nar-rativas e #cções: a invenção de si. Porto Alegre: EDIPUCRS:EDUNEB, 2006. 21–40.

Leite, Sérgio Celani. *Escola rural: Urbanização e políticas educacionais.* São Paulo: Cortez, 1999. Print.

Passeggi, Maria da Conceição. "As duas faces do memorial acadêmico." *Odisséia* 9.13–14 (2006): 65–76. Print.

Souza, Elizeu Clementino de, et al. "La Reserche (auto)biographique et l'invention de soi au Bresil." Colloque International (1986–2007): Le Biographique, la Réflexivité et les Temporalités. Articuler Langues, Cultures et Formation. Université François-Rabelais, Tours. 25–27 June 2007.

Wanderley, Maria de Nazareth Baudel. "A emergência de uma nova ruralidade nas sociedades avançadas—o 'rural' como espaço singular e ator coletivo." *Estudos—Sociedade e Agricultura* 15 (2000): 87–146. Print.

Xavier Neto, L. P. "Educação do campo em eisputa: Análise comparativa entre o MST e o projeto escola ativa." *Encontro de Pesquisa Educacional do Norte-Nordeste Anais, 19.* João Pessoa-PB, Universidade Federal da Paraíba (UFPB), 2009. Print.

Index

Note: **Boldface** page numbers refer to figures and tables. Page numbers along with "n" refer to foot notes.

INDEX

INDEX